# The
# Storm
# of
# Steel

Ernst Jünger

Translated by Basil Creighton

Reprint of the 1929 ed. published by Chatto & Windus, London

ISBN: 9781696237727

v. I

# NOTE FROM THE PUBLISHER

Ernst Jünger's *The Storm of Steel* was originally published in 1920, under the title *In Storms of Steel: from the diary of a Shock Troop Commander, Ernst Jünger, War Volunteer, and subsequently Lieutenant in the Rifle Regiment of Prince Albrecht of Prussia (73rd Hanoverian Regiment)*. Although the 1st edition of the book did not sell well, it was notable for being one of the earliest accounts of the war. The text was largely lifted directly from Jünger's own unedited wartime diaries. The next major revision came in 1924, when Jünger began working with a new publisher. It is this version that was adapted by Basil Creighton, a world-renowned translator of German literature, into English as *The Storm of Steel* in 1929. This book is a reprint of that 1929 translation.

Jünger's views, and his interpretation of his experiences, changed many times throughout his life. He would complete 7 major revisions of *The Storm of Steel*, widely-regarded as his masterpiece. The 1929 translation, for decades the only version available in English, has subsequently been overtaken by translations based on later revisions of the book. At this time, the Creighton translation has been out-of-print for decades. Later editions of *The Storm of Steel* remove many of Jünger's reflections on leadership, nationalism, and the nature of heroism. Despite their removal, these passages can still offer readers a wealth of insights, insights that we hope to preserve by republishing this translation both in print and in digital form.

Whenever possible, we have taken efforts to preserve the elements of Creighton's original translation. Although subsequent translators have been critical of Creighton's work, it remains the most compelling and readable version of *The Storm of Steel*. For decades, this translation introduced generations of readers to one of Europe's greatest writers. We are very happy to allow new generations to enjoy the same experience.

# CONTENTS

# THE AUTHOR'S PREFACE TO THE ENGLISH EDITION

It is not impossible that among the English readers of this book there may be one who in 1915 or 1916 was in one of those trenches that were woven like a web among the ruins of Monchy-au-Bois. In that case he had opposite him at the time the 73rd Hanoverian Fusiliers, who wear as their distinctive badge a brassard with 'Gibraltar' inscribed on it in gold, in memory of the defence of that fortress under General Elliot; for this, besides Waterloo, has its place in the regiment's history.

At the time I refer I was a nineteen-year-old lieutenant in command of a platoon, and my part in the line was easily recognizable from the English side by a row of tall shell-stripped trees that rose from the ruins of Monchy. My left flank was bounded by the sunken road leading to Berles-au-Bois, which was in the hands of the English; my right marked by a sap running out from our lines, one that helped us many a time to make our presence felt by means of bombs and rifle-grenades.

I daresay this reader remembers, too, the white tom-cat, lamed in one foot by a stray bullet, who had his headquarters in No-man's-land. He used often to pay me a visit at night in my dugout. This creature, the sole living being that was on visiting terms with both sides, always made on me an impression of extreme mystery. This charm of mystery which lay over all that belonged to the other side, to that danger zone full of unseen figures, is one of the strongest impressions that `the war has left with me. At that time, before the battle of the Somme, which opened a new chapter in the history of the war, the struggle had not taken the grim and mathematical aspect which cast over its landscapes a deeper and deeper gloom. There was more rest for the soldier than in the later years when he was thrown into one murderous battle after another; and so it is that many of those days come back to my memory now with a light on them that is almost peaceful.

In our talks in the trenches, in the dugout, or on the fire-step, we often talked of the 'Tommy'; and, as any genuine soldier will easily understand, we spoke of him very much more respectfully than was commonly the case with the newspapers of those days. There is no one less likely to disparage the lion than the lion-hunter.

Indeed, the landscape in which we lived at the time had something about it of primeval Africa, with two mighty forces of nature locked in conflict there. It was only now and again that one caught the sight of a brownish-yellow fleeting shadow against the desolate countryside that stretched on and on before one's eyes; or heard, after creeping through the wire at night, a whisper or a cough from a post. The distant sound of transport, a cloud of smoke from a fire hidden from view, fresh chalk spoil thrown out on the tortured ground, the monotonous duel of the guns stretching on from week to month—those were the signs that we puzzled over as though they were the runes of a secret book or the spoor of some mighty and unknown beast that came nightly to drink.

As time went on, it grew more and more dangerous to lift a corner of the veil that fell like a magic hood over the spectre that was at once so near and so fatally far off. Raids undertaken to get a glimpse of the enemy's lines and some information about what was going on there became less frequent and more exacting as the volume and mass of war material increased. A more and more terrific barrage had to be put down before ten or twenty picked men, armed to the teeth, could make their occasional and exceedingly brief appearances in the opposing trenches. What the survivors brought back with them was the memory of a rapid and frantic glance into Vulcan's white hot cauldron.

Still, there were moments of another kind when the deep discord and the even deeper unity of this landscape came more clearly to one's mind. It was strange, for example, to hear at night the cry of the partridges from the waste fields, or at dawn the careless song of the lark as it rose high above the trenches. Did it not seem then that life itself was speaking out of the confidence of its savage and visionary heart, knowing very well that in its more secret and essential depths it had nothing to fear from even the deadliest of wars, and going its way quite unaffected by the superficial interchange of peace and war?

But then, too, did not this life, ruthless towards its creatures, superior to the pain and pleasure of the individual, looking on with indifference while its passive forces were melted down in the crucible of war, enter very clearly even into the soldier's simple mind? Many a time, in that quiet interlude after sunset before the first Verey light went up, this message was brought very near to the soul by the song of an outlying post waiting for the night relief. There was a deeper homesickness there than any peace in this world can set at rest.

Then the fire-step was manned once more, the relief moved off along the communication trenches, and the brisker rifle-fire of the night-time broke out; the ear was again on stretch to catch the pulse-beat of that other life under arms over there in the darkness. And often the Verey lights went up in dozens and the trench got lively when a patrol had crept up to our wire.

To-day there is no secret about what those trenches concealed, and a book such as this may, like a trench-map years after the event, be read with sympathy and interest by the other side. But here not only the blue and red lines of the trenches are shown, but the blood that beat and the life that lay hid in them.

Time only strengthens my conviction that it was a good and strenuous life, and that the war, for all its destructiveness, was an incomparable schooling of the heart. The front-line soldier whose foot came down on the earth so grimly and harshly may claim this at least, that it came down cleanly. Warlike achievements are enhanced by the inherent worth of the enemy. Of all the troops who were opposed to the Germans on the great battlefields the English were not only the most formidable but the manliest and the most chivalrous. I rejoice, therefore, to have an opportunity of expressing in time of peace the sincere admiration which I have never failed to make clear during the war whenever I came across a wounded man or a prisoner belonging to the British force.

# ORAINVILLE

The train stopped at Bazancourt, a small town in Champagne, and there we got out. With unbelievable awe we listened to the slow pulsation of the machinery of the front, a tune to which long years were to accustom us. Far away the white ball of a shrapnel shell melted into the grey December sky. The breath of the war passed by us with its peculiar horror. Did we imagine that nearly every one of us would be swallowed up in the days when that dull muttering over there broke out into unceasing thunder . . . one earlier, another later?

We had left the lecture-room, class-room, and bench behind us. We had been welded by a few weeks' training into one corporate mass inspired by the enthusiasm of one thought . . . to carry forward the German ideals of '70. We had grown up in a material age, and in each one of us there was a yearning for a great experience, such as we had never known. The war had entered into us like wine. We had set out in a rain of flowers to seek the death of heroes. The war was our dream of greatness, power, and glory. It was a man's work, a duel on fields whose flowers would be stained with blood. There is no lovelier death in the world . . . anything rather than stay at home, anything to make one with the rest. . . .

Our fevered thoughts cooled down as we marched through the heavy chalk loam of Champagne. Pack and ammunition and rifle weighted on us like lead.

At last we reached the village of Orainville, the rest-place of the 73rd Fusiliers, a little spot typical of that neighbourhood, consisting of fifty cottages built of brick or flint round a park-enclosed château.

The traffic in the village street was strange to eyes accustomed to peace conditions. There were only a few uneasy and unkempt civilians to be seen. Everywhere there were soldiers in worn and torn coats, with tanned faces and thick beards, who went to and fro with long swinging strides, or lounging in small groups at the cottage doors assailed us newcomers with chaff. At one place there was a cooker smelling of bean soup and surrounded by a ration-party clattering dixies. The Wallenstein-like romance was heightened by the incipient dilapidation of the village.

After spending our first night in a huge barn, we were paraded before the adjutant, Lieutenant (as he then was) von Brixen, in the courtyard of the château, and told off to our companies; mine being the 9th.

Our first day of the war was destined to make a very distinct impression on us. We were sitting in the schoolhouse, where we were quartered, having breakfast. Suddenly there was a series of heavy explosions close by and soldiers rushed from every house and crowded to the entrance of village. We followed their example without knowing why. Again there was the peculiar whisper and fluster overhead that we had never heard, drowned in a terrific crash. I was surprised to see the men round me crouching as if bent under terrific pressure.

Immediately after, black groups appeared in the empty village street, bearing black bundles on stretchers or on joined hands. A feeling of unreality oppressed me as I stared at a figure streaming from blood whose limbs hung loose and who unceasingly gave a hoarse cry for help, as though death had him already by the throat. He was carried into a cottage with the Red Cross flag over the door. What was all this then? The war had shown its claws and torn off its pleasant mask. It was so mysterious, so impersonal. One had scarcely given a thought to the enemy carrying on his secret and malignant existence somewhere behind. The impression of something arising entirely from beyond the pale of experience was so strange that it was difficult to see the connection of things. It was like a ghost at noon.

A shell had hit the entrance of the château and had struck a mass of stones and masonry into the doorway just as the inmates, terrified by the previous shell-burst, were flocking out. There were thirteen casualties—among them the bandmaster, Gebhard, whom I knew well by sight from the Promenade Concerts at Hanover. A horse standing tied up at the steps realized the danger before the human beings, and breaking loose galloped unhurt into the courtyard.

I could tell from talking to my companions that this episode had somewhat damped their martial ardour. It had affected me too. I seldom heard the rumble of a passing lorry without mistaking it for the sound of that deadly shell.

In any case, however, it was our fate all through the war to start at any sudden and unexpected sound. Whether a train clattered by, or a book fell on the floor, or a cry rang out at night, the heart always stood still for a moment in the belief that some great and unknown danger threatened. It was a sign of living four years under the shadow of death. The effect upon the dark regions that lie beneath the consciousness was so deep that at the least interruption of the usual course Death started up with warning hand, or as he does in those clocks where he appears above the dial at every hour with sand-glass and scythe. It was a sensation over which habit could not prevail, since the instinct of self-preservation remains always the same. The notion that a soldier becomes hardier and bolder as war proceeds is mistaken. What he gains in the science and art of attacking his enemy he loses in strength of nerve. The only dam against this loss is a sense of honour so resolute that few attain to it. For this reason I consider that troops composed of boys of twenty, under experienced leadership, are the most formidable.

On the evening of the same day came the moment we had so long desired, when, heavily laden, we set out for the line. Our way led through Betricourt, whose ruins stood up fantastically in the dusk, to a lonely ranger's lodge concealed in pine woods, known as the Fasanerie. This was the battalion reserve, and the 9th Company was in reserve till that night. The officer commanding Lieutenant R. Brahms.

We reported and were detained to our platoons, and soon found ourselves surrounded by bearded, mud-caked companions, who greeted us with a certain ironical good-humour. They asked us how things were going in Hanover and whether the war was going to end soon. Then the talk fell to laconic remarks about trenches, cookers, shell-fire, and other matters of trench warfare.

After a while there was a shout to 'turn out' at the entrance of our hut-like shelter. We fell in with our sections, and at the command 'Laden und sichern' we put a clip of live cartridges into the magazine with secret joy.

Then in silence and in single file we went across country through the night, in a landscape studded with clumps of woodland. Now and then a single shot rang out, or a rocket fizzed up and after a brief and ghastly illumination left the darkness blacker than before. The dull clank of rifles and entrenching tools was varied by the warning cry, 'Look out: wire!'

Then suddenly a rattle and a crash, and a curse: 'can't you open your mouth when there's a shell-hole coming?'

The corporal takes up the tale. 'Shut up, blast you! Do you think the French have mud in their ears?' We get on quicker. The dark of the night, the glimmer of a Verey light, the slow flicker of rifle-fire, induce a tremulous, alert state of the nerves; occasionally a chance bullet sings by, cool and thin, overhead and is lost in the distance. How often since then have I gone up the line in a mood half of excitement and half of melancholy through scenes of utter desolation!

Finally we were lost to the sight in one of those trenches that wind like white serpents through the night to the front line. Once there, I woke to find myself alone and shivering. I was staring intently over the parapet at a row of firs in front of the trench, among which my fancy conjured up shadowy figures on every side, while now and then a stray bullet crashed through the branches. The only change during these almost endless hours was that an older hand took me by a long, narrow sap to a post in front of the line, and there we occupied ourselves as I had done before, in keeping a look-out. For two hours after that I was allowed to sleep the sleep of exhaustion in a bare hole in the chalk. By dawn I was white and chalky as the rest. I felt as though I had lived this mole's life for months.

The regiment's front was opposite the village of Le Gauda in the chalk hills of Champagne. On the right was the destroyed Garnet wood; then the line zig-zagged through large fields of sugar-beet, among which the red trousers of those who had fallen in previous attacks were conspicuous, and ended in low ground where touch with the 74th had to be maintained by means of night patrols. The beck flowed over the weir of a destroyed mill, surrounded by gloomy trees. It was an eerie spot to be in when the moon threw shifting shadows between rifts of cloud and when strange sounds seemed to be mingled with the murmur of the water and the whisper of the reeds.

Trench life here was as exhausting as it well could be. The day began before dawn, when every man had to be standing-to. From 10 p.m. to 6 a.m. only two men from each section might be sleeping, which worked out at two hours sleep per man, and even this, owing to being wakened earlier or having straw to fetch and one thing or another to attend to, was often illusory.

Either we were on guard in the trench or else we went out to one of the numerous posts which were connected with the front line by long saps. These posts were intended to add security to the front line, but as trench warfare developed they were found too exposed and were given up.

This endless and terribly exhausting round of night guards was endurable in fine weather and even in frost. They were a positive torture when it rained, as it usually does in January. When the wet penetrated first the ground sheet pulled over your head, then coat and tunic, then trickled, hour after hour, down your skin, there resulted a state of depression that was impervious even to the cheering sounds of the relief wading along towards you. The first light of dawn shone on exhausted chalk-smeared figures that, with chattering teeth and white faces, threw themselves down on the dirty straw of the dripping shelter. Those shelters! They were holes hacked out in the solid chalk wall of the trench and covered with a layer of boards and a few shovels of soil. When it rained they dripped the whole day after. With a certain gallows humour they were called 'dripping wells,' 'men's baths,' and so on. If more than one desired to take their rest in them they were compelled to put their legs in the trench, where they formed excellent man-traps for passers-by. Under these circumstances there was little question of sleep during the day, even if there had not been two hours on guard, cleaning the trench, fetching food, coffee, and water, and a lot else.

It may be imagined that this unaccustomed life came very hard on us, particularly as the old soldiers were quite knowing enough to take advantage of us in every manner. They brought this habit with them from life in barracks, and in this way added some bitterness to days hard enough already. There was an end to it, however, when we had once been under fire together. The common soldier could not easily swallow the fact that we were volunteers. He took it to be a sort of bumptiousness on our part. I often encountered this notion during the war.

It was not much better when the company was in reserve. Our quarters were small mud huts covered with branches of fir trees near the Fasanerie or in Hiller wood, where the ground, deep in manure, gave at least the pleasant warmth of a hot-bed. Many a time one walked in a puddle inches deep.

though up to now I had known rheumatism only by name, it was not many days before I felt it in every joint through being always wet to the skin. Here, too, the nights were not for sleeping. They were used for deepening the numerous communication trenches.

A ray of light in this scene of dreary monotony was the arrival of the cooker every evening at the corner of Hiller wood. When the lid was taken off the dixies a wonderful smell of beans-and-bacon or something else as delightful was wafted aboard. But here too there was a dark spot: desiccated vegetables, reviled by fastidious gourmets as 'wire entanglements' or 'damaged crops.'

Under January 6th I even find in my diary the following indignant observation: 'In the evening the cooker waddled up and brought a filthy mess, probably stewed up out of frozen turnips.' On the other hand, under the 14th there is the enthusiastic entry: 'Wonderful bean soup, four rations, pangs of satiety. We had an eating competition and disputed which position was the best for putting it down. I was for standing to it.'

The days of rest at Orainville were the best. They were spent in having one's sleep out, cleaning equipment, and training. The company was quartered in a huge barn which had two step-ladder stairs as the only way in. We had stoves in spite of the building being full of straw. One night I rolled into one of them, and was only awakened by the attentions of several of my pals who were making violent efforts to extinguish me. To my horror I found my uniform was badly charred behind, and in consequence I had to go about for a considerable time in a species of frock-coat.

After a short while with the regiment we had pretty well lost the illusion with which we had set out. Instead of the dangers we had hoped for, only mud and work and sleepless nights had fallen to our lot, and the conquest of these called for a heroism that was little to our taste. The continuous exhaustion, too, was in part the fault of the higher command, which had not yet grasped the spirit of modern trench warfare. In a short war of movement the officer both can and must take it out of his men without regard; but in a war that drags on, this leads to physical collapse. The immense number of posts and the continual digging were for the most part unnecessary and even harmful. Trenches are not the first thing, but the courage and freshness of the men behind them. 'Battles are won by iron hearts in wooden ships.'

Certainly in the trenches we heard a few bullets whistle, and now and then had a few shells over from the Rheims forts; but these small experiences of war were far beneath our expectations. All the same, we were often reminded of the murderous reality that lay behind these apparently aimless incidents. For example, on the 8th January a shell hit the Fasanerie and killed Lieutenant Schmidt, the adjutant of the battalion.

On the 27th January, in honour of the Kaiser, three hurrahs rang out, and along the whole length of the front 'Hail to thee conqueror's wrath' was sung to the accompaniment of the enemy's rifle-fire.

During these days I had a most unpleasant experience which nearly brought my military career to an inglorious conclusion. The company was on the left flank, and towards dawn, after a night entirely without sleep, I and another had to do double sentry-go in the low-lying ground. Owing to the cold, I had, against orders, thrown my blanket over my head and was leaning against a tree. My rifle was resting on a bush close behind me. Suddenly there was a noise behind me. Out went my hand . . . the rifle was gone. The officer on duty had slipped up behind me and got hold of it without being observed. As a summary punishment he sent me armed with a pickaxe towards the French posts, about a hundred metres away, a Red Indian idea that nearly cost me my life. For during the course of my remarkable penalty patrol, a patrol of three volunteers crept forwards through the rushes and was seen and shot at by the French. One, called Lang, was hit and never seen again. As I was standing close by, I got my share of one of those platoon salvoes then so much in favour, and the twigs of the willow beside me whistled round my ears. I clenched my teeth and stood where I was, out of pure cussedness. I have never been able to forgive this N.C.O. —who soon after was severely wounded and got his discharge—for this dirty trick.

We were all heartily pleased when we heard that we were at last to be taken out; and we celebrated our departure from Orainville by a tremendous beer-drinking in the huge barn. On the 4th February '15 we were relieved by a Saxon regiment and marched to Bazancourt.

That month, the hardest of the whole war for me, was a good schooling all the same. It made me thoroughly familiar with the whole round of trench duties and fatigues in their severest form. This experience stood me in good stead later, when without it I might as an officer have demanded the impossible of my men.

# FROM BAZANCOURT TO HATTONCHÂTEL

At Bazancourt, a dreary little town in Champagne, the company was quartered in the school, which, owing to the really surprising feeling for order shown by the regiment, very soon had the appearance of a peace-time barracks. There was an orderly sergeant to turn us out in the morning, hut fatigue and roll-call by sections at night. Every morning we marched out for a few hours' drill on the waste and untilled fields round about. After a few · days I left this busy scene of military duties and exercises. I was detailed to attend an O.T.C. course in Recouvrence.

Recouvrence was a remote little village hidden among delightful chalk hills. A certain number of the more youthful of us were sent there from the division to receive a thorough military training from a staff of officers and N.C.Os. detailed by each regiment. Those of us who came from the 73rd had good reason, in connection with this course, to be grateful to Lieutenant Hoppe, an extremely capable officer, who, unfortunately, was killed soon after.

Life in this secluded spot was a strange mixture of the rigours of military training and the freedom of a university. During the day we were licked into military shape in accordance with all the rules of the art of war. At night we gathered together with our instructors, and in quite as radical a manner emptied enormous barrels of beer furnished by the canteen at Montcornet. When in the early morning hours we streamed out from our various messes, the village street had the unusual appearance of a students' Walpurgis night. Our C.O., a captain, had, however, the very educational habit of taking in hand the duties of the day following with a redoubled energy.

Once we were actually kept at it for forty-eight hours at a stretch. The reason was this: It was our respectful custom to offer the captain a safe-conduct to his billet at the close of a carousal. One evening a godlessly tipsy fellow, a true Simplicius Academicus, who always reminded me of Magister Lankard, was entrusted with this important duty. He was soon to announce with beams of joy that instead of taking the 'old 'un' to bed he had accommodated him with a stall in a byre.

Punishment was not long delayed. We had scarcely reached our quarters in hopes of a brief repose when the alarm sounded. With curses we strapped on our equipment and ran to the place appointed. There stood the 'old 'un' waiting for us in as evil a temper as can be imagined and displaying an unusual energy.

He greeted us with the shout, 'Fire alarm! The guardroom's on fire!'

Before the eyes of the astonished inhabitants the fire-engine was trundled out of its shed and the hose screwed on, and the guardroom was then deluged with a magnificent stream of water. The 'old 'un' stood on some stone steps like a grim Jupiter Pluvius and took charge of the proceedings, urging us on from above to unstinted exertions. Sometimes his thunder broke over the head of some soldier or civilian who peculiarly aroused his anger and he gave the order for him to be instantly removed. The unfortunate was hurried with all speed behind the nearest house and so removed from his sight. When the morning dawned we still stood with sinking knees at the pump. At last we were dismissed to get ready to go on parade.

When we got to the parade-ground the 'old 'un' was there before us, brisk and spruce, and ready to devote himself with peculiar ardour to our instruction.

We treated the little episode for what it was—a cheerful interlude between two acts of war.

Our intercourse with each other was very free and easy, for we all came from the same social class. Three or four of us used to live and mess together. I still have a grateful memory of the scrambled eggs and fried potatoes for supper. On Sundays we had a rabbit or a fowl. As I was mess secretary, our landlady laid before me a number of chits she had had from requisitioning soldiers. The substance of most of them was that Fusilier So-and-So had kissed the daughter of the house and in return requisitioned twelve eggs. Unfortunately this amusing bouquet, culled from the fields of folk-humour, is too obscene to quote from.

The inhabitants were surprised that common soldiers like us all spoke French more or less fluently. Sometimes a comic situation arose from it. I was sitting one morning in the village barber's, with a friend called Clement. There were several villagers waiting, and one of them said to the barber, who was just setting to work on Clement with this razor: 'Eh, coupez la gorge avec!' at the same time drawing his hand across his throat. To his consternation Clement replied quietly: 'Quant à moi, j'aimerais mieux la garder,' displaying thereby the equanimity that well befits a soldier.

In mid-February we of the 73rd were taken aback by the news of the heavy losses our regiment had suffered near Perthes, and we regretted having spent those days away from our fellows. On the 21st March, after a brief examination, we went back to the regiment, which was at Bazancourt once more. At this date there was a parade and a farewell address by General von Emmick on the occasion of our leaving the 10th Corps. 24th March we were entrained and conveyed to the neighbourhood of Brussels, and there we were brigaded with the 76th and the 164th in the 111th Infantry Division.

Our battalion was quartered in Hérinnes (Flemish: Herne), a small town in a pleasant Flemish countryside, and here on the 29th March I spent a very happy twentieth birthday.

Though the Belgians had plenty of room in their houses, our company was, from false scruples, stuck in a great draughty barn, with the raw sea winds of that district blowing through it in those cold March nights.

It was always: 'Belgium must not be treated as the enemy's country.' That was a very natural consideration to show; but when once the military necessity of marching through it had been accepted, it was absurd to boggle over the petty consequences. It is in a war more important than may perhaps be thought that the men should sometimes have beds to sleep in. And when no beds are empty, then some must be emptied. The soldier must have the first consideration. We sometimes make ourselves ridiculous with our misplaced human kindness, and might have taken more care of our dignity.

The population, half Flemish and half Walloon, was very friendly towards us. I had many talks with the owner of an estaminet, a keen socialist and freethinker, who invited me to celebrate Easter Sunday with him, and even refused payment for what I drank. Such encounters are almost unbelievably welcome and beneficial after the rough companionship of the ranks.

Towards the end of our time there the weather was fine, and tempted us to go for walks in the delightful and well-watered country round. The scene was made the more picturesque by the many naked figures seated all along the poplar-fringed stream with their laundry on their knees, engaged in a zealous hunt for lice.

As I had so far been more or less free from this plague, I assisted a friend, Priepke, to deal with his woolen vest, which was as populous as the habit of Simplicius Simplicissimus of yore. So we wrapped it round a large stone and sank it in a stream. As our departure from Herne followed very suddenly upon this, it is likely that the garment enjoys a quiet resting-place there to this day.

On the 12th of April 1915 we entrained at Hal, and, to defeat the spies, were taken by way of the north wing of the front to the neighborhood of the battlefield of Mars-la-Tour. The company had their customary barn quarters in the village of Trouville, one of the usual squalid hamlets of Lorraine, whose flat-roofed windowless houses look like a lot of stone boxes thrown together in a heap. On account of the danger from aircraft we had to keep ourselves close in the overcrowded place. In the neighbourhood are the famous fields of Mars-la-Tours and Gravelotte. A few hundred metres from the village the road from the frontier to Gravelotte was cut and the French boundary-post lay smashed on the ground. In the evenings we often had the melancholy satisfaction of a walk over the boundary to Germany.

Our barn was so ruinous that we had to pick our way with care over what remained of the boarded floor, or else we found ourselves on the ground underneath.

One evening, as our platoon was busied, under the presidency of our esteemed corporal, Kerkhoff, in dividing out our rations on a manger, one of the huge oak beams of the timber roof came crashing down. By good fortune it caught between two cob-walls just above our heads. We got off with a fright, but our beautiful ration of meat disappeared for good beneath a shower of rubble. We had scarcely settled down again after this ominous disaster when there was a thundering knock at the door and the voice of the sergeant-major warned us to fall in. At first, as always on such occasions, there was a moment's silence. Then a regular stirabout: 'My helmet! where's my haversack? I can't get my boots on! You've got hold of my cartridges! Oh, shut up!'

Finally, however, all was ship-shape and we marched to the railway station of Chamblay, whence we were conveyed in a few minutes to Pagny-sur-Moselle. In the early morning we climbed to the heights above the Moselle and came to a halt in Prény, a romantic hill village, surmounted by the ruins of a castle. This time our barn was a stone one filled with scented mountain hay, and through its window slits we look out on the vine-clad slopes of the Moselle and the little town of Pagny in the valley, which was often shelled and bombed. Sometimes a shot hit the Moselle and flung up a great column of water.

The warm weather and the magnificent country worked on us like magic, and we went for long walks whenever we had time off. We were in such high spirits that at night we had to indulge in ragging before we could settle down to sleep. A favourite game, among others, was pouring water or coffee into the open mouths of the snorers.

On the evening of the 22nd April we left Prény, and after a march of over thirty kilometres reached the village of Hattonchâtel without a single man falling out, and this with full pack. We pitched tents in the forest on the right of the famous Grande Tranchée. Everything pointed to our being put into the fighting the following day. Field dressings, second tins of bully, and artillery flag signals were given out.

At night, in that mood of foreboding known to soldiers of every time, I sat a long while on the stump of a tree overgrown with blue anemones, before I crept over the others to my bed in the tent; and that night I had a confused dream in which a death's-head played the leading part. Priepke, to whom I told it in the morning, hoped the skull was a French one.

# LES EPARGES

The young green of the woods shown in the morning light. We went by concealed ways to the narrow gorge behind the front line. It had been given out that the 76th Regiment was attacking after twenty minutes' artillery preparation, and that we were to stand by in reserve.

Precisely at 12 noon our artillery began a violent bombardment that echoed and re-echoed through the forest gorges. It was here we understood for the first time that dreaded word, drum-fire. We sat on our knapsacks and waited in suspense. An orderly dashed up to the company commander. Hurried words. 'The three first lines are in our hands. Six guns captured.' We broke into a cheer and the spirit of the offensive woke in us.

At last came the longed-for orders and we moved off in file in the direction of the faint crackling of rifle-fire. It was war.

Beside the path in a dense plantation of firs there were dull crumps, and earth and twigs came showering down. The laughter was a trifle forced when one of us, overcome by his nerves, flung himself on the ground. Then the warning cry of death came flitting along the ranks from in the front, 'Stretcher forward!'

Soon we passed the point where we had broken through. The wounded had already been sent back. Blood-stained fragments of equipment and flesh were caught on the bushes all round . . . a strange and oppressive sight that made me think of the red-backed shrike that spits its prey on the thorns.

The Grande Tranchée was full of troops hastening forward. Wounded men implored water and cowered against the wall of the trench, prisoners carrying stretchers went panting rearwards, chargers careered madly through the fire. On every side shells churned on the soft ground. Heavy branches fell to earth. Right in our way lay a dead horse with gaping wounds and, beside it, smoking entrails. A bearded Landwehrsman leaned against a tree. 'Boys, now for it. The French are on the run.'

We were in the battle-tossed empire of the infantry. In a circle all round the break-through, the artillery fire made a clean sweep of the trees. On the tortured ground lay the dead and dying that the attack had cost us, their faces toward the enemy and their grey coats scarcely visible against the ground. A gigantic fellow whose red beard was smeared with blood stared into the sky, his fingers clutching the loose soil. Another, younger, lying in a shell-hole, stirred and turned over. The shallowness of death was already on his face. He did not seem to like our looking at him. With a listless movement he drew his cloak over his head and lay still.

From here we went on in file. Shells were screaming over all the time. Where they struck there was a flash and the soil of the clearing was whirled aloft. 'Stretcher-bearers!' We had our first casualty. A shrapnel bullet had severed Fusilier Stoller's carotid artery. Three bandages were saturated instantly, and within a few seconds he had bled to death. Near by were two guns that could not keep quiet and drew on us even heavier fire. A gunner lieutenant, who was looking for wounded, was knocked over in a column of smoke that went up at his feet. He picked himself up with marked composure and came slowly back. We were greatly impressed.

It was getting dusk when orders came to advance. We went by an endless communication trench through thick undergrowth much wrecked and torn by shell-fire. The trench was strewn with kit and equipment thrown down by the flying French. Near Les Eparges we had to dig ourselves in in rocky ground, for there were no other troops in front of us. At last I sank down into a bush and fell asleep. Often as I dozed I could see high overhead the shells of some artillery or other describe their ellipses in a train of sparks.

'Here, get up, you! We're moving forward.' I woke on grass wet with dew. As we were swept with machine-gun fire, we made haste back into our communication trench again and took possession of an abandoned French position on the outskirts of the forest. My attention was caught by a sickly smell and a bundle hanging on the wire. Jumping out of the trench in the early morning mist, I found myself in front of a huddled-up corpse, a Frenchman. The putrid flesh, like the flesh of fishes, gleamed greenish-white through the rents in the uniform. I turned away and then started back in horror: close to me a figure cowered behind a tree. It wore the shining straps and belt of the French, and high upon its back there was still the loaded pack, crowned with a round cooking utensil. Empty eye-sockets and the few wisps of hair on the black and weathered skull told me that this was no living man. Another sat with the upper part of the body clapped down over the legs as though broken through the middle. All round lay dozens of corpses, putrefied, calcined, mummified, fixed in a ghastly dance of death. The French must have carried on for months without burying their fallen comrades.

Before midday the sun broke through the mist and sent out a pleasing warmth. After I slept for a bit on the floor of the trench I walked along its deserted bays. Taken by the attack of the day before, it was heaped high with mountains of provisions, munitions, equipment, weapons, and newspapers. The dugouts resembled plundered pawnbrokers' shops. Here and there lay the bodies of those who had fallen at their posts; their rifles were still on the parapet. A trunk with head and neck shot away was clipped in among some riven woodwork. White cartilage shone out from the red and blackened flesh.

It was hard to understand. Near-by a young fellow lay on his back, his glazed eyes and his fingers fixed in their last aim. It was a weird sensation to look into those dead and questioning eyes. It gave me a shudder that all through the war I never quite lost. His pockets were turned inside out, and beside him lay his pitiful plundered purse. . . .

Although I made up my mind to omit all comments from this book,[1] I should like all the same to say a word or two about this first glimpse of horrors. It is a moment so important in the experience of war. The horrible was undoubtedly a part of that irresistible attraction that drew us into the war. A long period of law and order, such as our generation has behind it, produces a real craving for the abnormal, a craving that literature stimulates. Among other questions that occupied us was this: what does it look like when there are dead lying about? And we never for a moment dreamt that in this war the dead would be left month after month to the mercy of wind and weather, as once the bodies on the gallows were.

And now at our first glance of horror we had a feeling that is difficult to describe. Seeing and recognizing are matters, really, of habit. In the case of something quite unknown the eye alone can make nothing of it. So it was that we had to stare again and again at these things that we had never seen before, without being able to give them any meaning. It was too entirely unfamiliar. We looked at all these dead with dislocated limbs, distorted faces, and the hideous colours of decay, as though we walked in a dream through a garden full of strange plants, and we could not realize at first what we had all round us. But finally we were so accustomed to the horrible that if we came on a dead body anywhere on a fire-step or in a ditch we gave it no more passing thought and recognized it as we would a stone or a tree. . .

I strolled along the devastated trench without being troubled by enemy fire. It was the brief respite before mid-day that often on many a battlefield I learned to welcome as a breathing-space. I used this time now to have a look at everything quietly and comfortably. The enemy accoutrements, the darkness of the dugouts, the miscellaneous contents of the haversacks, everything was new and puzzling. I put French cartridges in my pockets, unbuckled a silk-soft groundsheet, and carried off a water-bottle covered with blue cloth, and after three steps threw all away again. I was induced by a fine striped shirt, lying near an officer's ransacked valise, to pull off my uniform and change my linen, and I was delighted by the fresh, clean feel on my skin. In those days no one imagined going on leave during a war or being able to have a change of clothes. We fought till we were wounded, and wore the old shirt till the acquisition of a new one allowed us to throw it away. It was the length of the war that drove us back at last to humdrum ways. Even Colonel von Oppen, who had sworn a mighty oath that there were three things he would never do during the campaign—have his beard trimmed, change his patched cloak for a new one, or take a pen in his hand—had at last to forswear himself.

Now that I was rigged out afresh, I looked for a sunny nook in the trench

---

[1] Its aim is to deal with the experience of war purely. I have attempted to deal with its psychology in other work. (*War as Inward Experience*, E. S. Mittler & Son, Berlin.)

and, sitting on a piece of timber, I opened a round tin of beef and had lunch. Then I lit a pipe and read the numerous French newspapers lying all round. Most of them, as I saw from the date, had been sent into the trenches the day before from Verdun.

Visibility was now good, and a German battery in a small wood just behind the trench began firing. It was not long before the enemy made the appropriate answer. Suddenly I was frightened out of my wits by a mighty crash behind me, and a cone of smoke rose high up in the air. Unused as I still was to the multiple din of the war, I was not able to disentangle the whistle and hum of our own guns from the rending crash of the enemy shells that fell with ever briefer pauses. And what puzzled me most of all was why it went on from all sides, as though the whizzing shells crossed each other's paths in a senseless maze above the maze of little trenches in which we were dispersed. I could see no occasion for all this activity, and it disturbed and puzzled me. I was still without experience of fighting, and saw it as a recruit. The battle seemed to me to proceed as strangely and disconnectedly as though it went on upon another planet. At the same time I had no fear. For I felt that I was not seen, and I could not believe that any one aimed at me or that I should be hit. Indeed, when I rejoined my section I surveyed our front with complete calm. It was the courage of ignorance.

Towards mid-day the artillery fire rose to a wild dance. It broke round us without pause. White, black, and yellow smoke mingled their clouds. The shells with black smoke, called 'Americans' or 'coal-boxes' by the old soldiers, exploded with a fearful detonation. In between one heard the familiar twittering of the falling fuses, like the song of canaries. It was odd that the birds in the forest did not appear to be in the least put out by this hundredfold clatter. They sat peacefully above the swaths of smoke in the shattered branches, and in the brief intervals of silence we could hear their love-calls and untroubled songs. Indeed, it seemed that they were urged on to song by the sea of noise that tossed around them.

I sat with another man on a bench fixed into the wall of the trench. Once there was a report on the boarded loophole through which we were looking, and rifle bullet passed between our heads and plunged into the soil.

We were having casualties all the time. I could not tell what went on in the other parts of the trench, but the constant call for stretchers showed that the shelling was beginning to take effect. Now and then some one hurried by with a fresh white bandage that shone out on head or neck or hand, and disappeared to the rear. According to the superstition of the trenches, there was no time to be lost in getting safely out of it with a light wound, for as it was often the forerunner of a serious one.

My comrade, a volunteer named Kohl, displayed that North German cold-bloodedness which seems peculiarly designed for such situation. He bit and squeezed at a cigar that never after all would burn, and he looked very sleepy. His composure was not disturbed when suddenly there were reports as of a thousand rifles behind us. The shell-fire had ignited the forest, and huge flames climbed crackling up the trees.

At this moment a man appeared at the corner of our fire-bay and told us to follow on the left. We did so, through clouds of smoke. It was a ration party, just got back, and hundreds of abandoned pots and pans were cooking on the parapet.

Who could eat now? A crowd of wounded with blood-soaked bandages pressed on past us, showing the state of their nerves in their white faces. Above, all along the edge of the trench, stretcher after stretcher passed along quickly to the rear. The feeling that we were in a tight corner began to take hold of us. 'Look out for my arm!' 'Look alive, man; keep touch!'

The trench ended in a wood. We stood aimlessly under giant beeches. Our company commander, a lieutenant, came up through the underground and called for the senior N.C.O. 'Swarm out and take up a line facing west. Then report to me in the dugout in the clearing.' With a curse the N.C.O. took over.

The impression made on the men by this occurrence was a standing lesson to me during the whole time I was in command myself. Later I got to know this officer, who distinguished himself on many occasions, and I learned that matters of importance had detained him. All the same, an officer should never be parted from his men in the moment of danger on any account whatever. Danger is the supreme moment of his career, his chance to show his manhood at its best. Honour and gallantry make him the master of the hour. What is more sublime than to face death at the head of a hundred men? Such a one will never find obedience fail him, for courage runs through the ranks like wine.

We deployed and, wondering what to expect, took cover in a row of flat pockets hollowed out by some predecessor or other. We were calling out to each other and joking, when we were cut short by a noise that shook us to the marrow. Twenty metres behind us clods of earth were whirled through a cloud of white smoke and rattled through the tree tops. Time after time the explosions rolled through the forest. With glazed eyes we stared at one another, and our bodies clove to the earth in utter impotence and prostration. Shell followed shell. Suffocating gases hung in the undergrowth, dense vapour wrapped the tree tops, trees and branches came crashing to the ground, loud cries rang out. We jumped up and ran wildly, hunted by lightnings and stunned rushes of air. We ran from tree to tree seeking cover and chasing round the great trunks like hunted game. A dugout into which many ran got a direct hit that sent the heavy timber sky-high.

With the N.C.O. I ran panting to a mighty beech, like a squirrel pursued with stones. Automatically, and starting back at one shell-burst after another, I ran on after him, while he turned round now and again and stared at me with wild eyes and shouted: 'What about these ones, eh? what about these?'

Suddenly there was a flash among the interlacing roots, and a blow against my left thigh threw me to the ground. I thought I had been hit by a lump of earth. Then I saw from the stream of blood that I was wounded. Later I discovered that a splinter as fine as a hair had given me a flesh wound after expending its force on my purse. The shaving cut from the thick leather was as thin as a sheet of paper.

I threw down my pack and ran to the trench we had left. From all sides the wounded converged upon it out of the shell-swept wood. The trench was frightful. It was blocked with severely wounded and dying men. One, stripped to the waist and with torn sides, leant against the trench wall. Another, from the back of whose head a triangular rent hung down, uttered piercing, agonizing cries without ceasing. . . . And still shell upon shell.

My nerve broke down utterly. Without regard for any one I ran anyhow through the throng, and at last, falling back once or twice in my haste, climbed up out of the hellish tumult of the trench so as to have free passage in the open. I tore along like a bolting horse through the thick undergrowth, across tracks and clearings, till at length I found myself in a part of the wood near the Grande Tranchée.

Close by was a dressing-station, a dugout covered with branches. Here I spent the night among a crowd of other wounded. A worn-out doctor stood in the midst of groaning men, bandaging, injecting, and giving directions in a quiet voice. I pulled the cloak of one of the dead over me and fell into a deep sleep, disturbed by strange and feverish dreams. I woke once in the middle of the night and saw the doctor still at work by the light of a lantern. A Frenchman uttered every moment a piercing yell, and near me some one grumbled irritably: 'Just like a Frenchman! Oh well, if they couldn't yell they wouldn't be happy.' Then I fell asleep again.

When I was carried out the next morning a splinter bored a hole through the canvas of the stretcher between my knees. I was taken across the Grande Tranchée, which was still heavily bombarded, to the chief dressing-station, and then moved into the church of the village of St. Maurice. Near me in the jolting ambulance lay a man with an abdominal wound who implored his comrades to shoot him with orderly's revolver.

A hospital train stood under steam in St. Maurice Station, and in two days we reached Heidelberg. As I saw the slopes above the Neckar wreathed in cherry blossom I felt a vivid pang of home-sickness. How beautiful a country, worth bleeding for and dying for!

The battle of Les Eparges was the first I was in, and it was not at all what I had expected. I had taken part in a great military operation without coming within sight of the enemy. It was later that I experienced hand-to-hand fighting, that supreme moment of warfare when the infantryman comes into the open and when the chaotic vacancy of the battlefield has its murderous and decisive interludes.

# DOUCHY AND MONCHY

My wound was healed in fourteen days. I was sent to the reserve battalion at Hanover, and reported there as a cadet. After going through a course at Doberitz and getting further promotion, I went back to the regiment in September 1915.

I left the train at St. Leger, the headquarters of the division, and marched with a detachment of recruits to Douchy, the headquarters of the regiment. On our front the autumn offensive was in full swing. Over a wide stretch of country the front line was marked by a swaying cloud of smoke. Over our heads were aeroplanes and the tac-tac-tac of their Lewis guns. Apparently we were spotted from a captive balloon, for at the entrance of the village the smoke of a bomb rose in a black cone in front of us. I turned aside and led the column into the village by another route.

Douchy, the headquarters of the 73rd, was a village of moderate size, and had not so far suffered a great deal from the war. It lies in the undulating country of Artois, and during our year and a half's fighting in this part of the front it served us as a second depôt and as a rest-place where we could recuperate after hard times in the front line. How often we heaved a sigh of relief at the sight of a lonely light gleaming on a wet night at the entrance of the village! There one had at any rate a roof over one's head and an undisturbed nook of one's own. One could sleep without having to turn out every four hours and without being pursued even in one's dreams by the constant expectation of a raid. The first day of rest was like being born anew, when after a bath one puts on clean clothes and well-brushed uniform. There were drill and games on the fields about, to loosen the joints and awaken a sense of comradeship among men who had spent the long and lonely nights on guard. From this we got fresh zest for new and arduous days. At first the companies used to march up in turn to the front every night. This exhausting double shift was later given up by order of Colonel von Oppen, who showed in this his habitual commonsense. The security of a position depends on the freshness of its defenders and their fighting spirit, not the length of the communication trenches and the depth of the firing line.

Douchy had many innocent recreations to offer us. There were numerous canteens well provided with eatables and drinks. There was a reading-room, a café, and later even a cinema in a large barn most skilfully converted. The officers had a splendidly-equipped casino and a skittle-alley in the vicarage garden. Often companies held festive evenings at which officers and men vied with each other in drinking in the good old German style.

As the civilian population still lived in the village, all the space available had to be made full use of. The gardens were partially occupied with huts and temporary dwellings of one sort and another; a large orchard in the centre of the village was used for the church parade; another was made into a pleasure garden and called the Emmich Platz. Here in huts covered with branches were the barber and the dentist. A large meadow near the church served as a burial ground. Nearly every day one company or another marched there to bury one or more of their number.

Thus in the course of a year the buildings appropriate to a garrison town overgrew the dilapidated village like a mighty parasite. The peaceful picture was scarcely recognizable. Dragoons watered their horses in the village pond, infantry training went on in the gardens, and all over the meadows soldiers lay and sunned themselves. Nothing was kept up that did not serve a military purpose and all that did was in perfect order. Hedges and fences were broken down or removed altogether to give better communications, while, on the other hand, at every corner there were huge signposts, shining and resplendent. While roofs fell in and all that was burnable went by degrees for fuel, the telephone and electric light were installed. The cellars were used as the starting-points for deep dugouts so that the occupants of the houses could have shelter during bombardments, and the spoil was heaped callously in the gardens. A political economist could have studied here a small working model of the Communist state, for in the whole village there were no boundaries and no personal possessions.

The French inhabitants were in huts on the outskirts of the village towards Monchy. They were mostly timid, pitiful figures, who had suffered bitterly from the war. Children played without a thought on the threshold of the ruinous houses, and old men went with bent heads through the busy scenes that with brutal ruthlessness made the place where they had lived their lives no longer recognizable. The young people had to present themselves every morning before Lieutenant Oberländer, the town-major, whose rule was a strict one, in order to have their tasks allotted them in the cultivation of the land within the village boundaries. We only came in contact with the natives when we took our clothes to be washed or bought eggs and butter. Intimate relations were very rare. Love had no place in this stark and devastating machinery.

There were two French boys, orphans, one eight, the other twelve years old, who became attached to the troops in the most extraordinary way. They wore nothing but field grey, spoke fluent German, and saluted all officers in the prescribed manner. They spoke of their fellow-countrymen contemptuously and called them 'Schangels' as they heard the soldiers doing. Their great desire was to go into the line with their company. They were proficient in drill and fell in on the left of the company at roll-call, and when they wished to accompany the canteen orderlies on an expedition to buy provisions at Cambrai they duly asked for leave. When the 2nd Battalion went to Quéant for a few weeks' training, one of the two, called Louis, was, by order of Colonel von Oppen, to remain behind in Douchy, so that no occasion or false reports should be given to the civil population. During the march he was nowhere to be seen, but when the battalion arrived he jumped out of one of the transport waggons, where he had hidden himself. Unfortunately, some of the more thoughtless of the men used to take them into the canteen for the amusement of teaching them to drink. Later, I believe, the elder was sent to an N.C.O. course in Germany.

Scarcely an hour by road from Douchy lay Monchy-au-Bois, the village where the two companies in reserve were quartered. This place was the occasion of bitter fighting in the autumn of 1914. At length it remained in German hands, and the fighting came to a standstill in a shallow ellipse round the ruins of the once prosperous place. The houses were now burnt and shot to bits. The waste gardens were churned up by shells and the fruit trees split and riven. The wilderness of stone had been adapted for defence by trenches, barbed wire, barricades, and concrete emplacements. The streets could all be swept with machine-gun fire from a central concrete emplacement, the Torgau Redoubt. There was another, the Altenburg Redoubt, an entrenched post on the right of the village, which concealed one platoon of the reserve company. There was a quarry out of which in times of peace limestone had been got for building, and this was an important part of the defences. It had been discovered only by chance. A company cook, whose bucket had fallen into a well of spring water, went down after it and discovered a hole that seemed to connect with a large cave. The matter was looked into, and a second entrance was broken through into a bomb-proof refuge that held a considerable body of men.

On the lonely hill on the road to Ransart there was a ruin that once had been an estaminet. It was called Bellevue because of the extensive view from there over the front. In spite of its danger it had great attractions for me. The eye could travel for miles over the ruined landscape, whose dead villages were connected by roads where no vehicle moved and no living being was to be seen. Further back were the faint outlines of Arras, the forsaken city, and further to the right gleamed the chalk-mine craters of St. Eloi. The waste and overgrown fields, with great cloud shadows flitting over them, checkered and crossed the network of trenches with yellow lines. Only here and there the smoke of a shell wavered up, as though propelled by a ghostly hand, and fluttered loose in the air; or the ball of a shrapnel hovered over the desert land like a great flock of wool, and slowly dissolved away. The face of the earth was dark and fabulous, for the war had expunged the pleasant features of the countryside and engraved there its own iron lines that in a lonely hour made the spectator shudder.

The forlornness and the profound silence, broken now and then by the deep tones of the guns, were emphasized by the sad marks of devastation. Torn packs, broken rifles, pieces of equipment, and among them, in grim contrast, a child's plaything; shell fuses, deep shell-holes, water-bottles, torn books, broken utensils, holes whose mysterious darkness suggests a cellar in which, perhaps, the bones of the unfortunate tenant have been gnawed clean by the never idle swarms of rats; a peach-tree, whose supporting wall has gone, stretching out its branches for help. The skeletons of the domestic animals still tied by their heads in their stalls, trenches cut through the deserted gardens where, smothered among weeds, are seen onions, wormwood, rhubarb, and daffodils; in the neighbouring fields stacks through whose thatch the corn is shooting; and all this traversed by a half-obliterated communication trench and scented by the odour of burning and decay. The soldiers who walks among the ruins of a place like this and thinks of those who lately lived their peaceful lives there, may well be overtaken by sad reflections.

The line, as I said above, ran in a narrow half-circle round the village, with which it was connected by a number of communication trenches. Our front was divided into two segments, Monchy South and Monchy West. These were again subdivided into the six company sectors A to F. The circular form of the position offered the English an excellent opportunity of flanking fire, and they made good use of it, inflicting heavy losses.

I was sent to the 6th Company, and went into the line a few days after my arrival, as a section leader. An unpleasant welcome awaited me, owing to English 'toffee-apples.' C sector, held by the 6th Company, was the most exposed of the whole of our front. Our company commander at the time was Lieutenant R. Brecht, who had hurried across from America at the outbreak of the war, and a better man in defence of such a position could not be found. His fighting spirit was never behindhand, and it brought him at last a glorious death.

Our life in the trenches passed very methodically. The following is a description of a normal day.

A day in the front line begins at dusk. At seven a member of my section wakes me from the afternoon sleep in which I have indulged in view of trench duty at night. I buckle on my belt, stick a Verey-light pistol in it and some bombs, and leave my more or less comfortable shelter. A first patrol of the familiar section of the trench assures me that all posts are properly manned. The password is exchanged in a low voice. Meanwhile night has fallen, and the first Verey lights have taken their silver course up the sky. Eyes stare intently along our front. A rat rustles among the jam tins thrown over the top. A second joins it with a squeak, and soon the scene is alive with flitting shadows that stream from the ruined cellars or disused dugouts of the village. Rat-hunts are a favourite diversion in the dreary round of trench duty. A piece of bread is laid as a bait and a rifle carefully sighted on it, or the explosive is taken from the duds, strewn in their holes, and ignited, till, with shrill squeaks, their singed bodies shot forth. Repulsive, nauseous creatures!

Their rustling multitudes carry with them a penetrating effluvium, and I can never help think of their secret doings among the dead in the cellars of the village.

A few cats, too, have been drawn to the trenches from the destroyed villages in search of human company. A large white tom-cat, with one forepaw shot off, was a frequent ghostly visitant of No-man's-land, and seemed to be on terms with both sides.

But I was speaking of trench duty. Such distractions are welcome; and it is easy to be talkative, if only to fill in the endless hours of darkness. That is why I, too, have stopped beside one of the men, a veteran of many scraps, or another N.C.O., and drink in with rapt interest all the little nothings he can tell me. As N.C.O. it is often my fortune in turn to be led into amiable talk with the officer on duty, who feels a bit lonely himself. He will even talk to me like a brother, and in a low and earnest voice pour out all his hopes and secrets. Nor am I behindhand, for the pressure of the hard black walls of the trench weighs on me too, and I have a longing for a little warmth and something human in all this unnatural loneliness.

The talk flags. We are tired out. Phlegmatically we stand in a fire-bay, leaning against the trench and staring at the glow of each other's cigarettes. . . .

In frost, one tramps freezing to and fro, and the hard ground rights with all the foot-beats. Very often it is raining. Then with upturned collar one stands under the penthouse entrance of a deep dugout and watches the monotonous descent of the drops. Suppose the step of a superior officer is heard approaching along the sopping trench. One leaps out, of course, and going a little further on whips suddenly round, and saluting with a crack of the heels, reports 'Sergeant on duty. All in order in the trench.' For standing in the dugout entrances is forbidden.

The thoughts go wool-gathering. One looks at the moon and thinks of snug and happy days at home, or of the great town far away behind where at this moment people are streaming from the cafés, and where the chief streets, with their busy night life, are brightly lit with arc lamps. It seems as though one must have dreamed all that ages ago.

Then something rustles in front of the trench. There is a sound of wire clinking. In a second every dream is shattered and the senses are sharpened till they hurt. You clamber on to the fire-step and let off a Verey light. Not a sound nor a sign. It must have been a partridge, or a hare.

One often hears the enemy at work on his wire. At once shot after shot is fired in the direction of the sounds, and not only because such are the orders, but because there's a certain satisfaction in it. We, too, take out wire nearly every night, and have many casualties doing it. Then we curse the beastly swine the English.

Then, perhaps, there's a whistling, whispering noise following upon a dull report. 'Trench mortar over!'

You rush for the nearest dugout steps and hold your breath. Trench-mortar bombs explode with a very different and far worse noise than shells. There's something rending about them and treacherous, and something personally malignant. They're insidious beasts, and rifle-grenades are not much better. As soon as there are flashes from a particular spot behind the enemy front, all the posts leave the fire-steps and vanish. They know exactly from long experience where the guns are that are directed upon Section C.

At last the phosphorescent figures of your watch show that two hours have gone by. So you wake your relief without delay and get back to the dugout. Perhaps the ration party has brought letters or a parcel or a newspaper. It is a quite remarkable feeling to read the news from home and all its peaceful concerns while the shadow of the flickering candle flits to and fro across the low, rough timbering overhead. After I have scraped the worst of the mud from my boots with a bit of wood and given them a finishing touch on one of the legs of the primitive table, I lie down on the plank bed and pull my blanket over my head to enjoy four hours of sleep. Outside, the shots strike the parapet in wearisome iteration. A mouse flits over my face and hands without disturbing my sleep. I am left in peace even by smaller beasts, for the dugout was thoroughly disinfected only a few days ago.

I am torn from sleep twice more to take my turn of duty. During the last spell a light streak behind us in the eastern sky heralds the new day. The contours of the trench show up more sharply, and the impression made by the dawning light is one of unspeakable desolation.

A lark soars up. I feel that its thrills underline the situation too obtrusively, and I am annoyed. Leaning on the parapet, I stare at the strip of ground in front bounded by our wire in a mood of utter disenchantment. Surely these last twenty minutes might come to an end! At last there is a rattle of the dixies as the party sent for coffee comes back along the communication trench. It is seven o'clock and the round of night guards is ended.

I go into the dugout and drink some coffee and have a wash in a Bismarck herring-tin. I am so cheered up that the wish to lie down again has deserted me. And at nine I have to allot my section its tasks and set it to work. We are regular Jacks-of-all-trades, and every day the care of the trench makes its thousand claims on us. We sink deep shafts, construct dugouts and concerted posts, get wire entanglements ready, lay out drainage schemes, revet, prop, level, heighten, chamfer, and fill in latrines. In short, out of our resources we apply ourselves to every trade. And why not? What one can't do, another can. Not long since a miner took the pick from my hand as I was at work on our platoon dugout and said: 'Keep getting it out below, sir. It'll fall down of itself from on top!'

Fancy not having known such a simple thing as that all this while! But here, planted down in the middle of the empty waste where there's the sudden and unanswerable compulsion of seeking shelter from the shot and shell and wind and weather, of carpentering beds and tables, of building hearths and stairs, a man soon learns to use hands. He sees the value of the handicrafts.

At one o'clock dinner is brought up the line in large vessels that once were milk-cans and jam-drums, from the kitchen in a cellar at Monchy. After dinner . . . a little sleep or reading while gradually the two hours' daily trench duty draws nearer. They pass a great deal more quickly than those of the night. One observes the well-known enemy position through field-glasses or periscope, and often gets a shot at a head target with the help of the latter. But caution is necessary, for the English too have sharp eyes and good glasses.

One of a post suddenly collapses in a stream of blood, shot in the head. His fellows tear the field-dressing from his tunic and bind him up.

'There's no use in doing that now, Wilhelm.'

'He's still breathing, man.'

Then the stretcher-bearers come and take him to the dressing-station. The stretcher bumps heavily against the corners of the fire-bays. Scarce gone . . . and all is as it was before. Somebody throws a shovelful of soil over the red patch and every one goes about his business. One has got callous. Only a new recruit leans, whitefaced, against the revetting of the trench. He is trying to see the hang of it all. It had been so sudden, such a terrible surprise, such a brutal and unspeakable assault. It can't be possible, can't be real. Poor fellow, there's something quite different in store for you. . . .

Often, too, it is quite jolly. Many of us take quite a sporting interest in the job. With a malicious satisfaction we observe the hits of our shells on the enemy trenches. 'There's a hit, my boy!' 'God! See it go up!' 'Poor Tommy!' They delight in shooting off rifle-grenades or sending light mortar bombs over, very much to the disgust of frailer spirits. 'Leave off that nonsense, man. We get stink enough without that.' But nevertheless these hotheads are for ever puzzling out the best possible ways of slinging over bombs with home-made catapults or of making the ground in front of the trench murderous with explosive machines. Perhaps they cut a narrow passage through the wire in front of their posts in order to entice an enemy patrol, by this bait of an easy way through, straight up to their rifles. Another time they creep out over the top and tie a bell on to the wire and this long string with which can be pulled in order to excite the English posts. Even the war is a joke to them.

Afternoon coffee time is sometimes positively cheerful. Often the N.C.O. is bidden to give one of the officers his company on these occasions. It is done with great punctiliousness. 'May I permit myself?' 'Most obedient thanks.' A delightful quality of the Prussian officer is this precision of politeness in all situations. It gives something firm and characteristic even to the youngest of them.

On the tablecloth of hessian there is even the glimmer of two china cups. Afterwards the batman puts a bottle and two glasses on the rickety table. Conversation proceeds more confidently. Strange to say, here too it is the love of one's neighbour that affords the welcome topic of conversation. A vigorous gossip of the trenches has evolved, and this is the mainstay of these afternoon visits. It might almost be a little garrison. Superiors, comrades, and those under one's command are subjected to a rigorous criticism. A new and engrossing rumour has just run through the platoon commanders' dugouts of all six companies from the right flank to the left. The observation officers who traverse the regimental front with telescope and sketchmap are not guiltless of it. Indeed, the company sector is by no means a sealed compartment. Rather it is a busy thoroughfare. Staff officers appear in the quiet morning hours and diffuse activity, very much to the annoyance of the front-line swine, who has just got down to it after the last spell of trench duty, and at the horrid cry, 'Divisional general in the trench!' hurls himself button and buckled again up the dugout steps. Besides these there are the pioneer officer and the trench-construction officer, all of whom behave as though the trenches existed only to display their special tasks. The artillery observation officer who wants to put down a trial barrage is greeted with particular coldness, for no sooner has he retreated again with his telescope and periscope than the English artillery is announced and of course the infantry meets the bill as usual. Then the officers in command of entrenching detachments roll up. They plant themselves in the platoon commander's dugout till nightfall and drink rum and smoke and play Polish lottery, and at last leave as clean a table as the brown rats. It is late when a little fellow flits like a ghost through the trench, creeps up behind the posts and shouts 'Gas attack!' in their ears, and then quietly ticks off the seconds it takes to get their masks on. It is the gas officer. Lastly, at midnight, there's a knocking on the plank door of the dugout. 'Have you dossed down already? Here . . . sign on quick for twenty knife-rests and six dugout frames.' The carrying party has come. So it is that—at least in quiet times—there's an everlasting coming and going, till at last the dwellers in the dugout are tempted to sigh, 'If only they'd shell a bit and then at least there'd be some peace.'

'May I take my leave, sir? Duty in half an hour.'

Outside, the heaped-up earth of parapet and parados gleams in the last rays of the sun and the trench lies already in deep shadow. Soon the first Verey light will go up, the night guards are mounted, and the new day of the front-line soldier has begun.

# TRENCH WARFARE DAY BY DAY

Thus it was that our days passed in a fatiguing monotony, broken only by the short spells of rest at Douchy. Yet there were many pleasant hours even in the line. I often sat at the table of my little dugout, whose rough planked walls, hung with weapons, had a look of the Wild West, and enjoyed a pleasant feeling of being comfortably tucked away, as I drank a cup of tea, read, and smoked while my batman was busy at the tiny stove and a smell of toast rose in the air. No one who has fought in the trenches has missed this mood. Outside, along the fire-bays went the stamp of heavy, regular steps; a challenge rang out in monotone when some one passed along the trench. The dulled ear scarcely detects the never-ceasing rifle-fire, or the short whack of a bullet striking, or the Verey lights that sizzle near the opening of the air-shaft. It was then I took out my notebook from my map-case and wrote down in brief the events of the day. So, as time went on, a conscientious chronicle of C sector took shape as a part of my diary, a chronicle of one tiny snippet of the long front where we were at home and where at last we knew every overgrown bit of trench, every shelter whose roof had fallen in. Around us in heaped-up mounds of earth lay the bodies of fallen comrades. On every foot's-breadth a drama had been enacted. Behind every traverse fate lay in ambush, day and night, to snatch a victim. And yet all of us felt a strong attachment to our sector and had almost grown to be a part of it. We knew it when it ran as a black band across a landscape covered with snow, when at mid-day the flowery wilderness around pervaded it with drowsy scent, or when the eerie paleness of the full ghostly moon caught in its web those dark corners where the squeaking companies of rats carried on their secret existence. On the long summer evenings we sat on its fire-steps while the balmy air carried the busy hammerings or the songs of home across to the enemy; we fell over timber and broken wire when Death drummed with his steel club on the trenches and a heavy vapour crept out from their shattered walls. Often the general wanted to give us a quieter part of the regimental front. Each time the company begged as one man to stay in sector C. I am setting down here a short selection from which the notes that I wrote down on these nights at Monchy.

7.10, 1915—Standing at dawn near my section's post on the fire-step opposite our dugout when a rifle bullet tore one of the men's caps from front to back without hurting him. Just at this time two pioneers were wounded on our wire. One shot through both legs. One shot through the ear.

During the morning the left-flank post was shot through both cheek-bones. The blood spurted in thick streams from the wound. To finish the bad luck, Lieutenant Ewald came to our sector to-day to photograph sap N, which is only 50 metres from the trench. As he turned to get down off the fire-step a shot shattered the back of his head. He died instantly. Besides this, one of the men had a slight shoulder wound.

19.10.—The sector of the middle platoon was shelled with 15-centimetre shells. One of the men was blown against the boarding of the trench. He suffered severe internal injury, and a splinter cut the artery of his arm. In the early morning mist, while repairing our wire in front of the right flank, we found a French corpse that must have been months old. In the night we had two casualties wire-carrying. Gutschmidt was shot through both hands and one thigh. Schäfer through the knee.

30.10.—Owing to heavy rain in the night the trench fell in in many places, and the soil mixing with the rain to a sticky soup turned the trench into an almost impassable swamp. The only comfort was that the English were no better off, for they could be seen busily scooping the water out of the trench. As we were on higher ground, they had the benefit of the superfluous water we pumped out as well. The collapse of the trench walls brought to light a number of those who fell in the last autumn's fighting.

2.11.—I took an entrenching party from the Altenburg Redoubt to C sector. One of them, Landstrumsman Diener, climbed on to a ledge in the side of the trench to shovel earth over the top. He was scarce up when a shot fired from the sap got him in the skull and laid him dead on the floor of the trench. He was married and had four children. His comrades lay in wait a long while behind the parapet to take vengeance. They sobbed with rage. It is remarkable how little they grasp the war as an objective thing. They seemed to regard the Englishman who fired the fatal shot as a personal enemy. I can understand it.

24.11.—A man of the machine-gun company got a bad head wound while in our sector. Half an hour later one of our company was hit in the cheek.

29.11.—Our battalion went back for fourteen days to the little town of Q. that lay in the divisional area, and was destined later to get such a sanguinary name. We went for training and to enjoy the blessings of life behind the line. While there I got my commission as lieutenant and was posted to the 2nd Company, where I was to see many cheery times, and stiff ones too.

We were invited to many a heavy drink by the town-majors of Q. and neighbouring places, and had a little glimpse into the almost boundless sway that these village potentates exercised over their subjects and the inhabitants. The King of Q., as he called himself, a captain, was greeted on his appearance at table every evening with uplifted right hands and a thundering shout, 'Long live the King!' He played the capricious monarch till dawn, and punished every breach of his etiquette and its very intricate formulations with drinks all round. We front-line fellows, in our innocence, came out of it very badly.

Next day he was to be seen after lunch, in thin disguise, proceeding through his domains in a dogcart to pay his visits on neighbouring Kings and do copious honor to Bacchus. Thus he made worthy preparations for the evening bout. He called it 'making a raid.' Once he got into a dispute with the King of J., and sent a mounted military policeman to declare war. After several engagements in the course of which two detachments of officers' grooms pelted each other with lumps of earth from small trenches furnished with wire entanglements, the King of J. unwisely regaled himself with Bavarian beer in the Q. canteen and was surprised and taken prisoner while visiting a secluded spot. He had to ransom himself with a large barrel of beer. Thus ended the battle of these mighty ones.

The inhabitants were under strict discipline. Trespasses and transgressions were speedily visited by the town-majors with fines or imprisonment. Much as I am the disciple of the logical gospel of force, I was disgusted by the painful exaggerations of it I witnessed in those days, such as the compulsion upon all inhabitants, women included, to salute officers. Such regulations are pointless, degrading, and injurious. Such was our method, however, all through the war. Punctilious over trifles, undecided in the face of the severest injuries from within.

On 11.12 I went over the top to the front line to report to Lieutenant R. Wetje, commanding the 2nd Company, which was in C. sector. It gave me a shock, as I jumped down into the trench, to see how it had altered during our fortnight's absence. It had fallen in until it was nothing but a large trough filled with mud a yard deep, in which its occupants splashed sadly about in an amphibious existence. As I sank in to my hips my thoughts recurred with sorrow to the King of Q. and his round table. We poor front-line swine! nearly all the dugouts had fallen in and the deep dugouts were flooded. For the next weeks we had to work without respite merely to get firm ground beneath our feet. For the time being I lived with Lieutenants Wetje and Boje in a dugout whose roof, in spite of a ground-sheet suspended beneath it, dripped like a watering-can. Every half-hour the batmen had to bail out the water with buckets.

One morning, when, thoroughly wet through, I went up out of the dugout into the trench, I could scarcely believe my eyes. The field of battle that hitherto had been marked by the desolation of death itself had taken on the appearance of a fair. The occupants of the trenches on both sides had been driven to take to the top, and now there was a lovely traffic and exchange going on in schnaps, cigarettes, uniform buttons, etc., in front of the wire. The crowds of khaki-coloured figures that streamed from the hitherto so deserted English trenches had a most bewildering effect.

Suddenly there was a shot that dropped one of our fellows dead in the mud. . . . Whereupon both sides disappeared like moles into their trenches. I went to the part of the trench opposite the English sap and shouted across that I wished to speak to an officer. Some of the English did in fact go back, and presently returned from their main trench with a young man who was distinguished from them, as I could see through my glasses, by a smarter cap. At first we conversed in English and then rather more fluently in French, while the men stood round listening. I put it to him that one of our men had been killed by a treacherous shot. He replied that this was the doing of the company on his flank and not of his men. 'Il y a des cochons aussi chez vous,' he remarked when some shots from the sector next to ours passed close to his head; and thereupon I made ready to take cover forthwith. We said a good deal to each other in the course of the interview in a fashion that can only be described as sportsmanlike, and would gladly at the end have made some exchange of presents in memory of the occasion.

It has always been my ideal in war to eliminate all feelings of hatred and to treat my enemy as an enemy only in battle and to honour him as a man according to his courage. It is exactly in this that I have found many kindred souls among British officers. It depends, of course, on not letting oneself be blinded by an excessive national feeling, as the case generally is between the French and the Germans. The consciousness of the importance of one's own nation ought to reside as a matter of course and unobtrusively in everybody, just as an unconditional sense of honour does in a gentleman. Without this it is impossible to give others their due.

In order to be on a clear footing again we made a solemn declaration of war within three minutes of breaking off our parley; and after 'Good evening' on his side and 'Au revoir' on mine, I had a shot, in spite of the regrets of my men, at his loophole. It was returned at once with one that nearly knocked the rifle from my hands.

This was the first opportunity I had of surveying the ground before the sap, for it was madness to show the peak of a cap at this dangerous spot. One thing I noticed was that there was the skeleton of a Frenchman just in front of our wire, whose white bones shone out from the rags of his blue uniform.

Shortly after this conference our artillery fired a few shells on the enemy trenches, whereupon, before our eyes, four stretchers were carried across the open without, to my delight, a single shot being fired from our side. From the English cap-badges we were left in no doubt after that day that we had the 'Hindustani' Leicestershires opposite us.

The weather towards Christmas became more and more dreary. We had to set up pumps in the trenches in order to make a show of keeping even with the water.

During this time of mud, too, our casualty rate rose considerably above the average. For example, I find in my diary under 12.12: 'To-day seven of our men were buried at Douchy and two more since have been shot dead'; and under 23.12: 'Mud and dirt get the upper hand. This morning at three o'clock a regular landslide came thundering down the entrance of my dugout. I had to set three men to work, and it took them all their time to bail out the water that poured like a mountain torrent into the dugout. The trench is water-logged beyond hope. We are up to our waists in ooze. It is enough to make one despair. On the right flank a dead body is coming to light, the legs only so far.

We spent Christmas Eve in the line. The men stood in the mud and sang Christmas carols that were drowned by the enemy machine-guns. On Christmas Day we lost a man in No. 3 platoon by a flanking shot through the head. Immediately after, the English attempted a friendly overture and put up a Christmas tree on their parapet. But our fellows were so embittered that they fired and knocked it over. And this in turn was answered with rifle grenades. In this miserable fashion we celebrated Christmas Day.

On the 28.12 I was the commandant of the Altenburg Redoubt. It was on this day that one of my best men, Fusilier Hohn, had an arm torn off by a shell splinter. Another, Heidotting, was badly wounded in the thigh by one of the many stray bullets that buzzed round this low-lying strong post. My trusty August Kettler, too, was hit by a shrapnel bullet on the road to Monchy, where he was going to fetch my rations—the first of my many batmen. It got him in the windpipe and stretched him out. When he had started off with the dishes I called after him, 'August, don't you stop one on the way!' 'No fear, sir.' And now I was summoned and found him lying on the ground quite close to my dugout drawing every breath with a raucous noise through the wound at the base of his neck. I had him taken back, and he died in hospital some months later. On this occasion, as on many others, what I found particularly painful was that the wounded man could not say a word and only stared with helpless eyes like a tortured beast at those who had tried to help him. It always made one feel more than usually powerless in the face of another's troubles.

The way to Monchy from the Altenburg Redoubt cost, all told, a profusion of blood. It followed the further slope of a slight depression that lay 500 metres perhaps behind our front line. The enemy, who no doubt was aware from aeroplane photographs that the track was much used, made it his business to comb it out with machine-gun fire at short intervals or to sling plenty of shrapnel at it. Although there was a trench running beside it, and though there were strict orders to use this trench, everybody made a practice of going along in the open with the usual indifference of the old soldier to the risk of a bullet. As a rule it was all right, but one or two victims were claimed daily, and this with time mounted up to a good number. Besides this, the builders of the Altenburg Redoubt had placed the latrine in the very lowest spot of the valley, where the stray bullets from every quarter of the compass appeared to forgather, so that it was often compelled to fly for the open clasping of a newspaper in one hand and one's clothing in the other. Nevertheless, this indispensable institution was left undisturbed in its perilous position, a speaking example of the general indifference to danger.

January, too, was a month of unremitting labour. Each platoon, with shovels, buckets, and pumps, first removed the mud from the immediate neighbourhood of their dugout, and then, when they had solid ground under their feet, proceeded to establish communications with the sections on either side. In Adinfer wood, where our artillery was situated, forestry detachments were employed in stripping young trees of their branches and splitting them in long sections. The walls of the trench were slopped off and entirely revetted with this material. Numerous culverts and sump pits and gullies were constructed, till by degrees the conditions of life were bearable again.

On the 28th January 1916 a man in my platoon got a body wound from a splinter of a bullet that was shattered to bits against his loophole plate. On the 30th another got a bullet in the thigh. On the 1st February, the day of our relief, the communication trenches were being heavily shelled. A shrapnel shell fell just at the feet of Fusilier Junge, my one-time cleaner of the 6th Company. It did not explode, but flared up and he had to be carried away with severe burns.

About the same time a N.C.O. of the 6th Company, whom I knew well and whose brother had been killed a few days before, was fatally injured by a 'toffee-apple' which he had picked up. He had unscrewed the fuse, and observing that the powder was smouldering he put the end of his cigarette into the opening. Of course, the 'toffee-apple' exploded and wounded him in over fifty places. It was like this we were continually suffering losses through the carelessness that comes from constantly having to do with explosives. Lieutenant Pook was an uncomfortable neighbour for this reason. He inhabited a lonely dugout in a tangle of trenches behind the left flank, and there he had shepherded together a number of enormous duds. He occupied himself with unscrewing their fuses and then examining them. I always gave this uncomfortable dwelling a wide berth whenever I had to pass by it.

On the night of 3rd February we had arrived in Douchy once more after a fatiguing spell in the line. Next morning I was sitting in my billet on the Emmichs Platz in the mood appropriate to the first day of rest, comfortably drinking coffee, when suddenly a monster of a shell, the herald of a heavy bombardment, exploded at my very door and blew the window in to the room. With three bounds I was in the cellar, whither the other occupants of the house had also betaken themselves with astonishing speed, and there we presented a lamentable picture. As the cellar was half above ground and separated from the garden only by a thin wall, we all crowded into the short, cramped neck of a shaft. My sheep-dog crept whimpering between our tightly-packed bodies with an animal's instinctive desire for the darkest corner. Far away in the distance one heard the heavy reports at regular intervals, followed within a few seconds by the whistling howl of the heavy lumps of metal hurtling through the air and ending in crash after crash as they exploded all round our little house. Each time an unpleasant rush of air came through the cellar window, clods of earth and splinters rattled on the tiled roof, and in the stalls the terrified horses snorted and reared up. The dog whimpered, and a fat bandsman, as each shell came whistling over, cried aloud as though he was going to have a tooth pulled out.

At last the weather cleared and we could emerge again into the open air. The devastated village street was as lively as a disturbed ant-heap. My quarters had a sorry appearance. Close to the cellar wall the earth was torn up in several places, fruit trees were snapped off, and in the middle of a doorway lay a long and sinister dud. the roof was riddled with holes. A big splinter had carried off the chimney. In the company orderly-room next door a few sizable splinters had pierced the walls and a large wardrobe and torn nearly all the officers' uniforms that were kept there. Their owners were very much incensed, but I myself was among those who escaped.

On the 8th February, C sector was badly shelled. Already in the early hours our own artillery landed a dud into the dugout of my right-flank section. The inmates had an unpleasant surprise when it pushed in the door and overturned the stove. A witty fellow drew a caricature in which eight men were rushing for the shattered door over the smoking stove while the dud observed them from the corner with an evil wink. Besides this, at mid-day we had three dugouts smashed in. Fortunately, only one man was wounded slightly in the knee; for every one, even the posts, had been withdrawn into the deep dugouts. On the next day Fusilier Hartmann of my platoon got a mortal wound in the side. It was from a shell from the flanking battery. On the 25th February we had a very severe loss through the death of a very fine fellow and a great favourite. Just before the relief I got word in my dugout that Karg, a volunteer, had been hit in the deep dugout near-by. I went along and found, as so often before, a sad group standing round a motionless figure. The hands on the bloodstained snow were clenched and the glazed eyes stared into the sky. One more victim of the flanking battery. Karg, when the first few came over, was in a trench and at once jumped into the shaft of the deep dugout. A large splinter from a shell that struck the wall of the trench just opposite flew into the dugout entrance and hit him in the back of the head when he thought himself in safety. He died in an instant, unlooked-for death.

The flanking battery was, indeed, very active during those days. Almost hourly it fired a single unexpected salvo and the shell splinters swept the trench. In the six days from the 3rd February to the 8th it cost three dead and three severely and three lightly wounded. Though it was at the utmost 1500 metres from us on a hillside on our left flank, it was beyond the power of our artillery to silence it. The only means we had of diminishing its effectiveness lay in increasing the number of our traverses and heightening them so that the range of a shell-burst was confined to short lengths of trench.

With the beginning of March we had the worst of the mud behind us. The weather was dry and the trench freshly revetted; and now and then we had an hour or two of leisure and comfort. I sat every evening in my dugout at my little writing-table and read, or talked when I had a visitor. We were four officers with the company commander, and we passed our days together on the best of terms.

We met for coffee in the dugout of one or the other of us every day, or sat together in the evening over a bottle or two and smoked, played cards, and comported ourselves like soldiers of fortune. Those pleasant hours in the dugout outweigh the memory of many days of blood and dirt and exhaustion. They were, too, only possible during long periods of, comparatively speaking, quiet trench warfare, during which we became completely at home with each other and fell into almost peace-time habits. Our chief pride lay in our building activities, to which the gentry further back contributed very little. We sank a shaft of thirty steps near the other deep dugout into the soft chalky ground, and connected the two by a gallery at right angles to the shaft. By this means we could go in comfort six metres underground from the one flank of our platoons to the other. My pet enterprise was a gallery sixty metres long running from my platoon headquarters to the company commander's dugout, provided on the right hand and on the left with chambers of ammunition and living-rooms. These places were of the utmost value during the subsequent fighting.

When, after morning coffee (one even got the paper pretty regularly), we met each other washed and shaved in the trench footrule in hand, we compared progress in our respective parts of it, while the talk turned on dugout frames, pattern dugouts, hours of work, and such matters. At night when I lay down on my plank bed I had always had the pleasant consciousness of having in my sphere fulfilled the expectations those at home had of me. I had given all my energies to the defence of my two hundred metres of the front line, and cared for the well-being of my sixty men.

It was only now when there was time for it that I was able to experience this feeling to the full. In the winter months we had not a thought in the trenches but of digging and 'Will this damned business never end?' It is not danger, however extreme it may be, that depresses the spirit of the men so much as over-fatigue and wretched conditions. People who have leisure can afford themselves every luxury, even that of heroic feelings. That is true for the people as a whole. Its moral worth can only reach its full height when the pressure of work is not crashing upon any section of it. On the 1st of March, as I was standing behind a ground-sheet with Landwehrsman Ikman, who was killed not long after, a shell burst straight in front of us. The splinters flew about us without a hit. When we took a closer look we found that numerous fragments of steel a length and sharpness that turned the stomach had ripped the ground-sheet. The men called these things rattles or grapeshot, because there was nothing to be heard of them but a shower of splinters that suddenly whistled round you.

On the 14th March there was a direct hit from a 15-centimetre shell in the sector on our right. It killed three men and severely wounded three more. One of them disappeared without leaving a trace. Another was burnt black. On the 18th the sentry in front of my dugout was hit by a shell splinter that tore off one cheek and the top of one ear.

On the 19th, Fusilier Schmidt II, on the left flank of my platoon, got a bad head wound. On the 23rd, Fusilier Lohmann was killed near my dugout by a shot in the head. On the same evening one of the posts reported that an enemy patrol was on our wire. I left the trench with a few men, but nothing came of it.

On the 7th of April, on the right flank of the platoon, Fusilier Kramer was wounded in the head by the splinter of a bullet. We had a great many casualties owing to the ease with which the English bullets flew into fragments on the least impact. At mid-day the neighbourhood of my dugout was plastered with heavies for hours together. My skylight was smashed for the umpteenth time, and at every detonation there was a hail of hard lumps of soil through the opening. We drank our coffee, however, unmoved.

Later we had set a duel with a harebrained Englishman who showed his head over the parapet of a trench 100 metres away at the utmost, and got a succession of bull's-eyes on our loophole. I and several others answered his fire, when a perfect shot got the edge of our embrasure and filled our eyes with dust and gave me a very slight skin wound in the neck from a splinter. Nevertheless, we did not give in, but kept bobbing up and taking a short aim and disappearing again. A moment later a bullet struck Fusilier Storch's rifle and burst, covering his face with blood from at least ten wounds. The next shot tore apiece from the edge of our embrasure. Another smashed the glass we used for observation. We had the satisfaction, however, after several shots had struck a parapet in front of his face, of seeing him disappear for the last time. Just after, I got the plate behind which this mad fellow had kept appearing time after time with three shots of K. ammunition, and sent it flying.

On the 9th of April two English fliers flew up and down just above our position. The entire trench strength rushed into the trench and opened a furious fire. I had just said to Lieutenant Sievers, who was standing beside me, 'If only the flanking battery doesn't look lively!' when the fragments of steel flew about our ears, and we jumped for the nearest dugout stairs. I advised him to come further in, when, smack! a splinter as broad as your head fell, still smoking, at his feet. Just afterwards we had a few shrapnel shells as well that burst over our heads. A man was hit by a pin's-head splinter on the shoulder, and small as it was the wound was painful. I replied with a few rifle-grenades, for it was an unwritten law of the infantry to confine themselves to the rifle. When it came to explosives, the retaliation was always at the least in the ratio of two to one. Unfortunately, the enemy was so plentifully supplied with munitions that at first it took our breath away.

After these excitements we drank a few bottles of red wine in Sievers's dugout, and I became unawares so elated that, in spite of the brilliant moonlight, I walked home over the top. Losing my direction, I soon found myself in an enormous mine-crater, and heard the English at work in their trenches close by. After I had made myself a nuisance by throwing them two bombs, I betook myself with all speed back to our trench, and on the way fell foul on one of our foot-angles consisting of four iron spikes. During this time a fairly lively activity prevailed in front of the wire, and sometimes it was not without a certain savage humour. One of our fellows on patrol was shot at because he stammered and could not get the password quickly enough. Another time one of the men, returning at midnight after a festive evening in the kitchen at Monchy, climbed out over the entanglements and opened fire on his own trench. When his ammunition was exhausted he was hauled in and soundly thrashed.

# THE OVERTURE TO THE SOMME OFFENSIVE

In mid April 1916 I was detailed to attend an officer's training course at Croisilles, a little town behind the divisional front. The course was under the personal charge of the general director of the division, Major-General Sontag. Theoretical and practical instruction was given in a whole series of military matters. The lessons in tactics on horseback with Major Jarotzky were particularly attractive. We made a number of expeditions to see the great organization that had been conjured up practically out of nothing in the back areas; and it gave us an idea, accustomed as we were to look down on all that went on behind the fighting line, of the immense amount of work that went on in rear of the fighting troops. We saw the slaughter-houses, the commissariat depôt, and the equipment for the repair of guns at Boyelles, the sawmills and pioneer park in Bourlon wood, the dairy and the pig farm and plant for turning carcasses to account at Inchy, the aviation park and bakery at Quéant. On Sundays we motored to the neighbouring towns of Cambrai, Douai, and Valenciennes, 'in order to see women for once.'

I had not been at all pleased to leave the front line and my platoon, to which I had grown more and more attached; but still I used the time to rid myself completely of war and its clamour. I had books sent me, and I read and wrote and rode and went long walks and made a collection of beetles, and in order to fight my rooted tendency to solitude I was glad to spend my evenings in the mess, where there soon grew up that cheerful, careless spirit that is characteristic of a body of Prussian officers.

It would not be right, in a book so full of bloodshed that I am afraid the ready may weary of it, to suppress a little adventure in which I played a somewhat comic part. When our battalion in the winter had been the guests of the King of Q., I had, as a newly commissioned officer, to inspect the guard for the first time. As I was leaving the place in search of a small guard posted in a railway station, I lost myself, and had to ask the way at a little cottage standing alone. The only occupant was a seventeen-year-old girl called Jeanne, whose father had died not long before. She now kept house there alone. After giving me the information I asked, she smiled and said: 'Vous êtes bien jeune. Je voudrais avoir votre avenir.' I gave her the name of Jeanne d'Arc, because of the martial spirit that inspired those words and when I was back in the trenches I often thought of the bare and lonely cottage.

One evening, at Croisilles, I suddenly had the impulse to ride over there. I had a horse saddled, and the town was soon behind me. It was an evening of May, as though designed for a romantic excursion. The clover lay in dark red billows over the meadows, whose hedges were white with may and the chestnuts were like giant candelabra standing lit up in the dusk before the villages. I rode through Bullecourt and Ecoust without ever dreaming that two years later I should be going over the top in an attack on the ruins of these very villages that now lay so peacefully with their ponds and hills behind.

At the little station where I had inspected the guard, civilians were still unloading gas-containers. I stayed watching them a while, and next the cottage gleamed out at me between its lilacs and red hawthorn, with its dark red tiles and the round lumps of moss. I knocked on the shutters, for they were already closed.

'Qui est lá?'

'Bon soir, Jeanne d'Arc.'

I was given as friendly a welcome as I could have hoped. When I tied up my horses I went in, and was invited to supper: eggs, white bread, and butter, which was most appetizingly put on a cabbage-leaf. My small hostess meanwhile displayed the ease of manner that one finds so often in France among quite simple girls.

So far there would have been no fault to find, but later, when I was leaving, a military policeman flashed a torch at me and asked for my credentials. My talk with the civilians, the care with which I had observed the unloading of the gas-drums, and the unfamiliarity of my appearance in a district where there were few soldiers billeted, had all combined to awake a suspicion of espionage. Of course, I had forgotten my paybook, and so I was haled before the King of Q., who was as usual still in conclave at the round table.

King and court alike behaved towards me with humour and discretion, and I was welcomed as one of the company. This time I saw the King in another light. The hour was late, and he discoursed of primeval tropical forests in which he had been employed for years laying a railway. He spoke well and vividly. We saw coast towns, with low white buildings gleaming out over the sea, caravans vanishing within forests aswoon with heat, blue butterflies spreading their iridescent wings, and clusters of crimson orchids blooming in festoons from trees that hung over mighty torrent-beds.

The strange figure of the King was indeed a sign that even the strictest army organization cannot so entirely mop up the personal element in life that nothing remains of man but his functions. Here was an oddity luxuriating from the grey soil of the war, and I was too little of the soldier pure and simple to be annoyed at it.

Hence too came the charm of my little adventure, to which there were other chapters to be added. Its charm lay in the contrast between its tender rural colours and the brazen background. The little pleasures that life offered borrowed an unimagined enhancement from the unceasing thunder of the guns and from the destiny whose oppression never left one's mind. the colours were more affecting. The wish to knit oneself with life in enjoyment was more urgent. For the thought crept into everybody's mind: 'Perhaps this is the last spring you will see.' This gave an indescribable intensity to every expression of life, and after such an experience one can understand the peculiar wish of Stendhal, 'La perfection de la civilization serait de combiner tous les palisirs délicats du 19me siècle avec la présence plus fréquente du danger.' Or, as Schiller expresses it in a manlier way without the taint of decadence:

'Be the summons to-morrow, yet to-day let us taste
The crest of each moment too precious to waste.'

On the 16th of June we were dismissed to our units after a brief address by the general, from which we learned that the enemy were getting ready for a big offensive on the western front, and that the left flank of it would be just opposite our part of the line.

It was clear to us after joining the regiment that something was in the air, for we were told by the others of the increasing activity of the enemy. The English had twice—without success, to be sure—attempted a raid in force against C sector. We had retaliated, after heavy preparation, by an attack of three officer patrols on the so-called trench triangle, and had taken a good number of prisoners. During my absence Lieutenant Wetje was wounded in the arm by a shrapnel bullet, but was again in command of the company soon after my return. My dugout had altered also. A direct hit had reduced it by half. The English, on the raid above mentioned, had smoked it out with bombs. The officer in command in my place succeeded in escaping by the skylight, but his batman was killed. The blood was still to be seen in large brown stains on the lining boards.

On the 20th June I was detailed to discover by listening in front of the enemy trench whether mining was going on, and at 11 o'clock I clambered through out pretty high wire entanglements with Fähnrich Wohlgemut, Lance-corporal Schmidt, and Fusilier Parthenfelder. We covered the first stretch stooping, and then crawled on close together through the long grass and weeds. Memories of school reading-books came back to me as I crept on my belly though the dewy grass and thistle stems, painfully anxious to avoid cracking the least twig, for fifty metres in front the English trenches rose as a black streak in the half-light. The bullets of a distant machine-gun fell almost perpendicularly round us; here and there a Verey light went up and threw its cold illumination on the desolate plots of ground.

Once there were two loud crackling sounds behind us. Two shadows passed along swiftly between the trenches. Just as we made ready to jump on them they vanished. Immediately after, the thunder of two bombs in the English trench told us it was two of our men who had crossed our path. We crawled on.

Suddenly the Fähnrich clutched my arm: 'On the right, quite close—gently, gently.' Directly after, I heard sundry rustlings in the grass ten metres to our right. With one of those lightning intuitions that come to one on such occasions I saw the whole situation. We had been crawling the whole time along the English wire. They had heard us and now had come out of the trench to examine the ground in front of them.

Such moments on the prowl by night are unforgettable. Eyes and ears are stretched to their utmost. The sound of the enemy's feet coming nearer through the tall grass assumes the remarkable and portentous distinctness that takes almost the entire possession of one. The breath comes in gasps and it is all you can do to suppress the noise of it. The safety-catch of your revolver goes back with a little metallic click—a sound that goes through the nerves like a knife. The teeth grate on the fuse-pin of the bomb. The fray will have to be short and murderous. You are aquiver with two violent sensations—the tense excitement of the hunter and the terror of the hunted. You are a world in yourself, and the dark and horrible atmosphere that broods over the waste land has sucked you in utterly to itself.

A succession of indistinct figures rose up close behind us. Whispering voices came to us. We turned our heads in their direction. I heard Parthenfelder, a Bavarian, bite on the blade of a dagger.

They came still a few steps nearer, but then began to work on the wire, apparently without having observed us. Without taking our eyes off them we crawled slowly back. Death, after towering up between the two parties in eager expectation, took himself off in disgust. After a time we got on to our feet and were soon safely back in the trench.

The happy issue of our excursion inspired us with the thought of taking a prisoner, and we resolved to see about it the next evening. In the afternoon, when I had just lain down to get a little rest in view of our plans for the night., I was scared out of my wits by a terrific crash close to the dugout. The Englishmen were sending 'toffee-apples' over which, in spite of the moderate report they made when fired off, were of such weight that the splinters from them smashed the stout tree-trunk posts of the revetment clean through. I clambered cursing from my *coucher* and into the trench, intending to jump down the nearest deep dugout with a shout of 'Bomb left!' as soon as I saw one of those black fellows describe his circular course through the air. We were so generously provided with trench-mortar bombs of every caliber and description during the next weeks it became second nature when going along the trench to keep one eye aloft and the other on the nearest deep dugout entrance.

That night, then, I once more prowled about between the trenches with three companions. We crawled on all-fours right up to the English wire and there took cover between scattered clumps of grass. After a while several

English appeared dragging a roll of wire. They stopped just in front of us and began cutting the roll of wire with wire-clippers and talking in whispers. We crept nearer together in order to hold a muttered consultation. 'A bomb in the middle of them and then grab him.'

'But there are four of them, man!'

'Don't talk rot!'

'Mind, mind!' My warning came too late; as I looked up, the English crept like lizards under their wire and disappeared in the trench. We now felt somewhat uneasy. The thought that they would lose no time in bringing a machine-gun into action gave me a nasty taste in the mouth. The others, too, had the same anxiety. With much rattling of weapons we retreated on our bellies. There was a great stir in the English trench, hushed voices and a lout pattering of feet to and fro. Swish—a Verey light! All round us it was light as day while we endeavoured to hide our heads in clumps of grass. Another Verey light. Painful moments. If only one could sink into the earth or be anywhere else than ten metres in front of the enemy's trench. One more, and then ping . . . ping . . . the unmistakable report of rifle-shots at short range. They've spotted us.

Without more ado we shouted to each other our intention of making a dash for it, and jumping up we raced for our own lines in a hail of bullets. After a few steps I stumbled and fell into a small and shallow shell hole, while the three others, thinking I was done for, careered past me. I flattened myself to the ground and let the bullets sweep over me through the long grass. The burning pieces of magnesium from the falling Very lights, many of which burned out close to me, were not much pleasanter. Gradually the fire slackened, and after a quart of an hour I crept from my refuge, slowly at first and then as fast as hands and knees would carry me. As the moon had set meanwhile, I lost all sense of direction, and had not the least idea where either the English or Germans were. Not a glimpse could I see of Monchy Mill on the horizon. Now and then a shot from one side or the other whistled by with a very ugly sound. At last I lay down in the grass and determined to wait for dawn. Suddenly I heard a whisper close by me. Once more I put myself in fighting trim, and then prudently uttered a few sounds that might proceed equally from an Englishman or a German, and determined to reply to the first word of English with a bomb. I was glad to find that they were my own fellows, who were just unbuckling their belts to carry in my corpse on them. We sat together for a bit in the shell-hole and rejoiced over our fortunate reunion. Then we returned to our own trench, from which we had been absent three hours.

I was out again on trench duty at five. In No. 1 platoon I found Sergeant-major H. in front of his dugout. I was surprised to see him at this early, and he told me that he was lying in wait for an enormous rat whose gnawing and scratching prevented him from sleeping. He took the opportunity of showing me his dugout, which was absurdly diminutive, and which he had christened the 'bantam's perch.'

While we were standing together there was a dull report which certainly did not betoken anything out of the way. H., who on the day before had very nearly stopped a large mortar-bomb and was consequently very nervous, went like a flash for the nearest dugout steps and, taking the first thirteen sitting, put the remainder to good use in three somersaults. I stood above in the entrance and laughed till I cried over this painful interruption of a rat hunt. The poor victim meanwhile was tenderly rubbing various parts of his body and attempting to put back a dislocated thumb. The unlucky fellow told me that he had been sitting at his supper when the mortar-bomb arrived, and not only had his food been entirely smothered in dust, but on that occasion as well he had fallen downstairs.

After his enlivening interlude I had repaired to my dugout, but I was not destined to-day, either, to have the refreshment of sleep. From early morning we were bombarded by trench-mortars with ever-lessening intervals. Towards mid-day it got too lively for me altogether. With the help of a few men I got our Lanz mortar into action and started firing on the enemy trenches. It was, I must say, but a poor return for the heavy stuff with which we were so generously favoured. We crouched on the sun-cracked ground in our little gun-pit, and sweating sent over bomb after bomb. The English were not at all put out, so I had recourse with Lieutenant Wetje to the telephone, and after mature consideration sent off the following S.O.S.: 'Helen is spitting into our trenches. Nothing but great big bits. We want potatoes all sizes.'

We had recourse to this rigmarole in case the enemy might be listening in. Very soon there came the comforting reply from Lieutenant Deichmann that the fat sergeant-major with the stiff moustache and a few of his younger brothers were coming forwards. Immediately after, the first of our two-hundredweight bombs hurtled into the enemy's trench with an incredible detonation. It was followed by a few salvos from the field artillery, and after that we had peace for the rest of the day.

At noon next day, however, the ball was opened in an even livelier fashion. At the first shot I went by my underground gallery to the second line, and from there to the communication trench where we had made our mortar emplacement. We opened fire, and for every 'toffee-apple' that came over we returned a Lanz. After we had exchanged about forty bombs it appeared that the enemy had marked us down and was aiming for us. Soon they fell to right and left of us. But we kept on firing till one came straight for us. We pulled through our trigger-line once more at the last moment and then ran for it. I had just reached the muddy trench blocked with wire when the brute exploded close behind me. The rush of air sent me flying over a bundle of barbed wire into a shell-hole full of green slime, with a shower of hard clods hurtling after me. I got up half-stunned. I was in evil plight.

Breeches and boots were ripped with barbed wire. My face and hands and uniform were plastered with mud, and one knee was bleeding from a long scratch. Somewhat put out of action, I crept back along the trenches to get a little rest.

Apart from this the enemy's fire had done no great harm. The trench was blown in here and there, a Priester mortar was smashed, and the 'bantam's perch' was disposed of by a direct hit. Its unfortunate owner had already bestowed himself in a deep dugout. Otherwise he would no doubt have seized the opportunity for a third fall downstairs.

The firing continued all afternoon without a break, and towards evening rose to the pitch of drum-fire with innumerable cylinder bombs. Our fellows called these cylinder-shaped missiles 'clothes-baskets,' and it often looked as though the sky was raining baskets. We sat in the deep dugout entrances in tense expectation, ready to receive all comers with rifle and bomb. However, after half an hour the fire slackened off again. During the night there were two more outbursts. The men on guard remained unmoved on the fire-steps. As soon as the fire ceased we made a brilliant display of light rockets, and every man hurried out of the deep dugouts to assure the enemy by a furious burst of rifle-fire that the spirit of the Hanover Fusiliers was not to be broken.

In spite of this crazy bombardment we lost only one man, Fusilier Diersman, whose skull was smashed by a mortar bomb that struck the parapet in front of him. Another man was wounded in the back.

The day following this disturbing night there were many bursts of firing to warn us of an approaching attack. The trench was shot all to bits during these days, and, owing to the broken timber of the revetment, was almost impassable. A number of dugouts were smashed in besides.

Brigade headquarters sent forward an intelligence report: 'Intercepted English telephone message: The English gave precise information of the gaps in our wire and asked for steel helmets. Whether steel helmets is a code word for trench heavies is not yet known. Be prepared!'

We decided to stand-to during the succeeding night. It was made known that everyone who did not answer with his name at the word 'Hallo' would instantly be shot. Every officer had a red light in his pistol so that the artillery could have prompt warning.

The night was even crazier than its forerunners. In particular, a concentration of fire at 2.15 a.m. beat anything that preceded it. A perfect hail of heavies fell in a circle all round my dugout. We stood in fighting order on the steps of the deep dugouts. The light of the candle-end flickered on the moist and mildewed walls. A bluish vapour streamed in at the entrances. The earth flew from the edges of the trench. Wumm! 'Damn the thing!' 'Match, somebody!' 'Be ready!' One's heart beats in one's throat, trembling fingers loosened the pins of the bombs. 'That's the last one!' 'Outside!' As we crowded out, one more with a delay action fuse went up and slung us backwards. Nevertheless, while the last of the iron fowl came dropping in, every fire-step was already manned. We opened rapid fire, and the ground in front, wreathed in swathes of smoke, was brightly lit up with light-rockets.

When the firing had ceased we had one more loss. Fusilier Nienhuser suddenly fell from the fire-step and rolled bumping down the dugout steps into the middle of a group of his fellows assembled at the bottom. When we examined him we found a small wound on the forehead and a puncture over the right nipple from which blood was flowing. It was impossible to say whether the wounds or the fall had killed him.

At the close of this night of alarms we were relieved by the 6th Company. We moved off down the communications trenches to Monchy in that peculiar brand of ill-humour that is produced on exhausted nerves and sleepless eyes by a bright morning sunshine. From there we proceeded to the reserve line, lying along the edge of Adinfer wood. A magnificent panorama of the battle of the Somme in its opening stages was spread before us. The front-line sectors were veiled in clouds of white and black smoke, and one upon another the shell-bursts towered up into the sky. Above them the brief flash of exploding shrapnel could be seen by the hundred.

When at last we were hoping for a little sleep that night, orders came to load heavy trench-mortar ammunition in Monchy, and we had to wait the whole night and to no purpose for a railway waggon that had got hung up somewhere, while the English made numerous attempts on our lives, fortunately without result, by high-angle machine-gun fire and shrapnel exploding right over our heads. I was particularly annoyed by one artist with the machine-gun who fired at such an angle that the bullets, from mere force of gravity, came straight down on us. It was no good taking cover from them behind a wall.

During this night the enemy gave me an example of the closeness of his observation. In the second line, about 2000 metres from him, a heap of white chalk was thrown up from a deep dugout that was being excavated for an ammunition dump. The English, unfortunately, were right in concluding that this heap would be removed the following night, and sent over a salvo of shrapnel, by which three men were severely wounded.

Next morning I was roused from sleep once more, with orders to take my platoon as a working party to C sector. My sections were distributed among the 6th Company, and I then returned with a few men to Adinfer wood and set them to work felling timber. On the way back to the line again I went into my dugout for half an hour's rest. All to no purpose, for I was not to have a moment's peace these days. I had scarcely pulled off my boots when I heard our own artillery start a peculiarly lively fire from the edge of the wood. At the same moment my batman, Paulicke, appeared at the top of the dugout steps and shouted down, 'Gas attack!'

I snatched up my gas-mask, pulled on my boots, buckled my belt, and, running outside, saw an immense gas-cloud hanging in heavy white swathes over Monchy, and rolling towards Point 124 in the low ground.

As most of the platoon were in the front line, and as an attack was very probable, there was only one thing to be done. I jumped over the entanglement in front of the reserve line and was soon in the middle of the gas cloud. I put on the mask, but quickly tore it off again. I had run so fast that I could not get enough air though the intake. The eye-pieces, too, were misted over in a second, so that I could see nothing. As I felt pains in the chest I tried at least to get through the cloud of gas as quickly as I could. On the edge of Monchy I had to pass through a barrage. The shells, interspersed with puff after puff of shrapnel, burst in an unbroken chain across the desolate country, which no one at the best of times ever traversed.

Artillery fire of that kind in the open country where there is freedom of movement has never, either actually or morally, the same effect as among buildings or in the trenches. In a moment I had the belt of fire behind me. But then I found myself in Monchy. A literal storm of shrapnel was breaking over it. Showers of bullets, splinters, and fuses whistled through the air, swept through the branches of the orchard trees in the garden wildernesses, and crashed against what remained of the ruined walls.

I found Sievers and Vogel, both officers of my company, sitting in a dugout in one of the gardens. They had made a blazing fire, and were bending over the flames to counteract the effects of the chlorine. I kept them company and did likewise until the bombardment slackened, and then went on to the front line by No. 6 communication trench.

As I walked along I saw numbers of small beasts lying dead on the bottom of the trench, killed by the chlorine, and I thought as I saw them 'Another barrage will come down any moment, and if you go fooling about like this you'll find yourself caught like a mouse in a trap.' Nevertheless, I went on with the utmost unconcern.

As it turned out, I was caught in a fresh and even wilder outburst just fifty metres from the company dugout. It seemed quite out of the question to pass even the short length of trench without being hit. By good luck I saw a little shelter that had been dug out in the side of the trench for despatch-riders . It was only the width of three dugout frames—not much, but always something. So there I crouched and let the storm go over me.

It seemed to me that I had chosen the hottest corner. Light and heavy 'toffee-apples,' Stokes bombs, shrapnel, 'rattles,' shells of every description, till at last I could no longer distinguish one from another as they came droning, moaning, and crashing all round me. I had to think of my good corporal in the forest of Les Eparges and his cry of horror: 'What do you think of these ones, eh?'

Now and then the ear was utterly dazed by a single, absolutely hellish crash accompanied by a sheet of flame. Then an unceasing and sharp swishing gave the impression again that hundreds of pound weights were flying after each other through the air with incredible velocity. Then came another dud, plunging with a short, heavy thump that shook the solid earth all round. Shrapnel exploded by the dozen, as prettily as crackers, scattering their little bullets in a heavy shower, with the empty cases whizzing after them. When a shell went up near-by, the soil rattled down in a torrent, and with it the jagged splinters as sharp as razors rent the air on all sides.

It is easier, nevertheless, to describe all this than to go through it, for the brain links every separate sound of whirring metal with the idea of death, and so the nerves are exposed without protection and without a pause to the sensation of the utmost menace. Thus I crouched in my little hole with my hand in front of my eyes, while all the possibilities of being hit passed through my imagination. I believe I have found a comparison that exactly conveys what I, in common with all the rest who went through the war, experienced in situation such as this. It is as if one were tied tight to a post and threatened by a fellow swinging a sledge-hammer. Now the hammer is swung back for the blow, now it whirls forward, till, just missing your skull, it sends splinters flying from the post once more. That is exactly what it feels like to be exposed to heavy shelling without cover. Fortunately for me personally, I always have the confidence at the back of my head that things will soon be better. One has the same feeling, too, at games; and though it may have no justification, it has at least the merit of reliving the nerves. And so this bombardment as well came to an end, and I was able to set out again, this time at top speed.

Every one in the front line, according to the regulations laid down for a gas attack and so often rehearsed, was busily greasing his rifle, which the gas had entirely blackened. A Fähnrich sorrowfully showed me his new sword-knot, whose brilliance had been turned to a blackish-green.

As there was no movement in the enemy, I withdrew with my platoon. In Monchy I saw a number of gas casualties sitting in front of the first-aid post. They were pressing their hands to their eyes and groaning and choking, while water ran from their eyes. Their condition was no laughing matter, for some of them died a few days later in frightful agony. We had had a gas attack of pure chlorine to go through. It has a corrosive and burning action on the lungs. I resolved from that day onwards never to go out without my mask, as I had done over and over again up to now, leaving, with incredible folly, my mask behind, and taking the case like a botanizing box with a piece of bread-and-butter inside. On the way back I went to buy something at the 2nd Battalion canteen, and there I found the wretched canteen-keeper in the midst of a heap of goods all smashed to smithereens. A shell had come through the roof and exploded among his stores and turned them into a remarkable medley of jam and tinned foods and green soap. He had promptly drawn up a statement of losses incurred, amounting to 82 marks and 58 pfennigs, with true Prussian exactitude.

In the evening my platoon, that had hitherto been a detached party in the second line, was brought forward into the village on account of the uncertain state of the front. We were given the underground quarry as our quarters. We made ourselves comfortable in its numerous recesses, and heaped up an enormous fire. .The shaft of the well served as chimney, as we could tell from the rage of certain company cooks who were nearly suffocated while drawing water. We had had a double ration of grog, and sat on lumps of chalk round the fire and sang and drank and smoked.

At midnight the salient in front of Monchy became an inferno. Dozens of alarm-bells were ringing, hundreds of rifles were firing, and green and white rockets went up without ceasing. Immediately on this our barrage came down, and a trail of fiery sparks could be seen each time a heavy trench-mortar fulminated. Through it all, wherever a human soul inspired the tumult, there rang out the long-drawn cry, 'Gas attack! Gas attack!'

A whitish wall of gas, fitfully illuminated by the light of the rockets, was moving over Monchy. As a strong smell of chlorine was noticeable in our cavern, we lit fires of straw at the entrances. The acrid smoke nearly drove us out of our refuge, and we were forced to clear the air by waving coats and ground-sheets.

Next morning we had the opportunity of marveling at the effects of a gas attack. Nearly every green thing was withered, snails and moles lay dead on every side, and any despatch-riders' horses that were in Monchy had water running from their mouths and eyes. The ammunition and the shell splinters that lay everywhere were covered with a beautiful green patina. Even Douchy, lying far to the rear, shared the effects of the gas-cloud. The civilians, who did not like it at all, assembled in front of Lieutenant-Colonel von Oppen's quarters and asked for gas-masks. They were put in lories and taken to places further in the rear.

We spent the next night in the quarry again. In the evening I got the message that we were to have coffee at 4.15, as an English deserter had declared that there was to be an attack at 5. And, in fact, I had scarcely been awakened by the return of the party sent for the coffee when the now familiar cry, 'Gas attack!' rang out. There was the sickly smell of phosgene in the air, and the drum-fire on the Monchy salient was terrific. It soon, however, died down.

A lively morning followed. Lieutenant Brecht emerged on the village street from communication trench No. 6 with a blood-stained bandage round one hand, accompanied by one of his men with fixed bayonet and an English prisoner. He was received in west headquarters and told the following story:

The English had released gas- and smoke-screens at 5, and at the same time smothered the trench with trench-mortar fire. The men as usual left their cover before the firing stopped, and we had thirty killed. Then two strong raiding parties appeared out of the smoke. One of the two had forced their way into the trench and taken off a wounded N.C.O. The other was held up on the wire. The only one of them who got through was taken prisoner by Lieutenant Brecht, who had led a planter's life in America before the war, and who seized him by the throat and shouted, 'Come here, you son of a bitch!' The sole representative was now entertained with a glass of wine. With half-frightened, half astonished eyes he looked up the village street that, deserted moments ago, was now crowded with ration-parties, stretcher-bearers, despatch-carriers, and all whom curiosity could collect. The prisoner was a tall young fellow with yellow hair and the face of a child. 'A pity,' thought I, as I looked at him, 'to have to shoot such a fellow as that.'

Soon a long train of stretchers arrived at the dressing-station. From the South sector, too, there were many casualties, for in company sector E also a strong raiding party had got into the trench. About fifty stretchers on which lay groaning men with blood-soaked bandages were set down in front of some huts of corrugated iron. Inside, the doctor, with his sleeves rolled up, was busy at his job.

A young fellow, whose blue lips on a face as white as a sheet looked very bad, was muttering, 'It's all up. . . . I shan't ever again . . . I've got . . . to . . . die.' A fat Medical Corps sergeant looked at him with pity, and to comfort him kept murmuring, 'Now now, my boy, now now!'

Although the English had prepared for this minor attack, of which the chief object was to divert some of our reserves from the front of the Somme offensive, by numerous trench-mortar bombardments and gas attacks, they succeeded in taking only one wounded man prisoner, and they left a number of dead in front of our wire. Certainly, our losses also were considerable. The regiment that morning had forty killed, including three officers.

At noon of the next day we went back at last to our beloved Douchy for a few days, and the same evening we celebrated the happy outcome of the little affair with a few well-earned bottles of wine.

On the first of July we had the sad duty of burying some of the dead in our burial-ground. Thirty-nine plain wooden coffins were lowered into the grave. The address by the Pastor Phillippi was so affecting that the men cried like children. The text was, 'You have fought a good fight,' and he began with the words, 'Gibraltar—that is your motto; and truly you have stood like a rock in a raging sea!'

The great value of ceremonial observances was made clear to me on this affecting occasion. We have often, one time and another, left ten times the number of dead on the field and yet not been so deeply touched by the loss as we were that day beside the open graves.

I learned during these days to value at their true worth the men with whom I had still three more years of fighting to go through.

You will not find a man in the whole army who can be relied upon so implicitly to do his duty simply and without fuss as the man of Lower Saxony.

When there was the need to prove, 'Here stands a man, and if need be here he falls . . .,' not one of them ever wavered. It showed great self-mastery to leave the security of the deep dugout and face the storm of fire during those days in the trenches when the trench-mortar bombs were exploding by the hundred and when the flanking battery swept us with shrapnel and when bits and splinters were hurtling all ways. In the open field there may be some simple pleasure in showing your courage, but it is another thing to clench your teeth and to go to your post alone in the night and under fire. It is just this quality of courage that I have always marveled at in those quiet, fair-haired Saxons.

On the evening of the 3rd of July we went back to the line. It was comparatively quiet, though there were still signs of there being something in the wind. The machine never ceased to throb and hammer. We often intercepted suspicious telephone conversations about gas-containers and mines addressed to an English R.E. officer in the front line. From early morning to dusk enemy aeroplanes kept our trenches under fire. The average daily bombardments were much heavier than usual. In spite of this we were relieved on the 12th July without having any unpleasant experiences, and went into reserve at Monchy.

On the evening of the 13th July our dugouts in the garden were under fire from a 24-centimetre naval gun. The heavy shells came whistling over and exploded with a really frightful noise. During the night we were awakened by lively firing and a gas attack. We sat in the dugout round the stove with our masks on. Vogel, who could not find his, ran to and fro in great distress, while some of his comrades, who bore him no love, took a malicious joy in declaring that the smell of gas was getting stronger every moment. At last I gave him my spare re-fill, and he hugged the smoking stove for an hour like an image of misery and coughed and held his nose with a piteous air and pulled away at the mouthpiece.

On the same day I had two casualties in my platoon—Hasselmann with a rifle wound in the arm, and Maschmeier with a shrapnel bullet in the neck.

No attack followed that night. Nevertheless, it was a bad business and cost the regiment twenty-five dead and many wounded. On the 15th and 17th we had two more gas attacks to go through. On the 17th we were relieved, and were twice shelled in Douchy—once while Major von Jarotzky was addressing the assembled officers in an orchard. It was irresistibly comic, in spite of the danger, to see how the company flew apart, nearly falling on their noses in their extreme haste to get through the fences and vanish like lightening wherever cover was to be found. In the garden of my billet a little girl of eight years old was killed by a shell while rummaging for rubbish in a pit.

On the 20th July we were back on the line. On the 28th I arranged with Wohlgemut and the volunteers, Bartels and Birkner, to go on patrol. We had no other object in view than to make a little tour on the other side of the wire and see what No-man's-land might bring forth; for trench life had begun by degrees to be monotonous again. In the afternoon Lieutenant Brauns of the 6th Company, who was relieving me, paid me a visit in the dugout and brought one or two bottles of good wine with him. It was half-past eleven when we broke up the meeting, and then I went into the trench, where I found my three comrades standing together in the dark corner of a traverse. After picking out a few dry bombs I climbed over the wire in the best of spirits, while Brauns shouted after me: 'Give 'em hell!'

It was not long before we had stalked the enemy wire. Close in front of it in high grass we discovered a stout and well-insulated wire. I thought the discovery might have some importance, and I told Wohlgemut to cut a piece off and take it back with him. While he was employed with a cigar-cutter in default of a better instrument, there was a clink of wire immediately in front of us, and a party of English appeared and began to work on the wire without observing us in the grass.

With the annoying experience of previous patrols in my mind I breathed an almost inaudible 'Wohlgemut, bomb in the middle of them!'

'Better leave them to get to work, sir!'

'An order's an order, Fähnrich.'

The spirit of the Prussian drill-yard did not fail to breathe its spell even in this wilderness. I heard the dry rasp of the fuse-pin as he pulled it out, and I had the doomed feelings of a man who has let himself in for a very uncertain adventure. I saw Wohlgemut lob the bomb along the ground in order to show himself as little as possible. It stopped in some weeds almost at the feet of the English, who clearly had noticed nothing. A few moments of intense expectation went by. Then a bang and a flash lit up the reeling figures. We sprang like tigers into the white cloud of smoke with the shout, 'You are prisoners!'

In less than a second all was confusion. I held my pistol against a face that shown out like a white mask in the darkness, a shadow squeezed backwards into the wire and cried out. Close to me on my left Wohlgemut fired his revolver, while the volunteer, Bartels, in the excitement of the moment blindly slung a bomb in the midst of us.

At the first shot the magazine of my revolver dropped out, and I stood shouting at an Englishman who squeezed himself in horror closer and closer against the barbed wire. Again and again I pressed the trigger, but not a shot rang out. It was a nightmare. There was now a tumult in the trench. Shouts were followed by the rattle of a Lewis gun. We jumped back. I took cover in a shell-hole and turned my revolver on a shadow behind me. This time it was lucky I could not fire, for it was Birkner behind me, though I thought he had long since got back.

After this we made a dash for our own trench, but in front of our wire the bullets came so thick that I had to jump into a crater full of water and laced over with wire. Swinging on a barbed hammock over the face of the waters, I listened with mixed feelings to the dense hail of bullets sweeping past, while bits of wire and splinters plunged into the lip of the crater. After half an hour, when the firing had died down, I worked my way over our entanglements and jumped into the trench, where a joyful welcome was ready for me. Wohlgemut and Bartels were there already, and after another half-hour Birkner turned up too. There was a general rejoicing over our lucky escape. The only regret was that a prisoner had again slipped through our fingers. When I lay down on the bed-boards in the dugout I realized that my nerves had been touched. My teeth were chattering, and, exhausted though I was, I could not sleep. Next morning I could scarcely walk. I had torn one knee on the wire, and the other had a splinter in it from the bomb Bartels had chucked at me.

These brief and sporting interludes were, all the same, a good tonic for the nerves and a relief from the monotony of trench life.

On the 11th of August a black horse was galloping to and fro behind the English lines in front of Berles-au-Bois. A Landwehrsman brought it down with three shots. The English officer from whom it had run away must have made a very sorry face at this sight. During the night the case of a rifle bullet hit Fusilier S. in the eye.

In the village, too, the casualties were more and more frequent. The walls were levelled by artillery fire, and there was less and less cover against the random bursts of machine-gun fire. We began to connect up the village with trenches and to build up walls at the most dangerous spots.

The 12th of August was the long-desired day when I got my second leave. However, I had scarcely got home and made myself comfortable when a telegram came after me: 'Return immediately. Further orders form the town-major, Cambrai.'

Three hours later I was sitting in the train. On the way to the station I met three girls in light summer dresses, with tennis-rackets in their hands, laughing as they went. it was a brilliant farewell life gave me, and one that I often thought of when I was back in the line.

On the 21st I was once more in the well-known neighbourhood. The roads, owing to the departure of the 111th Division and the arrival of the new one, were thronged with troops. The 1st Battalion lay in Ecoust-St.-Mein, which we stormed two years later. I spent the night in the attic of an empty house with eight other officers.

In the evening we sat up a long while drinking coffee that two Frenchwomen made for us in a neighbouring house. It was the strongest drink we could procure. We knew that we were on the verge this time of a battle such as the world had never seen. Soon our excited talk rose to a pitch that would have rejoiced the hearts of any freebooters, or of Frederick's

Grenadiers. A few days later there were very few of that party still alive.

# GUILLEMONT

On the 23rd August we were transported in lorries to Le Mesnil. Our spirits were excellent, though we knew we were going to be put in where the battle of the Somme was at its worst. Chaff and laughter went from lorry to lorry. We marched from Le Mesnil to dusk at Sailly-Saillisel, and here the battalion dumped packs in a large meadow and paraded in battle order.

Artillery fire of hitherto unimagined intensity rolled and thundered on our front. Thousands of twitching flashes turned the western horizon into a sea of flowers. All the while the wounded came trailing back with white dejected faces, huddled into ditches by the gun and ammunition columns that rattled past.

A man in a steel helmet reported to me as guide to conduct my platoon to the renowned Combles, where for the time we were to be in reserve. Sitting with him at the side of the road, I asked him, naturally enough, what it was like in the line. In reply I heard a monotonous tale of crouching all day in shell-holes with no one on either flank and no trenches communicating with the rear, of unceasing attacks, of dead bodies littering the ground, of maddening thirst, of wounded and dying, and of a lot besides. The face half-framed by the steel rim of the helmet was unmoved; the voice accompanied by the sound of battle droned on, and the impression they made on me was one of unearthly solemnity. One could see that the man had been through horror to the limit of despair and there had learnt to despise it. Nothing was left but supreme and superhuman indifference.

'Where you fall, there you lie. No one can help you. No one knows whether he will come back alive. They attack every day, but they can't get through. Everybody knows it is life and death.'

One can fight with such fellows. We marched on along a broad paved road that showed up in the moonlight as a white band on the dark fields. In front of us the artillery fire rose to a higher and higher pitch. *Lasciate ogni speranza!*

Soon we had the first shells on one side of the road and the other. Talk died down and at last ceased. Everyone listened—with the peculiar intentness that concentrates all thought and sensation in the ear—for the long-drawn howl of the approaching shell. Our nerves had a particularly severe test passing Frégicourt, a little hamlet near Combles cemetery, under continuous fire.

As far as we could see in the darkness, Combles was utterly shot to bits. The damage seemed to be recent, judging from the amount of timber among the ruins and the contents of the houses slung over the road. We climbed over numerous heaps of debris—rather hurriedly owing to a few shrapnel shells—and reached our quarters. They were in a large shot-riddled house. Here I established myself with three sections. The other two occupied the cellar of a ruin opposite.

At 4 a.m. we were aroused from our rest by the fragments of bed we had collected, in order to receive steel helmets. It was also the occasion of discovering a sack of coffee-beans in a corner of the cellar; whereupon there followed a great brewing of coffee.

After breakfast I went out to have a look round. Heavy artillery had turned a peaceful little billeting town into a scene of desolation in the course of a day or two. Whole houses had been flattened by single direct hits or blown up so that the interiors of rooms hung over the chaos like the scenes on a stage. A sickly scent of dead bodies rose from many of the ruins, for many civilians had been caught in the bombardment and buried beneath the wreckage of their homes. A little girl lay dead in a pool of blood on the threshold of one of the doorways.

The square in front of the ruins of a church had been particularly hard hit. Here was the entrance to the catacombs, a very ancient underground passage with recesses here and there in which were crowded the staffs of all the units engaged. It was said that the civilians had opened up the entrance with pickaxes when the bombardment began. It had been walled up and kept secret from the Germans during the whole of their occupation. The streets were reduced to narrow paths winding circuitously round and over heaps of timber and masonry. Quantities of fruit and vegetables were going to waste in the churned-up gardens.

A plentiful supply of 'iron rations' provided us with a dinner that we cooked in the kitchen, and concluded, needless to say, with strong coffee. I then settled myself in an armchair upstairs. From letters scattered about I saw that the house belonged to a brewer, Lesage. Cupboards and chests of drawers were thrown open; there was an overturned washstand, a sewing-machine, and a perambulator. The pictures and the looking-glasses on the walls were all broken. Drawers had been pulled out and emptied, and a yard deep all over the floor were underclothes, corsets, books, papers, bedroom tables, broken glass, bottles, notebooks, chair legs, coats, cloaks, lamps, curtains, window-frames, doors torn from their hinges, lace, photographs, oil-paintings, albums, broken boxes, hats, flower-pots, and torn wall-paper, all tangled up together in wild confusion.

The view through the broken windows showed the square utterly deserted, and ploughed up by the shells, which had strewn it with the branches of the limes. The artillery fire that raged around the place without ceasing deepened the gloom of this appalling picture. Now and then the gigantic crash of a 38-centimetre shell dominated the tumult; whereupon a hail of splinters swept through Combles, clattering through the branches of the trees, or striking on the walls of the few houses that were still left standing, and bringing down the slates from the roofs.

In the course of the afternoon the firing increased to such a degree that single explosions were no longer audible. There was nothing but one terrific tornado of noise. From 7 onwards the square and the houses round were shelled at intervals of half a minute with 15-centimetre shells. There were many duds among them, which all the same made the houses rock. We sat all this while in our cellar, round a table, on armchairs covered in silk, with our heads propped on our hands, and counted the seconds between the explosions. Our jests became less frequent, till at last the fool hardiest of us fell silent, and at 8 o'clock two direct hits brought down the next house.

From 9 to 10 the shelling was frantic. The earth rocked and the sky boiled like a gigantic cauldron. Hundreds of heavy batteries were concentrated on and round Combles. Innumerable shells came howling and hurtling over us. Thick smoke, ominously lit up by Verey lights, veiled everything. Heads and ears ached violently, and we could only make ourselves understood by shouting a word at a time. The power of logical thought and the force of gravity seemed alike to be suspended. One had the sense of something as unescapable and as unconditionally fated as a catastrophe of nature. A N.C.O. of No. 3 platoon went mad.

At 10 this carnival of hell gradually calmed down and passed into a steady drum-fire. It was still certainly impossible to distinguish one shell from another. At 11 orders came down to parade in the square. There we joined the two other platoons preparatory to marching into the line. There was a fourth platoon under Lieutenant Sievers detailed to carry rations forward. They surrounded us while we hastily got together on this risky spot, and loaded us with things to eat, of which in those days there were still plentiful supplies. Sievers pressed a pan full of butter on me, and shaking my hand at parting wished me luck.

Then we moved off in single file. Every man had the strictest orders to follow closely on the man in front. We had scarcely got out of the place before the guide found he had missed the way. We were compelled to turn back under heavy shrapnel fire. Next we were following, mostly at the double, a white band laid down over the open ground to give the direction. It was shot into bits. Often we had to come to a halt at the worst moment, when our guide lost his way. To lie down was forbidden, in case we lost touch.

In spite of this, Nos. 1 and 3 platoons suddenly vanished. On again! We got to a sunken road, much shelled, where the sections stowed themselves. 'Lie down' was the order. A nauseous and oppressive scent warned us that this road had claimed many a victim. After a run that threatened death at every step we reached a second sunken road in which battle headquarters were concealed. Then we went the wrong way and had to turn back, nerve-racked and crowding on each other. Five metres, at the utmost, from Vogel and myself a medium-heavy shell struck the rear bank of the road with a dull crash and shot a volley of great clods on us, while its dead fragments flew in a shower over our backs. At last the guide found the way again. He had come upon a surprising landmark—a group of dead bodies.

On and on! Some of the men collapsed as they ran, for we were compelled to force the last ounce from their exhausted bodies. Wounded men called to us on left and right from the shell-holes and were disregarded. On and on, with our eyes fixed on the man in front, along a knee-deep trench formed of linked up shell-holes of enormous size, where the dead were almost touching. Our feet found little purchase against their soft and yielding bodies. Even the wounded who fell by the way shared the same fate and were trodden beneath the boots of those who still hurried on.

And always this sickly smell. Even my orderly, little Schmidt, my companion in many a dangerous patrol, began to reel. I snatched the rifle from his hand, though even at such a moment his politeness made him resist me.

At last we reached the front line. It was held by men cowering close in the shell-holes, and their dead voices trembled with joy when they heard that we were the relief. A Bavarian sergeant-major briefly handed over the sector and the Verey-light pistol.

My platoon front formed the right wing of the position held by the regiment. It consisted of a shallow sunken road which had been pounded by shells. It was a few hundred metres left of Guillemont and a rather shorter distance right of Bois-de-Trônes. We were parted from the troops on our right, the 76th Regiment of Infantry, by a space about 500 metres wide. This space was shelled so violently that no troops could maintain themselves there.

The Bavarian sergeant-major had vanished of a sudden and I stood alone, the Verey-light pistol in my hand, in the midst of an uncanny sea of shell-holes over which lay a white mist whose swathes gave it an even more oppressive and mysterious appearance. A persistent, unpleasant smell came from behind. I was left in no doubt that it came from a gigantic corpse far gone in decay.

As I had no idea how far off the enemy were, I warned my men to be ready for the worst. We all remained on guard. I spent the night with my batman and two orderlies in a hole perhaps one yard square and one yard deep.

When day dawned we were astonished to see, by degrees, what a sight surrounded us.

The sunken road now appeared as nothing but an enormous sea of shell-holes filled with pieces of uniform, weapons, and dead bodies. The ground all round, as far as the eye could see, was ploughed by shells. You could search in vain for one wretched blade of grass. This churned-up battlefield was ghastly. Among the living lay the dead. One company after another had been shoved into the drum-fire and steadily annihilated. The corpses were covered with masses of soil turned up by the shells, and the next company advanced in the place of the fallen.

The sunken road and the ground behind was full of German dead; the ground in front of English. Arms, legs, and heads stuck out stark above the lips of the craters. In front of our miserable defences there were torn-off limbs and corpses over many of which cloaks and ground-sheets had been thrown to hide the fixed stare of their distorted features. In spite of the heat no one thought for a moment of covering them with soil.

The village of Guillemont was distinguished from the landscape around it only because the shell-holes there were of a whiter colour by reason of the houses which had been ground to powder. Guillemont railway station lay in front of us. It was smashed to bits like a child's plaything. Delville wood, reduced to matchwood, was further behind.

Day had scarcely dawned when an English flying-man descended on us in a steep spin and circled round incessantly like a bird of prey, while we made for our holes and cowered there. Nevertheless, the observer's sharp eyes must have spied us out, for a siren sounded its deep, long-drawn notes above us at short intervals. After a little while it appeared that a battery had received the signal. One heavy shell after another came at us on a flat trajectory with incredible fury. We crouched in our refuges and could do nothing. Now and then we lit a cigar and threw it away again. Every moment we expected a rush of earth to bury us. The sleeve of Schmidt's coat was torn by a big splinter.

At the third shot the occupant of the next hole to mine was buried by a terrific explosion. We dug him out instantly, but the weight of earth had killed him. His face had fallen in and looked like a death's-head. It was volunteer Simon. Tribulation had made him wise. Whenever the course of the day, when the airmen were about, any one stirred from his cover, Simon was heard scolding and his warning fist appeared from behind the ground-sheet that curtained his earth.

At three in the afternoon the men came in from the left flank and said they could stick it no longer as their shelters were shot to bits. It costs me all my callousness to get them back to their posts.

Just before ten at night the left flank of the regimental front was heavily shelled, and after twenty minutes we came in for it too. In a brief space we were completely covered in dust and smoke, and yet most of the hits were just in front or just behind. While this hurricane was raging I went along my platoon front. The men were standing, rifle in hand, as though carved in stone, their eyes fixed on the ground in front of them. Now and then by the light of a rocket I saw the gleam of helmet after helmet, bayonet after bayonet, and I was filled with pride at commanding this handful of men that might very likely be pounded into the earth but could not be conquered. It is in such moments that the human spirit triumphs over the mightiest demonstrations of material force. The fragile body, steeled by the will, stands up to the most terrific punishment.

Sergeant-major H., the unfortunate rat-catcher of Monchy, who was with the platoon on our left, intended to fire a white Verey light. By mistake he fired a red one, and this signal was taken up on all sides. At once our barrage came down to a tune which delighted us. One shell after another went howling over our heads and crashed into sparks and splinters over the ground in front of us. A mixture of dust, suffocating gasses, and vaporous exhalations of corpses flung high in the air was blown back on us from the shell-holes. After this orgy of destruction, the fire returned to its customary level and stayed there all night and the next day. One man in the moment of agitation had released the whole mighty machinery of war.

H. remained what he was, an unlucky fellow. That same night he shot a Verey light into the leg of his boot while loading the pistol, and had to be carried back severely burnt. Next day it rained hard, and we were not sorry. With the laying of the dust the parched feeling was relieved and the great clusters of blue-bottles which the sun had brought out were driven away. I sat nearly all day in front of my earth on the ground, smoking, and eating, too, with appetite, in spite of my surroundings.

The next morning, Fusilier Knicke of my platoon got a bullet from somewhere through the chest. It hit the spine too and paralyzed his legs. When I went to see him he was lying in one of the shelter-holes quite resigned. In the evening when he was being carried back he had a leg broken on one of the many occasions when his bearers had to take cover the shell-fire. He died at the dressing station.

At mid-day a man of my platoon got me to have a shot at a single Englishman in Guillemont railway station. When I looked I saw hundreds of English hurrying forward along a shallow communication trench. They were not particularly upset by the rifle-fire we could bring to bear on them. This sight showed the unequal terms on which we fought, for if we had ventured on anything like it our men would have been shot to pieces in a few minutes. While on our side not a captive balloon was to be seen, on the English side there were thirty at once over one spot, observing every movement with argus eyes and at once directing a hail of iron upon it.

In the evening a big shell-splinter came hurtling for my stomach, but fortunately it was pretty well spent and fell to the ground after striking the buckle of my belt.

Two members of an English ration-party who had lost their way appeared at dusk on No. 1 platoon front. Both were shot down at point-blank range. One of them fell half into the sunken road, while his legs remained on the top of the ditch. None of the men would take prisoners, for how could we get them through the barrage? It was bad enough on our own men without prisoners to see to.

Towards one in the morning I was roused from a confused sleep by

Schmidt. I jumped up nervously and seized my rifle. It was our relief. We handed over what there was to hand over, and departed with all speed from this corner of hell.

We had scarcely reached the shallow communication trench when the first group of shrapnel burst among us. The man in front of me reeled from a wound in the wrist from which the blood spurted. He wanted to fall out and lie down. I caught him by the arm and got him to his feet in spite of his dazed condition, and did not let him go till I handed him over in the dressing station near battle headquarters.

It was hot work in both of the sunken roads, and we got quite out of breath. The tightest corner of all was when we found ourselves in a hollow where shrapnel and light shells were coming over all the time . . . Brrruch! Brrruch! the rain of iron crashed round us, scattering a shower of sparks in the darkness. Whoee! Another volley! We stopped, breathless, for I knew a fraction of a second in advance, from the sharpening intensity of sound, that the descending curve of the shell would end just where I stood. Immediately after there was a heavy crash at my very feet and the soft earth was flung high. This one of all others was a dud.

A better opportunity could not be wished for making the influence of an officer tell. Everywhere relieved and reliefs were hurrying through the shells and the darkness, some of them utterly lost and dazed with excitement and exhaustion. Everywhere voices rang out, in command, or in monotonous supplication from the shell-holes where the wounded were left to their fate. As we rushed by, I gave information to those who had lost their way, pulled men out of shell-holes, threatened to shoot any who wanted to fall out, kept shouting my name to keep my men together, and at last, as though by a miracle, I got my platoon back to Combles.

From Combles we still had to march beyond Sailly and the Government farm to the forest of Hennois, where we were to bivouac; and now our exhausted condition made itself felt in earnest. We shuffled bitterly along the road with hanging heads. Motor cars and ammunition columns crowded us to the ditch. In a kind of nervous distemper I was convinced that the transport rattling by pushed us to one side so roughly only out of spite, and more than once I surprised myself with my finger on the trigger of my revolver.

When our march was done we still had tents to pitch before we could throw ourselves down on the hard ground. During our time under canvas in this forest bivouac there were heavy downfalls of rain. The straw in the tents began to rot, and several of the men went sick. We five company officers were little put out by the dampness. Every evening we sat on our kit-bags under canvas, behind a battery of bottles.

We went back to Combles after three days, where I occupied, with my platoon, four smallish cellars. The first morning it was comparatively quiet, so I took a little walk through the devastated gardens and plundered an espalier of some delicious peaches. On my wanderings I got into a house surrounded by tall hedges, where a lover of beautiful old things must have lived. On the walls of the rooms there was a collection of painted plates, such as they love in northern France, holy-water basins, copperplate engravings, and Nativities carved in wood. There were stores of old china, and lovely old leather bindings were scattered about the floor, a fine old *Don Quixote* among them. It was a pity to leave all these treasures to destruction.

When I got back I found that the men had marauded the garden on their own account, and had now made a stew of bully and vegetables, in which there were potatoes, beans, carrots, artichokes, and many kinds of green vegetables. While we were eating, a shell hit the house, and three flew close by. But we paid little attention, for the surfeit of such sensations had blunted us. The house must have seen some casualties already, for a newly-carved cross stood on a heap of debris in the middle room, with a list of names carved in the wood. At noon on the next day I went to the house of the collector of china, and got a volume of the illustrated *Petit Journal*. It is to be found in nearly every French household, and it abounds in villainous bad taste. I then established myself in a room that still held together, lit a small fire of broken furniture, and began to read. I often had to shake my head, for I had stumbled on the numbers printed while the Fashoda affair was on. At about seven I turned the last page and went into a little room at the top of the cellar steps, where the men were cooking at a little fireplace.

I had scarcely joined them when there was a loud report in front of the door of the house, and at the same moment I felt a violent blow on my left calf. Shouting out that I was hit, I jumped down the cellar steps with my pipe still in my mouth.

A light was lit in a moment and the matter looked into. There was a ragged hole in my putties, from which blood ran on to the ground. On the other side there was the round swelling of a shrapnel bullet under the skin. The men bound me up and took me under fire to the catacombs, where our surgeon-major-general took me in hand. Lieutenant Wetje, who happened to be passing by, held my head while the bullet was cut out with knife and scissors. The surgeon congratulated me, for the bullet had passed between the shin and the fibula without any injury to the bone. 'Habent sua fata libelli et balli,' remarked the old corps student with a grunt, as he handed me over to an orderly to be dressed.

To my great joy many of my men came to say good-bye to me while I lay on a stretcher in a recess of the catacombs waiting for dusk. My honoured colonel, von Oppen, too, paid me a visit.

When evening came I was carried to the outskirts of town and put on a Red Cross waggon. The driver, without paying any heed to the cries of the occupants, went at full speed over the paved road, for it was being shelled, and neither shell-holes nor other obstructions could stop him. Finally we were taken on by motor to the village of Fins, and laid in the church, which was already crowded with wounded. A nurse told me that over 30,000 wounded had passed through Fins in the last few days. In the face of such figures I could not think much of the wound in my leg. From there I got to St. Quentin, whose windows shook in the incessant thunder of battle, and thence again in a hospital train to Gera, where I received the best possible attention in the garrison hospital.

I heard the subsequent fate of my company from my friends in the other battalions who were wounded after I was. It was put back into the line on the day after I got my wound, and suffered severe losses marching up and also during ten hours' drum-fire. It was then attacked from all sides owing to the large gaps in the line. Little Schmidt, Fähnrich Wohlgemut, Lieutenants Vogel and Sievers—in fact, nearly the whole company—had died fighting to the last. A few survivors only, Lieutenant Wetje among them, were taken prisoners. Not one man got back to Combles to tell the tale of this heroic fight that was fought to the finish with such bitterness. Even the English army command made honourable mention of the handful of men who held out to the last near Guillemont.

I was no doubt glad of the chance shot that withdrew me as if by a miracle from certain death on the very eve of the engagement. At the same time, strange as it may sound, I would willingly have shared the fate of my comrades and stood with them shoulder to shoulder while the iron dice of war rolled over us. Instead of this, I kept the unquenchable fame of these men as my reminder, in the worst moments of the sanguinary conflicts that were yet in store, that I must show myself always worthy to have been their comrade. . . .

It was the days at Guillemont that first made me aware of the overwhelming effects of the war of material. We had to adapt ourselves to an entirely new phase of the war. The communications between the troops and the staff, between the artillery and the liaison officers, were utterly crippled by the terrific fire. Despatch-carriers failed to get through the hail of metal, and telephone wires were no sooner laid than they were shot into pieces. Even light-signaling was put out of action by the clouds of smoke and dust that hung over the front of battle. There was a zone of a kilometre behind the front line where explosives held absolute sway.

Even the regimental staff only knew exactly where we had been and how the line ran when we came back after three days and told them. Under such circumstances accuracy of artillery fire was out of the question. We were also entirely in the dark about the English line, though often, without our knowing it, it was only a few metres from us. Sometimes a Tommy, feeling his way from one shell-hole to another like an ant along a track in the sand, landed in one that we occupied, and *vice versa* for our front line consisted merely of isolated and unconnected bits that were easily mistaken.

Once seen, the landscape is an unforgettable one. In this neighbourhood of villages, meadows, woods, and fields there was literally not a bush or a tiniest blade of grass to be seen. Every hand's-breadth of ground had been churned up again and again; tress had been uprooted, smashed, and ground to touch-wood, the houses blown to bits and turned to dust; hills had been levelled and the arable land made a desert.

And yet the strangest thing of all was not the horror of the landscape in itself, but the fact that these scenes, such as the world had never known, were fashioned by men who intended them to be a decisive end to the war. Thus all the frightfulness that the mind of man could devise was brought into the field; and there, where lately there had been the idyllic picture of rural peace, there was as faithful a picture of the soul of scientific war. In earlier wars, certainly, towns and villages had been burned, but what was that compared with this sea of craters dug out by the machines? For even in this fantastic desert there was the sameness of the machine-made article. A shell-hole strewn with bully-tins, broken weapons, fragments of uniform, and dud shells, with one or two bodies on its edge . . . this was the never-changing scene that surrounded each one of all these hundreds of thousands of men. And it seemed that man, on this landscape he himself had created, became different, more mysterious and hardy and callous than in any previous battle. The spirit and tempo of the fighting altered, and after the battle of the Somme the war had its own peculiar impress that distinguished it from all other wars. After this battle the German soldier wore the steel helmet, and in his features there were chiseled the lines of any energy stretched to the utmost pitch, lines that future generations will perhaps find as fascinating and imposing as those of many heads of classical or Renaissance times.

For I cannot too often repeat, a battle was no longer an episode that spent itself in blood and fire; it was a condition of things that dug itself in remorselessly week after week and month after month. What was a man's life in this wilderness whose vapour was laden with the stench of thousands upon thousands of decaying bodies? Death lay in ambush for each one in every shell-hole, merciless, and making one merciless in turn. Chivalry here took a final farewell. It had to yield to the heightened intensity of war, just as all fine and personal feeling has to yield when machinery get the upper hand. The Europe of to-day appeared here for the first time on the field of battle. . . .

The terrible losses, out of all proportion to the breadth of front attacked, were principally due to the old Prussian obstinacy with which the tactics of the line were pursued to their logical conclusion.

One battalion after another was crowded up into the front line already over-manned, and in a few hours pounded to bits.

It was a long while before the folly of contesting worthless strips of ground was recognized. It was finally given up and the principle of a mobile defence adopted. The last development of this was the elastic distribution of the defence in zones.

Thus it was that there were never again such bitterly-contested engagement as those that for weeks together were fought out round shot-shell woods or undecipherable ruins. The names of the tiniest Picardy hamlets are memorials of heroic battles to which the history of the world can find no parallel. There it was that the dust first drank the blood of our trained and disciplined youth. Those fine qualities which had raised the German race to greatness leapt up once more in dazzling flame and then slowly went out in a sea of mud and blood.

# AT ST. PIERRE VAAST

After fourteen days in hospital and as long on leave I went back to the regiment, which was now in the line near Deux Nœuds, quite close to the well-known Grande Tranchée. After my arrival it remained two days there, and the same time in the old mountain town of Hattonchâtel. Then we entrained at Mars-la-Tour for the Somme region once more.

We detrained at Bohain again and went into quarters at the village of Brancourt, near by. This was a neighbourhood we often touched upon in later days. It was agricultural, and yet there was a loom in nearly every house. The inhabitants did not appeal to me. They were dirty and of very low moral development. I was billeted on a cottage where lived a man and his wife and their daughter. I must own that in return for my money they made me most excellent dishes of eggs. The daughter told me over the first cup of coffee that she was going 'to drink a good cup of coffee with Poincaré after his return,' by which she meant, give him a piece of her mind. I have never heard any one so fluent in abuse as this *filia hospitalis*, particularly on the topic of a neighbour whom she accused of having lived in a certain street of St. Quentin. 'Ah cette p'lure, cette pomme de terre pourrie, jetée sur un fumier. C'est la crème de la crème,' she spluttered while she raged round the room stretching out her hands like claws in the vain search for an object on which to vent her wrath.

In the morning, when this rose of Brancourt was busied making butter or some other domestic matter, she looked unbelievably uninviting. Yet in the afternoon, when it came to parading the village street with pride or visiting her friends, the ugly grub had turned into the splendid butterfly. I always observed with some mistrust a large box of rice-powder that never left the table, for it seemed to me to be a complete substitute for soap and water.

One day the father begged me to forward an indictment to the town-major complaining of a neighbour who, not content with taking him by the throat and giving him a good beating, had shouted 'Demande pardon!' while threatening him with death.

Little observations of this kind gave me the comforting assurance that national pride, even in France, is not a quality of the masses. Two years later, when we returned to our native land after honourable and exacting warfare, the knowledge of this helped me to get over the remarkable reception that some of our own people gave us. 'Il y a des cochons partout!' as the English officer had justly remarked to me in front of the trenches at Monchy.

The 2nd Company was now under command of Lieutenant Boje. We spent our days here in the happy atmosphere of good fellowship. I must own that we often drank heavily until, indeed, we treated the whole world as no more than a laughable phantom that circled round our table. There were usually uproarious sounds from the room occupied by our batmen. Those who have never known the brief spells that separate one murderous battle from another may hold up their hands at us if they please. In any case we were glad to indulge ourselves and our men with every hour of debauch that life would yield while we were still within its circle.

I shall not be taken for a dipsomaniac, though I mention drink so often. I have never flouted the time-honoured and social rites of the bottle. At the same time, both before the war and since I have often gone for months without drinking at all. But at the front one came out of the line covered with mud and in a bad temper, to have the few days on rest taken up in training . . . and then the night came in the mess, and the present was blotted out and only memory and hope were lit up. All the devastation of every kind that surrounded one was seen in the light of humour and in a state of bliss, however fleeting it might be, and was finally lost altogether in the light-hearted independence of time that attends upon every toper. One broke through time, menacing and oppressive as it was, and rejoiced for an hour or two in a boundless world. The war left one with two memories, as I am sure every outspoken soldier of it will agree, that were always recurring: one, when one was faced with the worst moments it had to offer; the other, when the bottle went round as madly and merrily as ever it did in times of peace. It was only because these black and red threads were interlaced in fairly equal proportions that the experiences of war were not intolerable.

For the coming spell in the line I was appointed as scouting officer, and with a scout troop and two N.C.Os. was under the orders of the division.

On the 8th November the battalion moved in pouring rain to Gonnelieu. There the scout troop was detached to Lièremont and put under the command of the divisional intelligence officer, Captain Böckelmann. The captain, with us four scout officers, two observation officers, and his adjutant, was quartered in the priest's house. There we lived very happily together in comfortably furnished rooms.

Our predecessors took over the divisional front. We had to go up the line every second night. Our task was to ascertain where the front line ran and to see that communications were maintained, so that if the need arose we should be able to take the troops into the line and carry out orders in an emergency. My sphere of action was a sector left of St. Pierre Vaast wood and immediately in front of the so-called 'Nameless' wood. The first night, after nearly drowning myself in crossing a marsh flooded by the Tortille, I got into a thick cloud of phosgene shell-gas, and scurried back with weeping eyes to Vaux wood. On the way back I fell into one shell-hole after another, as I could see nothing through the misted eyepieces of the mask.

On the 13th November, hoping for better luck, I set out again on my second tour of the line. My orders were to ascertain that touch was maintained between the shell-holes that constituted the front line. I struggled to my goal along a chain of posts concealed in holes in the ground.

The shell-hole line deserved its name. A plateau in front of the village of Rancourt was pockmarked with innumerable miniature craters which here and there were occupied by two or three men. The monotony of the scene, where nothing was heard but the whistle and crash of shells, filled the mind with the dread of its utter desolation. After some time I lost touch with the line of shell-holes and went back in case I walked into the French. Soon after I came upon an officer I knew in the 164th Regiment, who warned me not to stay any longer now that dawn was breaking. So I hurried on through 'Nameless' wood, stumbling into deep shell-holes and over uprooted trees and through the almost impassable tangle of branches that covered the ground.

When I left the edge of the wood it was daylight. Before me lay an expanse of shell-holes without a sign of life. I stopped short, for, in modern battle, stretches of ground where not a man is to be seen are always suspicious.

Suddenly a shot from an unseen sniper got me in both legs. I flung myself into the nearest shell-hole and bound the wounds with my handkerchief, for, needless to say, I had forgotten my field-dressing. A bullet had passed through my right calf and grazed my left.

I crept back into the wood with the utmost caution, and from there limped over the shell-shot ground to the dressing-station. Shortly before this I had an example of the little incidents on which the chances of war turn. I was making for the cross-roads about a hundred metres ahead of me, when an officer in command of a working party whom I had known in the 9th Company called out to me. We had scarcely been talking for a minute when a shell struck the cross-roads where but for this chance encounter I should probably have been at that moment.

After dark I was carried on a stretcher to Nurlu. Captain Böckelmann was kindly waiting for me with a car. We were proceeding along the chaussée in the light of the enemy searchlights when the driver suddenly applied the brakes. A dark obstruction barred the way. It was an infantry section with its N.C.O., which had just fallen victim to a direct hit. It seemed as though death had united them in a peaceful sleep.

I had to be taken into the cellar of the priest's house, as Lièremont was just receiving its evening benediction. The same evening I was moved to the Villeret field hospital, and thence to the war hospital at Valenciennes.

The hospital was installed in the gymnasium near the station, and accommodated four hundred severe cases. A funeral procession with muffled drums left the main entrance day after day. The whole misery of the war was concentrated in the spacious operating-theatre. The surgeons carried on their sanguinary trade at a row of operating-tables. Here a limb was amputated, there a skull chiseled away, or a grown-in bandage cut out. Moans and cries of pain sounded through the room in the flood of remorseless light, while nurses in white hastened busily from one table to another with instruments and dressings.

The soldier who after such a sight goes back under fire with ardour unquenched has indeed withstood a test of nerve; for every fresh and terrible impression claws itself into the brain, and is added to the prostrating complex of imaginings that make the moment between the rush and the burst of a shell even more frightful.

Next to my bed a sergeant-major who had lost a leg lay dying. In his last moments he woke from delirium and got the nurse to read him his favourite chapter of the Bible. Then in a voice scarcely audible he asked all his ward companions to forge him for having so often awakened them from sleep by his delirious ravings, and then just before he died a few minutes later he tried to cheer us all up with an imitation of our orderly's comic dialect.

I was glad when after fourteen days I was able to leave this abode of piled-up agonies, with my wound half-healed. I had read with pride, meanwhile, of the magnificent and successful attack of the Fusiliers on St. Pierre Vaast wood.

The 111th Division were still holding the same front. There were several explosions as my train trundled into Epéhy. The ruins of goods trucks lumped together showed that it was no joking matter.

'What is going on here, I say?' asked a captain sitting opposite me. He had the fresh and rosy air of having been exported straight from home. Without wasting time by a reply I tore open the door and took cover behind the railway embankment. Fortunately they were the last ones, and only a few horses were wounded.

As I could not walk very well, I was given the post of observation officer. My field of observation was over the falling ground between Nurlu and Moislaines. I had a periscopic telescope built into a shelter, and with this I kept a look-out in the front line that I already knew well. My job was to ring up the division in case of heavy fire, coloured lights, or any other unusual events. All day long I crouched freezing on a chair behind the glasses in the November mist, with nothing to vary the monotony except an occasional call to test the wires. If the wire had been broken I had to have it mended by my breakdown squad. Apart from this I had nothing to do but wait for the moment of an attack.

The modern battlefield is like a huge, sleeping machine with innumerable eyes and ears and arms, lying hidden and inactive, ambushed for the one moment on which all depends. Then from some hole in the ground a single red light ascends in fiery prelude. A thousand guns roar out on the instant, and at a touch, driven by innumerable levers, the work of annihilation goes pounding on its way.

Orders fly like sparks and flashes over a close network, spurring on to heightened destruction in front and brining up from behind a steady stream of fresh men and fresh materials to fling into the flames. Every one feels that he is caught in a vortex which draws him on and on and thrusts him with unrelenting precision over the brink of death.

Every twenty-four hours I was relieved by another officer and betook myself to Nurlu, where fairly comfortable quarters had been rigged up in a large wine-cellar. I often think of those long, meditative November evenings which I spent smoking my pipe alone at the hearth of this barrel-shaped vault, while outside the mist dripped from the bare trees in the park and at long intervals a re-echoing broke the stillness.

On the 18th November the division was relieved and I went back to the regiment, now on rest in the village of Fresnoy-le-Grand. There I took over the command of the 2nd Company in place of Lieutenant Boje, then on leave. The regiment had four weeks of undisturbed rest in Fresnoy, and every one did his best to enjoy it to the full. Christmas and New Year were celebrated by the companies with great festivities at which beer and grog flowed in rivers. There were exactly four men left in the 2nd Company who had spent the previous Christmas with me in the line before Monchy. I was billeted on a French rentier, in whose house I shared the so-called 'salon' and two bedrooms with Fähnrich Gornick and my brother Fritz, who was spending six weeks with the regiment as cadet. We made ourselves very merry over the worthy married couple, who kept an argus-eyed watch over their plush furniture and alabaster vases and over their stack of wood in the yard, and who lived on terms of ceaseless animosity with the batman.

In this little retreat the bottle went round faster than ever. At night when walking late through the narrow streets one heard the sounds of carnival in every billet. Everything in wartime goes without reckoning, and hence came the preference of the soldier at the front for alcohol in its most concentrated forms. Our relations with the civilian population, too, were, to a great extent, of an undesirable familiarity; Venus deprived Mars of many servants.

Needless to say, we were at once put on a footing of old Prussian discipline, and it said a great deal for officers and men that after fourteen days the regiment was once more at its old level.

There was an inspection by the commander of the division, Major-General Sontag. On this occasion the regiment was honoured for its valiant conduct in the attack on St. Pierre Vaast wood, and distinguished by a number of decorations.

As I marched past the general at the head of the 2nd Company I observed that Colonel von Oppen appeared to make some remark about me to the general. A few hours later I received orders to report at divisional headquarters, where the general handed me the Iron Cross of the 1st class.

On the 17th January 1917 I was sent from Fresnoy on a four weeks' company commanders' course at Sisonne near Laon, where there was a

French manœuvering ground. Captain Funk, who was in command of our detachment, made the work exceedingly pleasant. He understood to an exceptional degree how to put the spirit above the letter and to interest us in the matters in hand.

The catering was certainly the sorriest I had ever experienced in the course of the war. During the whole four weeks there was seldom anything put on the table of our gigantic messroom but watery boiled swedes. At the same time the work was by no means light.

# THE SOMME RETREAT

On my return to the regiment, which had for some days been in the line near the ruins of Villers-Carbonnel, I was given temporary command of the 8th Company. Our rest-place was Devise.

On the march from there to the line one had to cross the plain of the Somme near the villages of Brie and St. Christ. The dreary devastation of these places in the midst of the melancholy marsh country used to put me in a peculiarly sorrowful mood as dark fragments of cloud chased across a moonlit sky, and the eerie interplay of light and shadow heightened the impression of chaos.

During the latter part of the time our front was exposed to numerous English attacks, connected with the great evacuation of the Somme area, for which we had made the most careful preparations. The enemy raided nearly every morning to ascertain whether we were still there. The following are a few of the experiences of those days.

1st March 1917. During the morning there was great artillery activity owing to the clear weather. In particular a heavy battery, with the help of balloon observation, pretty well flattened the section of the trench occupied by No. 3 platoon of my company. In the afternoon, in order to mark up any alteration of the line on my map, I splashed along to No. 3 platoon through the utterly waterlogged 'unnamed trench.' On the way I saw a giant yellow sun rush down to the ground trailing a black streamer behind it. An airman had attacked the unpleasant balloon and shot it down in flames. He got back in spite of a storm of fire.

In the evening Lance-corporal Schnau came to report that he had detected a sound of pickaxes, for four days past, underneath his section's dugout. I forwarded the report, and was sent a pioneer detachment with a listening apparatus, but our suspicions were not confirmed. Later we heard that our whole position had been undermined.

On the 5th of March a patrol approached our trench in the early morning and began to cut our wire. Lieutenant Eisen with a few men hurried off to warn the nearest post, and threw bombs. The enemy patrol then took to flight, leaving two men behind them. One, a young lieutenant, died immediately; the other, a sergeant, was severely wounded in the arm and leg. It appeared from papers found on the officer that he belonged to the Royal Munster Fusiliers. He was very well clothed, and his features, though distorted in death, were intelligent and energetic. It affected me to find the addresses of several London girls in his pocket-book. We buried him behind our trench, and put a simple cross at his head. I saw from this that all patrols need not end so fortunately as mine had done in days past.

Next morning, the English, after a short artillery preparation, attacked the front of the company, commanded by Lieutenant Reinhardt, with fifty men. The enemy crept up to the wire. Then one of them, who had a striker attached to his cuff, made a light-signal in order to silence the English machine-guns, and the whole party threw their last bombs and advanced on the trench. The men received them in such a masterful fashion that only one of them got into the trench. He ran straight through to the second line, and there, when he made no reply to summons to give himself up, he was shot. Only a lieutenant and a sergeant got through the wire. The officer, though he wore a steel shirt under his uniform, was accounted for by a bullet point-blank from Reinhardt's revolver that drove the whole steel plate into his body. The sergeant had both legs nearly torn off by a bomb; nevertheless, he clenched his short pipe between his teeth with stoical calm until he died. Here, as always, whenever we encountered the English we encountered brave men.

During the morning of this success I was strolling through the trench and saw Lieutenant Pfaffendorf, who was controlling the fire of his trench-mortar with a periscopic telescope from a fire-step. I had scarcely joined him when I saw an Englishman walking along over the top behind the third line of the enemy trenches. I seized the nearest rifle, sighted it at 600, got the man in the tip of the foresight, and then, aiming a bit in front of his head, I pulled the trigger. He went three steps, and then fell on his back as though his legs had been knocked from under him. After a few movements of his arms he rolled into a shell-hole, where, with the glass, we could see his brown sleeves showing up for a long while after.

On the 9th of March our front was properly plastered with shells. I was awakened in the early morning by the heavy firing, and, seizing my revolver, went, dazed with sleep, into the trench. When I pulled aside the ground-sheet at the top of the dugout steps, it was still as black as pitch. The bright flashes of the guns and the showers of earth woke me up in no time. I ran through the trench, but not a soul did I see till I came to a deep dugout, where a group of men crowded on the steps like hens crowding together in the rain, with no one in command. On such occasions the Prussian way is the best. Pitch into the men, and so get yourself going too. I took them with me, and soon made the trench look lively. I was delighted to hear little Hambrock's piping voice somewhere along the trench, occupied in the same way I was.

When the firing died down, I went back to my dugout in a bad temper, and there I was further ruffled by a telephone call from headquarters:

'What the hell is up? Why have you been all this time coming to the 'phone?'

Keeping in touch is no doubt most important, but fighting, after all, is action first and last.

After breakfast there was more of it. This time H.Es. were slowly but incessantly being 'plonked down' in front of our noses. At last it became boring, so I paid little Hambrock a visit by an underground gallery, and after seeing what he had to drink, sat down with him to a game of 'seven and four' we were a little upset once by a giant crash. It sounded as though a drunken gang came tumbling over each other down the steps. Lumps of earth clattered through the door and down the stove-pipe. The dugout shaft had got hit, and the timber revetment was shivered to matchwood. Sometimes a suffocating smell of bitter almonds blew down the shaft. Were they shooting prussic acid at us? Well, good luck to them. I had to leave the dugout once— indeed, I made four attempts in all, owing to constant interruption by the shells. Immediately after, the batman bounced in with the announcement that the latrine had disappeared beneath a direct hit. 'Well,' said Hambrock, 'you do have the devil's own luck!'

The fire ceased towards evening. I went along the trench in the mood I always experienced after being heavily shelled, a mood like the relief one feels after a violent storm. The trench looked pretty bad; stretches of it were entirely filled in. Five dugout shafts were smashed up. Several men were wounded. I went to see them and found them all fairly comfortable. There was one man killed. His body lay in the trench covered with a ground-sheet. A long splinter had torn his left hip away, though he was standing right at the bottom of the dugout steps.

In the morning we were relieved. On the 13th I was entrusted by Colonel von Oppen with the honourable task of holding the company front with a patrol of two sections until the whole regiment had crossed the Somme. Each of the four sectors of our front was to be held by a similar patrol under the command of an officer. The officers, starting from the right flank, were Reinhardt, Fischa, Lorek, and myself.

The villages we passed through as we marched to the front line had the appearance of lunatic asylums let loose. Whole companies were pushing walls down or sitting on the roofs of houses throwing down the slates. Trees were felled, window-frames broken, and smoke and clouds of dust rose from heap after heap of rubbish. In short, an orgy of destruction was going on. The men were chasing round with incredible zeal, arrayed in the abandoned wardrobes of the population, in women's dresses and with top hats on their heads. With positive genius they singled out the main beams of the houses and, tying ropes round them, tugged with all their might, shouting out in time with their pulls, till the whole house collapsed. Others swung hammers and smashed whatever came in their way, from flower-pots on the window ledges to the glass-work of conservatories.

Every village up to the Siegfried line was a rubbish-heap. Every tree felled, every road mined, every well fouled, every water-course dammed, every cellar blown up or made into a death-trap with concealed bombs, all supplies or metal sent back, all rails ripped up, all telephone wire rolled up, everything burnable burned. In short, the country over which the enemy were to advance had been turned into an utter desolation.

The moral justification of this has been much discussed. However, it seems to me that the gratified approval of arm-chair warriors and journalists is incomprehensible. When thousands of peaceful persons are robbed of their homes, the self-satisfaction of power may at least keep silence.

As for the necessity, I have of course, as a Prussian officer, no doubt whatever. War means the destruction of the enemy without scruple and by any means. War is the harshest of all trades, and the masters of it can only entertain humane feelings so long as they do no harm. It makes no difference that these operations which the situation demanded were not very pretty.

On the 13th I took over with my two sections the front that the 2nd Company now left to me. During the night a man with the ominous name of Kirchhof was killed by a shot through the head. This unlucky shot happened to be the only one fired by the enemy during several hours.

I did all I could to deceive the enemy as to our strength. A few shovelfuls of earth were thrown over the top, now at one point, now at another, and our machine-gun had to fire a few shots first from the left, and then from the right. Nevertheless, our fire sounded extremely thin when a low-flying scout crossed the line or a working party traversed our front behind the enemy's trenches. Consequently, patrols appeared every night at one point or another and set to work tampering with our wire.

On the last day but one I nearly met a sorrowful end. A dud shell from an anti-aircraft gun came hurtling down and exploded on the traverse against which I was innocently leaning. The rush of air sent me flying into the entrance of a deep dugout exactly opposite, where I came to in a state of utter stupefaction.

On the 17th, in the early morning, we could tell that an attack was imminent. In the English front line, usually unoccupied due to the mud, was to be heard the clatter of many feet. The laughter and shouting showed that they were a strong party and well fortified from within. Presently dark figures approached our wire. They dispersed under our fire, and one collapsed with a cry and was left behind. I withdrew my men to the entrance of the communication trench, and was kept busy in illuminating our front, now suddenly under artillery and trench-mortar fire, with Verey lights. As the white soon gave out, we made a fireworks display with coloured ones. When five o'clock came, the hour at which, according to orders, we were to evacuate the trench, we quickly blew up the dugouts with bombs, in so far as they were not already provided with infernal machines, some of which we had ingeniously constructed. During the last hours I had not dared to touch any box or door or bucket in case I might go up in the air.

At the appointed time all the patrols, some of them already involved in bombing engagements, retreated towards the Somme. We were the last to cross the river, and then the bridges were blown up by an engineer detachment. the drum-fire still raged away on our front, and it was some hours later when the first enemy patrols appeared on the Somme. We retired behind the Siegfried position, then still being constructed. The battalion was quartered in the village of Lehaucourt on the St. Quentin Canal. I occupied, with my batman, a comfortable little cottage where household goods were stored away in chests and cupboards. I should like to put on record, to show what sort of fellows ours were, that nothing I could say would induce my batman, the trusty Knigge, to make his bed in the warm sitting-room. He insisted all the time on sleeping in the cold kitchen. This attitude of reserve which is typical of the Lower Saxon made the relations between officers and men work very smoothly.

The first evening out on rest I invited a party of my fellow-officers to drink mulled wine spiced with all the spices left behind by the owner of the house; for our rearguard had earned the praise of all our superior officers, and fourteen days' leave as well.

# IN THE VILLAGE OF FRESNOY

My leave, on which I went a few days later, was this time not curtailed. I find in my diary this brief but eloquent record: 'Leave spent very happily. Need have no reproaches on that score after my death.' On the 9th April 1917 I returned to the 2nd Company, then quartered in the village of Merignies, not far from Douai. The pleasure of my return was dashed by an unexpected alarm which had for me the peculiarly unpleasant consequence that I had to ride the company charger to Beaumont. Through rain and sleet I rode at the head of the transport, that slipped all over the paved road, till we reached our destination at one in the morning.

When I had seen to my horse and the men as well as I could, I went in search of quarters for myself; but there was not an unoccupied corner to be found. At last a commissariat orderly had the excellent idea of offering me his bed, as he had to sit up for the telephone calls. While I was pulling off my boots and spurs he told me that the English had captured Vimy Ridge and a lot of ground from the Bavarians.

I could not help observing, in spite of his hospitality, that he was not at all pleased to find his quiet village headquarters turned into an assembly-point for the fighting troops.

The next morning the battalion marched in the direction of heavy firing to the village of Fresnoy. There I received orders to set up an observation post. I took a few men and explored the western outskirts of the village and found a cottage, in whose roof I had a look-out post made that commanded the front. We took the cellar as our dwelling-place, and in the course of making room there we came upon a sack of potatoes, a very welcome addition to our scanty provisions. My batman now roasted me potatoes every evening, with salt. Lieutenant Gornick also, like a true friend, sent me a large parcel of Leberwurst and some red wine. He had found them among the stores left behind in haste in Villerval, which had already been evacuated, but which Gornick was holding as an outpost with one platoon. I at once equipped an expedition furnished with perambulators and similar means of transport to secure this treasure. Unfortunately it returned empty-handed, as the English were already in full strength on the edge of the village. Gornick told me later that after the discovery of a large cellar of red wine a drinking bout had started, which, in spite of the attack then being made on the village, it had been extremely difficult to bring to a close.

On the 14th of April I was given the task of organizing an intelligence clearing-station in the village. For this purpose I had despatch-riders, bicyclists, telephone and light-signal stations, underground telegraph wires, carrier pigeons, and a chain of Verey-light posts placed at my disposal. I looked out a suitable cellar, with a deep dugout, and returned for the last time to my dwelling-place on the western edge of the village.

During the night I fancied I heard a crash now and then and shouts from my batman, but I was so dazed with sleep that I only murmured, 'Oh, let them shoot!' and turned over, though the whole place was thick with dust. Next morning I was awakened by little Schultz, Colonel von Oppen's nephew, who was shouting, 'I say—don't you know yet that your whole house has been blown to blazes?'

When I got up and surveyed the damage, I observed that a shell of the heaviest caliber had been planted on the roof, and that the observation post, indeed the whole house, was no more. If the velocity had only been a trifle slower the hit would have got us in the cellar and plastered the walls with us, so that in the nice saying of the trenches we might have been 'scraped off with a spoon and buried in the pot.' Schultz told me that his orderly said to him when he saw the ruins of the house: 'There was a lieutenant in there yesterday. Better have a look and see whether he is there still.' My batman was beside himself at the way I had slept through it.

During the morning we shifted our quarters into the new cellar. On the way we were nearly hit by the church tower, which the engineers were unobtrusively blowing up in order to deprive the enemy of an easy mark. In a neighbouring village they had forgotten to warn a post of two men who were keeping a look-out from the top of the tower there. By a miracle they were retrieved uninjured from the debris.

We furnished our roomy cellar very passably, for we collected what we required from mansion or cottage, and what we had no use for we burned in the stove.

During the first day there was a succession of duels to the death in the air. They ended nearly every time in the defeat of the English, as Richthofen's battle formation was circling over the neighbourhood. Often five or six machines were driven down or shot down in flames. Once we saw the pilot thrown from his machine and fall to the earth as a separate black speck. There were dangers, too, in staring up into the sky. A man of the 4th Company was killed by a falling splinter that hit him in the neck.

On the 18th April I paid a visit to the 2nd Company in the line. It held a salient in front of the village of Arleux. Lieutenant Boje told me that he had only had a single casualty for a long while, as the English shelling was so methodical that it allowed them to side-step and avoid it every time.

After I had wished him all the best, I had to leave the village at the gallop, on account of the continuous shooting by the enemy's heavy guns. I stopped 300 metres behind Arleux to watch the clouds that rose from each hit. They were red or black according to whether brick walls had been pounded or garden soil flung up; and among them was the delicate white of exploding shrapnel. When a few 'whizz-bangs' began falling on the footpaths that connected Arleux with Fresnoy, I abandoned the pursuit of further impressions and decamped at full speed, in case I might be 'slain,' as the stock phrase then was in the 2nd Company.

I was often making expeditions of this kind, sometimes as far as the little town of Hénin-Liétard, for during the first fourteen days, in spite of my large staff, there was not a single report to communicate.

From the 20th April Fresnoy was shelled by a 30.5 centimetre gun. The shells came over with a perfectly infernal hiss. After each hit the village was veiled in a huge reddish-brown cloud of picric-acid gas. Even the duds caused a small earthquake. A man of the 9th Company, who was surprised by one of them in the courtyard of the château, was flung over the trees in the park and broke most of his bones in the fall.

In the afternoon the village was shelled with all calibres. In spite of the danger I could not tear myself from the attic windows of my house. It was a breathless sight to see how small parties and despatch-carriers chased over the shelled area, often throwing themselves flat, while the ground was flung up on every side of them.

When I went into the village after this, one more cellar had been hit and set on fire. the salvage operations recovered only three bodies. Near the cellar lay one on its face, with the uniform in shreds. The head was torn off and the blood flowed into a puddle of water. When the stretcher-bearer turned the body over to remove any valuables I could not help seeing that on the stump of the arm there was only a thumb.

The enemy artillery became more active every day and left no doubt of an early attack. On the 27th April at midnight I had the following telephone message: '67 from 5 a.m.,' which meant in our code, 'Utmost readiness for an alarm at 5 a.m.'

So I lay down again, hoping to be all the better prepared for the expected exertions. However, as I was just falling asleep a shell hit the house and blew in the wall of the cellar stairs and threw the masonry into the cellar. We jumped up and hurried into the dugout.

As we crouched on the steps in the light of a candle, disconcerted and weary, the sergeant of night light-signaling section, whose post, together with two valuable signaling lamps, had been smashed up in the afternoon, came rushing in. 'Sir the cellar of No. 11 has had a direct hit and some of the men are still buried in the ruins.' As I had two cyclist and three telephonists in No. 11, I took some men and hurried to their help.

I found a lance-corporal and a wounded man in the dugout, and was given the following account. When the shells began to fall suspiciously near, four of the five occupants of the cellar decided to go down into the dugout shaft. One of them went straight away, one stayed where he was in bed, while the remaining three delayed to pull on their boots. The most prudent and the least, as so often in war, came off the best: the first had not a scratch, and the second had a splinter in the thigh. The three others were caught by the shell, which came through the cellar wall and exploded in the opposite corner.

After this narration I lit a cigar and went into the smoke-filled cellar. In the middle of it there was a heap of wreckage—bedsteads, straw mattresses, and various pieces of furniture, all in fragments and piled nearly up to the roof. After we had put a few candles on ledges of the walls, we set to work. Catching hold of the limbs that stuck out from the wreckage, we pulled out the dead bodies. One had the head struck off, and the neck on the trunk was like a great sponge of blood. From the arms stumps of another the broken bones projected, and the uniform was saturated by a large wound in the chest. The entrails of the third poured out from a wound in the belly. As we pulled out the last a splintered board caught in the ghastly wound with a hideous noise. The orderly made a comment on this, and was reproved by my batman with these words: 'Best hold your tongue. In such matters talking nonsense serves no purpose.'

I took an inventory of the valuables found on them. It was a horrible job. The candles flickered red in the vaporous air, and as the two men handed me pocket-books and silver objects it seemed as though we were engaged in some dark and secret work. The fine yellow plaster-dust fell on the faces of the dead and gave them the fixed look of waxed figures. We threw coverings over them and hurried out of the cellar, after taking up the wounded man in a ground-sheet. With the stoical advice to set his teeth, we carried him through a whirl of shrapnel fire to the dressing-station dugout.

When I got back to my dwelling-place the first thing I did was to have a few cherry-brandies. The experience I had been through had touched my nerve. Soon we were being violently shelled once more, and with the example before our eyes of what artillery fire can do in cellars we made all speed into the dugout shaft.

At 5.15 a.m. the fire increased to an incredible violence. Our dugout rocked and trembled like a ship on a stormy sea. All round resounded the rending of masonry and the crash of collapsing houses.

At 7 a.m. I received a message by light-signal addressed to the 2nd Battalion: 'Brigade requires immediate report on the situation.' After an hour a despatch-carrier brought back the news: 'Enemy taken Arleux and Arleux park. Ordered 8th Company to counter-attack. No news so far. Rocholl, Captain.'

This was the only message that my tremendous apparatus of transmission had to deal with during all three weeks of my time in Fresnoy—though certainly it was a very important one. And now that my activity was of the utmost value, the artillery fire had put nearly the whole organization out of action. Such were the results of over-centralization.

This surprising information explained why we had heard rifle-bullets, fired at no very great range, clattering against the walls of the houses.

We had scarcely realized the great losses suffered by the regiment, when the shelling was renewed with increasing fury. My batman was standing, the last of all, on the top step of the dugout stairs, when a crash like thunder announced that the English had at last succeeded in knocking in our cellar. The trusty Knigge got a squared building-stone on the back, but was not hurt. Above, everything was shot to blazes. Daylight came to us past two bicycles squeezed into the dugout entrance. We made ourselves as small as we could on the lowest step, while heavy explosions and the din of falling masonry convinced us of the insecurity of our refuge.

By a miracle the telephone was still working, so I explained the plight we were in to my chief at the division, and received orders to withdraw my men into the dressing-station dugout close by.

After packing up what it was most essential to take with us, we set about leaving the dugout by the second and only remaining exit. In spite of my preemptory order, backed up by unequivocal threats, the telephone staff, which was not much used to war, hesitated so long to venture out of the protection of the dugout into the shell-fire that this exit, too, was smashed in with a crash by a heavy shell. Luckily, no one was hit; only our little dog howled miserably, and from that moment was never seen again.

We pushed aside the bicycles that barred the way out through the cellar, and, creeping on all-fours over the heaps of debris, got into the open through a narrow crack in the wall. We did not pause to observe the incredible change that these few hours had produced in the village, but ran out of it as fast as we could. The last of us had scarcely left the yard gates when the house got another tremendous hit.

A compact belt of fire covered the area between the edge of the village and the dressing-station dugout. Light and heavy shells with direct and delay action fuses, duds, empty cases, and shrapnel combined to produce a nightmare of acoustic and optical effects. Through it, passing to right and left of the witch's cauldron seething in the village, the reserves were marching up.

In Fresnoy the shells were sending the earth in fountains as high as church towers. Each seemed bent on outdoing its predecessor. As though by magic, one house after another was sucked into the earth. Walls collapsed, gables fell, and bare rafters were flung through the air to mow the roofs of neighbouring house. Clouds of splinters danced above the whitish swathes of vapour. Eye and ear hung as though entranced upon this dance of destruction.

We spent two days in a painfully confined space in the dressing-station dugout, for besides my men there were the staffs of two battalions, two relief detachments, and the indispensable corps troops. Naturally, the constant coming and going in front of the entrances was observed by the enemy. Soon the range was got to a yard, and at intervals of a minute shells fell on the track outside, and there were casualties all the time. Indeed, the shouts for stretcher-bearers never ceased. I lost four bicycles which we had left outside, owing to this disagreeable bombardment. They were scattered to the four winds, in various states of contortion.

Stark and still, and wrapped in a ground sheet, Lieutenant Lemière, the commander of the 8th Company, lay at the entrance, his large horn spectacles still on his nose. His men had brought him there. He was shot in the mouth. His younger brother was killed a few months later in exactly the same way.

On the 30th April I handed over to my successor of the 25th Regiment, by whom we were relieved. We made our way to Flers, the rendezvous of the 1st Battalion. Leaving the much-shelled limekilns, 'Chez bon temps,' on our left, we went quickly on through the afternoon sunshine along the path to Beaumont. Our eyes rejoiced again in the beauty of the earth. We drew in the intoxicating breath of spring, thankful to have escaped the intolerably crowded confinement of the dugout. With the thunder of guns in our rear, my sympathies were with the poet:

'Surely the day that God has given
Has better uses than to kill.'

In Flers I found the quarter allotted me in the possession of some staff sergeant-majors, who, under the pretext that they had to keep the room for a certain Baron von X, refused to give it up to me. They failed, however, to reckon with the overstrained nerves of a worn-out front-line soldier. I told my men to smash in the door, and after a brief hand-to-hand engagement, under the eyes of the owner of the house, who, much alarmed, hastened on to the scene in his dressing-gown, we sent the gentlemen flying down the stairs. My batman carried politeness to such lengths that he threw their trench boots after them. After this assault I took possession of the warm bed, surrendering half of it to my friend Kius, who was wandering round without a billet. Sleeping in a bed after so long a time did us so much good that we woke next morning in all our 'pristine vigour.'

As the 1st Battalion had come off the lightest in the casualties of the recent days of fighting, we were in excellent trim as we marched to Douai station. From there we went by train to the junction of Busigny. We were to have some days' rest in Serain, a village in the neighbourhood. The population was friendly, and we had good quarters. On the very first evening the sound of happy forgatherings were to be heard from many of the houses.

These drink-offerings on the morrow of well-fought fights count among an old soldier's happiest memories. And though ten out of twelve had fallen, still the last two, as sure as death, were to be found on the first evening of rest over the bottle, drinking a silent health to their dead companions, talking and laughing over all they had been through. For dangers past—an old soldier's laugh. For those to come—a full glass, though death and the devil grin there, as long as the wine was good. Such has ever been the custom of war.

It was the officers' mess more than all that made me appreciate this. It was here, among the spirits of the undaunted dead, that the will to conquer was concentrated and made visible in the features of each weather-beaten face. There was an element at work here that the very horror of the war underlined and even spiritualized, an element one seldom found among the men with whom one lay in the shell-holes—sporting joy in danger, and a chivalrous impulse to see things out. And to say the least of it, I have never in this much-reviled circle heard one faint-hearted word.

My batman came next morning and read me the orders. From these it appeared that I was to take command of the 3rd Company. It was in this company, in the autumn of 1914, that Hermann Löns, the Lower Saxon poet, fell.

# AGAINST INDIANS

On the 6th May 1917 we were once more on the march to the now familiar Brancourt, and on the following day we went through Montbréhain, Ramicourt, and Joncourt into the Siegfried line, which we had left just a month before.

The first evening was stormy. Heavy rain pattered down without ceasing on to the flooded ground. Soon, however, a succession of bright, warm days reconciled us to our new station. I enjoyed the wonderful country undisturbed by the white puffs of shrapnel and the leaping cones of the shell-bursts; indeed, I scarcely noticed them. In those years of increased activity the signs of an offensive were as much a part of the spring as primroses and opening buds.

Our lines formed a crescent in front of the St. Quentin Canal. Behind us was the famous Siegfried line. I never could tell why we had to occupy the narrow, unfinished trenches in the chalk, when behind us lay this magnificent line.

The front line wound through an idyllic meadowland shadowed by small groups of trees and beautified now by tender colours of spring. We could move about with impunity behind and in front of the trench, for our front was protected by a belt of outposts pushed forward to a depth of a kilometre. These posts were a thorn in the enemy's side, and not a night went by for many weeks that he did not try to dislodge them either by cunning or force.

Our first spell in the line was, however, passed in welcome quiet. The weather was so fine that the men slept out on the grass. On the 14th May we were relieved by the 8th Company and, leaving the burning St. Quentin on our right, proceeded to our rest-place, Montbréhain, a large village that so far had suffered very little from the war and therefore had very comfortable quarters to offer. On the 20th, as company in reserve, we occupied the Siegfried line. The weather was gorgeous, and day after day we sat in the numerous arbours built in the side of the trench, or bathed in the canal, or boated on it.

The objection to occupying a trench otherwise so ideal lies in the frequent visits from superior officers, a pleasure very little esteemed in the line. In any case my left wing had no cause to complain of being too safe. It extended nearly to the village of Bellenglise, already seriously nibbled at, and on the very first day one of my men got a shrapnel-bullet wound in the right buttock. When I hastened to the scene of the disaster, he was seated in great content on his left side awaiting stretcher-bearers, and filling in the time with an enormous slice of bread and jam.

On the 25th May we relieved the 12th Company in Riqueval farm. This farm, formerly a large estate, was occupied in turns by each of the four companies in the line. There were three machine-gun positions at different points in our rear, and these had to be manned by sections in rotation. Theses strong points distributed behind the line, and covering each other like squares on a chess-board, were the first experiment in an elastic scheme of defence.

The rest of the men were sent forward on working parties every night.

The farm lay 1500 metres at most behind the front line. Nevertheless the buildings, surrounded by a well-timbered park, were still entirely intact. As there were deep dugouts under construction, there were plenty of men there. The red may-tree avenues in the park and the charm of the surroundings gave our life there something of the cheerful enjoyment which the Frenchman means by his 'vie de champagne,' in spite of the nearness to the front. A pair of swallows had nested in my bedroom. Before it was light they started on the noisy business of feeding their brood.

In the evenings I took my stick from the corner and wandered along the narrow paths that went up and down through the hilly country. The neglected fields were scented with wildflowers. Here and there single trees stood by the wayside. In peace time the labourers must often rested beneath them. They had an air of enchantment, standing alone in solitude, covered with blossom white or pink or red. It seemed that the war had thrown a heroic and melancholy light over the landscape, and without disturbing its loveliness added a ray to its brightness and a strength to its spell.

It is easier to go into the battle in the midst of such beauties of nature than when surrounded by a dead and cold winter landscape. Somehow, it comes to one quite simply that one's existence is part of an eternal circuit, and that the death of a single individual is no great matter.

On the 30th May this idyll came to an end as far as I was concerned, for the command of the 4th Company was taken over again by Lieutenant Vogeley, who had come out of the hospital. I rejoined my old 2nd Company, now under the command of a cavalry lieutenant, in the line.

Our front, extending from the Roman road to the so-called Artillery trench, was held by two platoons. The third, with company headquarters, was about 200 metres to the rear behind a small hill. There was a little wooden hut there, too, that I used to occupy with Lieutenant Kius, peacefully relying upon the poor shooting of the English artillery.

One side of it was built into the slope of a little hill facing the enemy; the three others trustingly offered themselves as a mark. Every day, when the morning's greetings came hurtling across, the following dialogue might be heard between the occupants of the upper and lower bunks:

'That you, Ernst?'

'Hm.'

'They're shooting, aren't they?'

'Well, let's lie where we are a little longer. I think those were the last ones.'

After a quarter of an hour:

'That you, Oskar?'

'Yes?'

'They are not going to stop to-day. I think that was a shrapnel bullet that came through the wall just now. We'd better get up. That artillery observer fellow cleared out long ago.'

We had always optimistically taken off our boots. By the time we were ready, the shooting had generally left off, and we could seat ourselves happily at the absurdly small table and drink coffee that the heat had turned sour, and light our morning cigars. In the afternoon, in scorn of the English artillery, we used to have sun-baths on a ground-sheet in front of the door.

Our cabin was extremely entertaining in other respects too. When one lay in sweet idleness on the wire mattress, gigantic earth-worms hung pendulum wise from the earth wall and shot into their holes with inconceivable rapidity at the least touch. A peevish mole sniffed about from his tunnel and added much to the enlivenment of our prolonged siesta.

On the 12th June I had to occupy the outpost on the company front with twenty men. It was late when we left the trench and went in the warm evening air by the footpath winding over the undulating ground. Dusk was so far advanced that the red poppies in the untilled fields blended with the vivid green grass to an extraordinarily rich tone.

We strolled silently along over the carpet of flowers. Each man was busy with his own thoughts; our rifles hung from our shoulders; and in twenty minutes we arrived at our destination. In whispers the post was taken over. Silently guards were mounted. Then the men we relieved disappeared into the darkness.

The outpost rested upon a short, steep hill. In the rear a wild and tangled wood melted into the night. It was separated from our steep bank by about a hundred metres of meadow ground. In front and to our right rose two hills over which ran the English lines. There was a ruin on one with the promising name 'Ascension farm.' A sunken road ran between these hills to the enemy.

And now, just as my posts had gone out, appeared Sergeant-major Hackmann with a few men of the 7th Company, just about to go on patrol. I attached myself to them as camp-follower, though I had no business to leave my post.

Using a method of advance invented by myself, we crossed two entanglements that barred our way and got over the crest of the hill without, to our surprise, having run into a single outpost. We could now hear English working parties to right and to left of us. It was clear to me after this event that the enemy had withdrawn his own posts so as not to involve them in fire which, as I shall shortly explain, he was about to open on ours.

My method of advance, mentioned just now, consisted in this, that over ground in which we might at any moment run up against the enemy each member of the patrol crept forward in turn. In this way, only one man at a time exposed himself to the risk of being shot from an ambush, while the rest, in a body behind, lay in readiness to attack. Naturally I took care to take my turn as leader, although my mere presence with the patrol was bad enough in itself. An officer in the front line often has to put himself technically in the wrong from considerations of a personal kind.

We stalked several working parties that, unfortunately, were separated from us by dense entanglements. The somewhat eccentric sergeant-major suggested giving himself up as a deserter and holding the enemy in parley until we had surrounded the first post. This plan was turned down after a brief discussion, and we crept back, disappointed, to the outpost.

There I sat down on the edge of the steep bank on my cloak, and, lighting a pipe as cautiously as possible, I gave rein to my thoughts. In the midst of the most beautiful castle in the air, I was suddenly alarmed by a peculiar rustling in the wood and the meadow. In the face of the enemy the senses are always on the look-out; and it is remarkable that, at such moments, quite ordinary sounds can give one the instant conviction, 'Something is up!'

At the same instant the nearest post came up to me: 'Sir, there are seventy Englishmen advancing to the edge of the wood.'

I was rather surprised by the numerical precision, but for the sake of prudence I hid myself, with the four men nearest me, on the edge of the bank in the long grass, in order to observe how matters developed. After a few seconds I saw a body of men gliding over the meadow. While the men covered them with their rifles I called out softly, 'Who goes there?' It was Teilengerdes, a N.C.O., an old veteran of the 2nd Company, who was trying to collect his agitated section.

I at once got them all in hand and formed them in line, with one flank on the wood and the other on the bank. In a moment, bayonets were fixed. When I was giving them directions and told a man who hung back to dress up with the rest, 'I am a stretcher-bearer,' was the answer. The fellow had his drill well in his head. Comforted by this triumph of Prussian discipline, I gave the word to advance.

While we were crossing the strip of meadow, a hail of shrapnel and a wild clatter of machine-gun fire began from the English side. We broke, against our wills, into a double, so as to reach the cover of the shoulder of the hill that lay to our front.

Suddenly a dark shadow rose in front of me. I seized a bomb and threw it. To my horror I saw in the flash of the explosions that it was the N.C.O. Teilengerdes, who had got in front unobserved and had just been tripped up by a wire. Fortunately he was not hurt. At the same time we heard the sharper explosion of English bombs not far off, and the shrapnel fire increased to an unpleasant intensity.

My firing-line broke and disappeared in the direction of the steep bank, which was under heavy fire. I with Teilengerdes and three more of the right sort stood my ground. Suddenly one of them rushed up to me: 'The English!'

Like a vision engraved for one second on my eyes I saw a double row of kneeling figures, at that moment, getting up and advancing over the meadow, which was lit up only by an occasional flash. I could clearly distinguish the figure of an officer on the right flank. Friend and foe were as though paralysed by this abrupt and unexpected encounter. Then we did the one thing left to us to do—turned and made off before the enemy recovered sufficiently to fire a shot. We jumped up and ran back to the bank. Though I tripped and fell over a treacherous wire stretched through the tall grass, I got back without further misadventure. The men were there, but they were in a state of great agitation, and it cost me all my energy to get them into line, even elbow to elbow.

I have always observed that the ordinary man whose sole preoccupation is his own danger is surprised by what seems to him an undivided attention to the matter in hand on the part of the officer in command, who among a thousand and one unnerving incidents of battle yet keeps his eye fixed upon the execution of his duty. This surprise makes an officer excel himself and spurs him on to always greater achievements. In this way officers and men call out energies in each other which would otherwise lie dormant. Indeed the moral factor is everything.

The enemy fire ceased of a sudden, and at the same time crackling and rustling sounds were heard in the undergrowth of the wood.

'Halt! Who goes there? Password.'

We kept on calling out for a good five minutes, and even shouted the old battle-cry of the 1st Battalion, 'Luttje Lage,' an expression signifying schnaps, and beer, known to every Hanoverian. Only a strange and incomprehensible shout came in reply. At last I took the responsibility on myself and gave the order to fire, though some of the men asserted that they had heard German words. The fire of twenty rifles swept the wood; bolts rattled; and soon the cry we heard changed to moans. This gave me a passing twinge of uncertainty. However, there were yellow flashes here and there in our direction, though they soon died away. One of the men was hit in the shoulder, and the stretcher-bearers bound him up.

'Cease fire!'

Slowly the command took effect and the firing ceased. The men had quite recovered their nerve. Once more there were calls for the password, and on my side the persuasive summons: 'Come here; you are prisoners. Hands up!'

Thereupon there were confused cries from the other side, which were interpreted by the men as 'Rache! Rache!' ('Revenge! Revenge!') A single figure detached itself from the border of the wood and came towards us. One of the men was idiot enough to shout 'Password' at him, at which he stopped and turned round.

'Shoot him dead!'

There were a dozen shots, and he sank into a heap beneath the tall grass.

This little episode gave us the feeling of satisfaction. Once more confused cries rang out from the edge of the wood. It seemed that the attacking party were encouraging each other to advance on their mysterious enemy.

In the utmost excitement we kept our eyes fixed on the dark strip of ground. It was beginning to dawn, and a light mist rose from the meadow-land.

Then a row of shadows rose out of the darkness. Five, ten, fifteen, a whole lot of them. Trembling fingers released the safety catches. They were fifty metres from us, thirty, fifteen . . . 'Fire!' For a minute the rattles rattled out. Sparks showered up whenever the storm of bullets encountered weapons or steel helmets.

'Suddenly there was a shout: 'Look out on the left!' Coming quickly on, a party of enemy was attacking us on the left flank. At the head of it was a giant with an outstretched revolver, swinging a white bludgeon.

'Left section! Left front!'

The men whipped round and received the new arrivals standing. Some of them, and among them their leader, fell at the first hurried shots. The rest vanished as swiftly as they had come. Now the moment to attack in turn. With fixed bayonets and a rousing 'Hurrah!' we stormed the wood. We threw a volley of bombs into the tangled undergrowth, and in a moment were once more in undisturbed possession of our outposts, without having encountered the pliant enemy.

We assembled in a cornfield and looked at each other. Our faces had an after-the-night-before look, and a lark that rose into the sky and began its trills was an added exasperation. We were in much the same mood as when, after a night of play, the cards are flung on to the table and the windows thrown open to let the cool morning air blow away the hanging cloud of cigar smoke.

While we handed round the water-bottles and lit cigars we heard the enemy retreating along the sunken road and the cries of the wounded they carried with them.

I decided to survey the field of battle. Strange sounds and cries of pain came from the meadow where we had routed the enemy with our rifle-fire. We found a number of dead in the long grass and three wounded who begged for mercy. They were convinced we would massacre them.

When I asked, 'Quelle nation?' one of them answered, 'Pauvre Rajput!'

They were Indians, who had come far over the sea to run their heads against the Hanover Fusiliers in this God-forsaken corner of the earth.

Their fine bodies were in an evil plight. At that short range the infantry fire has an almost explosive effect. Many had been hit for the second time when they had fallen, so that the track of the bullet passed along the whole length of their bodies. Not one had been hit less than twice. We took the wounded up and carried them to our trench. They cried out as if they were being stuck with spears, till the men had to stop their mouths and threaten them with their fists; and at this they seemed to be comforted in their anguish. One of them died while he was being carried in. He was taken on all the same, as there was a prize on the head of every prisoner, dead or alive. The two others strove to win our indulgence by shouting out all the time, 'Anglais pas bon!' Why these people spoke French I have never quite made out.

The company had heard the sounds of fighting and had had a heavy barrage put down on them. They welcomed us back to the trench in jubilation and with astonishment at our booty. I retired to our cabin with Kius and a half a dozen more whom he quickly enrolled, and was entertained in honour of the occasion with poached eggs.

Our achievement received the notice it deserved, and was mentioned in divisional orders with praise. With twenty men we had beaten back a detachment many times our number, though they had taken us in the rear and though our orders were to withdraw if attacked in force. Such successes can, of course, only be won by troops whose discipline and morale are of the first order. Of myself I could say with satisfaction that my command of the situation and my personal influence with my men had prepared a severe disappointment and an early grave for the officer who led the attack. We two had matched our wits in the same way as is customary in field exercises in training—except that we had not used dummy cartridges.

If these lines are read by any one belonging to the 1st Hariana Lancers I wish to express to him in this place my respect for a body of men who could claim as their commander such a one as he whom I had the honour to fight.

What does Nietzsche say of fighting men? 'You must have as enemies only those whom you hate, but not those whom you despise. You must be proud of your enemy, and then the enemy's success is your success also.'

The next evening I had orders again to occupy the outpost. It was impossible to occupy it by day, as it was in full view of the enemy. Kius and I with fifty men took each a side of the wood and met at the steep bank. There was nothing to be seen or heard of the enemy except that there was a shout and a Verey light and a shot from the sunken road which Sergeant-major Hackmann and I had reconnoitered. We marked this unwary individual down for our next expedition.

At this spot where we had beaten off the flank attack the night before were lying three dead. Two of them were Indians, and one a white officer with two gold stars on his shoulder-straps: a lieutenant, therefore. He had been shot in the eye. The bullet went out through the opposite temple and had smashed the rim of his steel helmet—which is now among my collection of sinister trophies. His right hand still grasped the club, stained with his own blood; his left a large Colt six-shooter. There were only two live cartridges left in the magazine.

The men plundered the fallen. I have always hated the sight; all the same, I did not interfere. What they took was otherwise doomed to waste anyway, and aesthetic or moral considerations seemed to me to be out of place in this dark meadow-ground over which all the callous relentlessness of war still brooded.

During the following days several more dead bodies were found in the undergrowth of the wood; this showed how heavy the enemy's losses had been, and made the outpost a rather unpleasant place to be in. As I was working my way alone through a thicket I heard a peculiar hissing and murmuring sound. I went nearer and came upon two corpses in which the heat had awakened a ghastly life.

On the 18th June the outpost was again attacked. This time the affair did not go off so well. The men broke and could not be rallied again. One, a N.C.O., Erdelt, jumped straight off the bank in the confusion. He rolled down and landed at the bottom among a party of Indians in ambush. He threw bombs, but was soon caught by the throat by an Indian officer and scourged in the face with a wire whip. His watch was taken from him and he was pushed and thumped and marched off by his captors. However, he managed to escape when the Indians threw themselves down on account of our machine-gun fire. After long wanderings behind the enemy's front he regained our lines, with thick weals across his face.

On the evening of the 18th June I went on patrol with little Schultz, ten men, and a light machine-gun. We set out from the outpost, now becoming by degrees somewhat oppressive, with the aim of paying the post that had lately made itself so obvious in the sunken road the honour of a visit. Schultz went with his party to the right of the sunken road, I to the left, with the understanding that if either party were fired on the other should run to its help. We worked our way forward on hands and knees through grass and thickets of broom, pausing now and then to listen.

Suddenly came the sharp rattle of a rifle-bolt. We sank into the ground. Every old hand knows the series of feelings that occupied the next seconds. For the moment one has lost the initiative and must wait and see what the enemy does next. A shot broke the oppressive stillness. I lay behind a broom-bush and waited. On my right some one threw bombs into the sunken road.

At once a whole line of fire flashed out in front of us. The sickening sharpness of the report showed that the fire came from only a few yards ahead of us, and, seeing that we had stumbled into too hot a corner, I gave the word to run for it. We all sprang up and sprinted for all we were worth, while rifle-fire was opened on us from our left as well. I gave up all hope of a safe return when I heard this unholy clattered. Unconsciously, I was in constant expectation of being hit. Death was out hunting.

Somewhere near us a detachment advanced to the attack with a small hurrah. Little Schultz confessed to me afterwards that he imagined a lean Indian behind him wielding a knife and already clutching him tight by the neck.

I tumbled once and brought down the N.C.O. Teilengerdes over on top of me. I lost my steel helmet, revolver, and bombs. Anything to get on! At last we reached the protecting bank and tore down it. Lieutenant Schultz reached it at the same time with his men. He announced quite out of breath that anyway he had paid out the cheeky post with bombs. Just after two men came in carrying Fusilier F., who was wounded in both legs. All the rest were unwounded.

The worst misfortune was that the man who had carried the machine-gun, a recruit, had fallen over the wounded man and left the thing behind. While we were holding a brief council of war and planning a second expedition, the artillery began firing. I was reminded very precisely of the night of the 12th, for this time too there was a hopeless stampede. I found myself alone on the bank with the wounded man, who, dragging himself forward by both his hands, implored me piteously not to leave him alone. 'Don't leave me, sir.'

I had to, little as I liked it, in order to take my part in putting the outpost in fighting trim. I got the men together in a row of shallow firing positions on the edge of the wood; but I confess I was thankful when the day dawned without further incident.

On such occasions I was always surprised and touched by the trusting reliance of the men on the ability of the officer to cope with the situation. 'Where shall we go, sir?' 'Help, sir, I'm wounded!' 'Where's the officer?'

To be in command at such moments and to have a clear head is its own supreme reward, just as cowardice is its own punishment. I have always pitied the coward, in whom battle arouses a series of hellish tortures, while the spirit of the brave man merely rises the higher to meet a chain of exciting experiences.

The next night found us at the same spot. Our object was to recover our machine-gun. However, a succession of suspicious noises as we crept on warned us that once more there must be a strong detachment on the watch for us.

It was decided, therefore, in accordance with a point of honour which like many others in the war made us inwardly curse, to recover the lost weapon by force. At 12 midnight, after three minutes' artillery preparation, we were to attack the enemy posts and look for the gun.

I put the best face I could on the sorry business, and in the afternoon I shot some ranging shots with some of the batteries.

At 11 at night I was once more with Schultz, my companion in misfortune, on the uncanny bit of ground where I had already passed so many exciting moments. The smell of corruption was scarcely endurable in the sultry air. We sprinkled the bodies with quicklime that we had brought with us in sacks. The covering of white shone out like grave-clothes in the darkness.

The enterprise opened with our own machine-gun fire whistling between our legs and pattering against the bank. On this account Schultz and I had a violent altercation, for he himself had given the machine-gunners their range. We were reconciled, however, when Schultz discovered me behind a bush in close confabulation with a bottle of Burgundy that I had brought with me to invigorate me for the precarious adventure and to calm my nerves, which had been on the stretch for nine days past.

The first shell came along to the minute and landed fifty metres behind us. Before we could express our surprise at this extraordinary shooting, a second was planted close behind us on the bank and showered us with earth. It was not for me even to emit a curse, for I myself had given the range for the guns.

After this cheerful opening we advanced more as a matter of honour than with any great hopes of success. Luckily, the enemy posts had apparently retired. Otherwise we might have had a very unpleasant reception. Unfortunately, we did not find the machine-gun, nor did we search for it very long.

On the way back, Schultz and I once more told each other what we really thought—I about the way he had directed his machine-gun fire, and he about the shooting of the guns. I had tested the range so accurately that the affair seemed incomprehensible. Later I learned that guns always shoot short at night, and that I ought to have added a few hundred metres when I gave the range. Then we sat down to the most important part of the business—the report. We did so well that every one was delighted.

The skirmishing came to an end the next day, for we were relieved by another division.

We went back to Montbréhain for a time, and marched from there to Cambrai, where we spent nearly the whole of July.

The outpost was finally lost on the night following our relief.

# LANGEMARCK

Cambrai is a quiet, sleepy little town whose name calls up many historical associations. The narrow, old-world streets twist about round the mighty town-hall, the weathered gates, and the many churches. Ponderous towers rear themselves from a maze of gables. Broad avenues lead to the park, which is adorned by a monument to the aviator Bléroit.

The inhabitants are peaceful, friendly folk who lead a comfortable bourgeois life in the large houses which are simple to look at but richly furnished. Many retired people settle here. The town is rightly called 'la ville des millionaires,' for there were over forty millionaires there just before the war.

The war broke its enchanted sleep with brutal suddenness and turned it into a focus of mighty battles. A new life hurried and rattled over its unevenly paved streets and clattered against the little windows where anxious faces were on the watch. Foreigners drank the treasured cellars dry, flung themselves on the great mahogany beds, and upset the contemplative civilians with something fresh every day. Now in their changed surroundings they could do no more than collect at corners or in doorways and hold whispered consultations over the latest fairy-tales of an eye-witness and the most certain news of the final and speedy victory of their fellow-countrymen.

The men lived in barracks and the officers in the Rue des Liniers. While we were there this street had the appearance of a students' quarter. Conversation carried on from one window to another, nightly sing-songs, and little romantic adventures were the order of the day.

We went every morning for training to the great square near the village of Fontaine, which was later to become famous. My job was a very interesting one, for Colonel von Oppen had entrusted me with the training of the storm troop.

My billet was extremely comfortable. It was in the house of a jeweler named Plancot-Bourlon, and he and his wife were both very friendly. They seldom allowed my mid-day meal to pass without sending me up something good from their own table. At night we drank tea together, played cards, and talked. One of the questions we most often discussed, naturally enough, was the very difficult one, why there had to be wars.

On these occasions M. Plancot used to tell stories of the citizens of Cambrai, who are never too busy for a joke. In peace time these stories sent streets, wineshops, and markets into roars of laughter, and they reminded me very forcibly of Tillier's wonderful uncle Benjamin.

A wicked fellow once sent to all the hunchbacks of the district requesting them to call on a certain solicitor with reference to an important inheritance.

At the appointed hour he and some of his friends watched from the window of the opposite house and enjoyed the delightful comedy—seventeen outraged and weeping hobgoblins storming the office of the unfortunate lawyer.

There was the story, too, of an old spinster who lived opposite, and who was distinguished by a long and slender neck strangely bent to one side. Twenty years before she had been notoriously eager to marry. Six young fellows presented themselves, and to each she gladly gave the permission to speak to her parents. The next Sunday a capacious coach drove up in which sat the six young men, each with a bouquet in his hand. In terror she locked the door and hid herself, and the suitors delighted the neighbourhood by playing the fool in the street.

Again: A notorious Cambresian went to the market and asked a peasant's wife, pointing to a soft round, and appetizing cheese covered with green mould:

'What is the price of this cheese?'

'Twenty sous, sir.'

He paid her the twenty sous.

'So the cheese is now mine?'

'To be sure, sir.'

'And I can do what I want with it?'

'Well, of course!'

Smack! he threw the cheese in her face and fled.

On the 25th of July we left the dear little town and entrained for Flanders. We had read in the papers that an artillery duel was raging there such as the world had never seen.

We detrained in Staden to the distant thunder of guns and marched through the unfamiliar landscape to our camp. On either side of the dead-straight road were green and fruitful fields, raised up in plots like flower-beds, and luscious, well-watered meadows surrounded by hedges. There were clean farmhouses scattered here and there, with low thatched or tiled roofs, and on the walls bundles of tobacco-plants hung out to dry. The countryfolk on the roads were of German type, and their rough speech had a pleasant, homely sound. We spent the afternoon in the farm gardens to avoid being seen from the air. Now and then the shells of heavy naval guns could be heard rushing hoarsely overhead from far back and then exploding not far from us. A number of men of the 91st Regiment who were bathing in one of the numerous little streams were killed. Towards evening I had to go with an advance detachment to the front line to prepare for the relief, and we went through Houthulst Forest and the village of Koekuit to the reserve battalion. On the way we had to 'break step' once or twice on account of some heavy shells. In the darkness I heard the voice of a recruit: 'The officer never lies down!'

'The man knows what he is about,' an older soldier informed him. 'Wait till a proper one comes, and he'll be the first to lie down!'

The man had noticed the principle I always followed: 'Only take cover when it is necessary, and then do it quickly.'

It is true that only the experienced can judge of the necessity, and feel the end of the shell's trajectory before the recruit has even recognized the light warning whisper in the air.

Our guides, who did not seem to be quite sure of themselves, took us along an endless box-trench. Such is the name for trenches that are not dug in the ground, because the water would stand in them at once, but built up above its level with sandbags and fascines. Then we went along the side of a terribly dishevelled wood, from which a few days before, according to our guides, a regimental staff had been driven by the small matter of one thousand 24-centimetre shells. 'Things seem to be done on a large scale here,' I thought to myself.

After we had wandered backwards and forwards through thick undergrowth, we came to a halt in a piece of ground overgrown with weeds and fringed by a marshy swamp in whose black pools the moonlight was reflected. Our guide had abandoned us, and all the white shells were falling somewhere and slinging up the mud that splashed back again into the water. At last the miserable guide returned to receive the full volley of our wrath and to announce that he had found the way. Nevertheless, he again led us astray until we came at last to a dressing-station over which shrapnel shells were bursting in couples at short and regular intervals. The bullets and empty cases rattled through the branches. The M.O. on duty gave us a sensible fellow, who took us on to the Mäuseburg, the headquarters of the reserve line.

From there I went straight on to the company of the 225th Regiment that our 2nd Company was to relieve. It took me a long search in the shell-pitted country before I found a few ruinous houses that were fortified inside by reinforced concrete. One had been smashed in the day before by a shell and the occupants squashed like mice beneath the falling roof-plate.

I spent the rest of the night at the company commander's overcrowded concrete block-house. He was an honest front-line swine who, with his orderlies, was passing the time over a bottle of schnaps and a good chunk of pork, with frequent intervals during which he listened to the steadily increasing shell-fire and shook his head. Then he would fall to bemoaning the good old days on the Russian front, and cursing the way his regiment had been pumped out. At last I fell asleep.

My sleep was heavy and oppressed. The H.E. shells falling all round the house in the pitchy darkness evoked a sense of indescribable loneliness and forlornness from the murdered landscape. Involuntarily I nestled up to a man who shared the same bunk. Once I was scared by a heavy thump. My men made a light and looked to see if the wall had been penetrated. It was found that a light shell had exploded against the outer wall.

I spent the next afternoon with the commanding officer of the battalion at the Mäuseburg, as there were still some important points on which I had to be informed. All this time 15-centimetre shells were falling round headquarters, while the captain, with his adjutant and the orderly officer, played an endless game of Skat over a sodawater bottle full of raw spirits. Sometimes he put his cards down to send off a report, or to discuss very seriously whether our concrete shelter was bomb-proof. We convinced him, in spite of the warmth with which he argued the contrary (the wish being clearly the father to the thought), that we were not fitted to sustain a direct hit from the air.

In the evening the customary artillery fire rose to frantic intensity, and in the front line there was an unceasing display of coloured lights. Dust-covered despatch-carriers brought in reports that the enemy was attacking. After weeks of drum-fire the infantry battle had begun.

I went back to company headquarters, and waited there for the arrival of the 2nd Company. It appeared at four in the morning during a very lively burst of shell-fire. I took command of my platoon at once and led it to a position covered with the fragments of a shell-destroyed house, a spot most unspeakably forlorn in the midst of an immense and dreary waste of shell-holes.

At six in the morning the Flanders mist lifted and gave us a glimpse of our ghastly surroundings. At once a swarm of low-flying enemy machines appeared, scrutinizing the battered ground and sounding sirens. Any scattered detachments of infantry that were above ground instantly endeavoured to hide themselves in shell-holes.

Half an hour later a terrific artillery fire set in. It raged round our refuge like a typhoon-scourged sea round an island. The hail of shells thickened to a throbbing wall of fire. We crouched together, expecting each second the crashing hit that would sweep us up with our concrete blocks and make our position indistinguishable from the desert of craters all round.

The whole day passed in bursts of heavy shell-fire like this, with pauses during which we prepared ourselves for the next bout.

In the evening an exhausted orderly turned up and handed me an order. From this I learned that the 1st, 3rd, and 4th Companies were to counter-attack at 10.30, and that the 2nd Company after being relieved was to swarm into the front line. In order to get a little strength to face the hours ahead, I lay down, never dreaming that my brother Fritz, whom I supposed to be still in Hanover, was in a section of the 3rd Company, and passing close to my hut in a hurricane of fire on his way to the attack.

My sleep was disturbed for a long while by the pitiful cries of a wounded man whom two Saxons had brought in. They had lost their way, and were utterly done up and had fallen asleep. When they awoke in the morning, their comrade was dead. They carried him to the nearest shell-hole, and after covering him with a few shovelfuls of earth they went back on their way, leaving one more to be added to the countless lonely and unknown graves of the war.

I woke at eleven out of a heavy sleep. I washed in my helmet, and sent for orders to the company commander. To my astonishment, he had already gone, without letting me or Kius or our platoons know anything of it.

This showed the consequence of putting officers of another arm in the service in command of front-line troops, only because of seniority, and though they did not know how even to handle a rifle. Let such fetishes be followed when human lives are not at stake.

While I still sat cursing on my bunk and considered what to do, an orderly appeared from battalion headquarters with the order to take immediate command of the 8th Company.

I learnt that the counter-attack of the 1st Battalion on the previous night had been repulsed with heavy loss, and that what was left had taken up a defensive position in a small wood called the Dobschüz wood, and to the right and left of it. The 8th Company had been given the task of swarming into the wood in support. It had, however, run into a barrage in the intervening ground and suffered heavy losses. As the company commander, Lieutenant Büdingen, was among the fallen, I was to lead the company on in a fresh advance.

After I had taken leave of my orphaned platoon, I made my way with the orderly across country. The desolation lay under a rain of shrapnel, and as we went along half-bent we were checked by a despairing voice. In the distance we could see a figure with bleeding arm-stumps raising itself from a shell-hole. We pointed to the hut we had just left, and hastened on.

I found the 8th Company crouching behind a row of concrete positions: an utterly dispirited little mob.

'Platoon commanders!'

Three N.C.Os. came forward and declared that a further advance towards Dobschüz wood was out of the question. It was indeed the fact that the shells were bursting on our front like a wall of fire. Next I had the platoons assembled behind three concrete positions. Each was about fifteen to twenty men strong. At this moment the fire lifted and came on to us. The scene was indescribable. At the concrete position on the left the whole section was blown into the air; the right got a direct hit and buried Lieutenant Büdingen, who was still lying there wounded, beneath its tons of masonry. We were in a mortar and beaten down by incessant concussions. Faces as white as death stared at each other, and the cries of those who were hit never ceased.

It was all the same now whether we stayed where we were, or went on or back. So I gave the command to follow me, and sprang out into the fire. After a few steps I was covered with earth and flung into a shell-hole by a shell which fortunately exploded straight upwards. I observed soon after, however, that the fire was not so heavy further on. When I had worked my way forward another two hundred metres, I looked about me. There was not a soul in sight.

Finally, two men emerged from the clouds of dust and smoke. Then one more. Then another two. With these five men I safely arrived at my goal.

I found Lieutenant Sandvoss, commander of the 3rd Company, and little Schultz seated in a half smashed-up concrete pill-box with three heavy machine-guns. I was greeted with a loud 'Hullo!' and a sip of cognac; and then the situation, by no means a pleasant one, was explained to me. The English were close in front of us, and both our flanks were in the air. We cordially agreed that this was a corner too tight for any but old veterans who had grown grey in the smoke of battle.

Without a word of warning Sandvoss asked me if I had heard anything of my brother. My feelings can be imagined when I heard that he had been in yesterday's attack and was missing. A moment later a man came and told me that my brother was lying wounded in a shelter close by, and pointed out to me a desolate blockhouse covered with uprooted trees. I hurried across a clearing which was covered by rifle-fire, and went in. What a meeting! My brother lay among a crowd of groaning stretcher-cases in a place that stank of death. He was in a sad plight. He had been hit by two shrapnel bullets in the attack, one of which had pierced the lung and the other his right shoulder. Fever shone in his eyes; it was only with difficulty that he could move or speak or breathe. He returned the pressure of my hand, and we began to talk.

It was clear to me that I could not leave him there, for at any moment the English might attack, or a shell put an end to the already damaged concrete shelter. It was a brother's duty to get him sent back at once. In spite of Sandvoss, who would not hear of any weakening our strength, I ordered the five men who had come with me to get my brother back to the Kolumbusei dressing-station, and from there to bring back with them men to rescue the other wounded also. We tied him in a ground-sheet, and stuck a long pole through it, which rested on two of the men's shoulders. I squeezed his hand again, and the sad procession started on its way.

From the edge of the wood I watched the swaying load on its way through another wood, among towering shell-bursts. As each one struck, I caught myself together, though the place where I was no safer. It is odd that another's danger makes a stronger impression than one's own. This may be explained partly by the confidence in his own luck that every one has. The belief that nothing can happen to himself makes each man underestimate the danger. It is only in another's case that one sees how overwhelming it is and how defenceless its victim.

After I had skirmished a little from the shell-holes on the forward edge of the wood with the English, who were coming on very slowly, I spent the night with my men and a machine-gun section among the ruins of the concrete pill-box. H.E. shells of quite extraordinary ferocity were going up all the time close by us. In the evening I was within an ace of being killed by one of them. The machine-gun began rattling off towards morning, when some figures approached in the darkness. It was a patrol of the 76th Regiment, come to get into touch with us. One of them was killed, there were many such mistakes during these days, but it was of no use to dwell on them.

At six in the morning we were relieved by a detachment from the 9th Company. They brought me orders to occupy the Rattenburg with my men. I had a casualty on the way, a Fahnenjunker wounded by a shrapnel bullet.

We found the Rattenburg to be a shell-shot house walled up with concrete slabs. It stood close by the marshy bed of the Steenbeek, which no doubt well deserved its name.

Somewhat done up, we entered into possession and flung ourselves down on the straw-covered bed boards. After a good feed and a pipe of tobacco we felt more ourselves again.

In the early hours of the afternoon we were heavily shelled with shells up to the heaviest calibres. Between six and eight one explosion overlapped another, and the building often trembled at the sickening thump of a dud and threatened to collapse. When the fire ebbed later on, I went cautiously over a hill that was covered in a close and whirring mesh of shrapnel to the Kolumbusei dressing-station, and asked for news of my brother. The doctor, who was examining the terribly mangled legs of a dying man, told me to my joy that he had been sent back in a fairly promising state.

Later in the night my ration-party turned up and brought the company, now reduced to twenty men, warm food, bully-beef, coffee, and bread, tobacco and schnaps. We ate heartily, circulating the bottle of '98 per cent.' without any irksome distinctions of rank. Then we turned in; but our rest, owing to the swarms of gnats that rose from the marshy banks of the stream, the shells, and the gas that was shot over occasionally, was not exactly undisturbed.

The result that I was so fast asleep the next morning that after a heavy bombardment had gone on for hours my men had to rouse me. They told me that men were coming back all the time, saying that the front line had been evacuated and that the enemy were coming on.

I first followed the old soldier's maxim, 'A good breakfast holds body and soul together,' and then, after lighting a pipe, went outside to see what was happening.

I could not see a great deal, as the surroundings were veiled in a thick haze. The artillery fire was increasing from moment to moment, and soon reached that pitch of intensity which the nerves, incapable of further shock, accept with an almost happy indifference. Showers of earth clattered incessantly on the roof, and the house itself was hit twice. Incendiary shells threw up heavy milk-white clouds, out of which fiery drops rained on the ground. A piece of this burning stuff came smack on a stone at my feet, and went on burning for a good minute. We were later told that men hit with it had rolled on the ground without being able to put it out. Shells with delay-action fuses burrowed into the ground, rumbling and pushing out flat disks of soil. Swathes of gas and mist crept over the battlefield, hugging the ground. Immediately in front we heard rifle and machine-gun fire, a sign that the enemy had advanced already.

Below, beside the stream, I saw some men walking through a constantly changing scenery of mud fountains shooting high into the air. I recognized the commanding officer, Captain von Brixen, supported by two stretcher-bearers, and with an arm bound up. I hastened towards him; he called out that the enemy was advancing, and warned me not to delay in getting under cover.

Soon the first bullets smacked into the shell-holes near by or were shivered against the broken masonry. More and more fleeing figures disappeared to our rear, while in front a storm of rifle-fire testified to the embittered defence put up by those who were holding on.

It was time to act. I decided to defend the Rattenburg, and made it plain to the men, among whom at this there were some rueful faces, that I had not the remotest thought of retiring. I posted the men at loopholes, and our one machine-gun was mounted on a window-sill. A shell-hole was chosen and a stretcher-bearer, who soon had plenty to do, was installed there. I, too, took a rifle I found lying about, and hung a belt of cartridges round my neck.

As my crowd was very small I tried to get reinforcements from the numbers of men who were passing by in disorder. Most of them obeyed my call willingly, glad to join up, while others whose nerve had gone hurried past after a hasty pause to see that there was nothing to be got by staying with us. In such cases a tender consideration has no place.

'Fire!' I called to the men who stood in front of me in the cover of the house, and a few shots rang out. Overcome by the eloquence of the rifle-muzzle, the shirkers, of whom in every battle there must always be some, came slowly nearer, though it was plain from their faces how little eager they were to give us their company. A canteen orderly whom I knew well made all kinds of excuses to get away. But I would not let go of him.

'But I have no rifle!'

'Then wait till there's a man shot.'

During a final crisis of artillery fire, in the course of which the ruins of the house were hit several times and the fragments of bricks pattered down on our helmets from high in the air, I was thrown down to the ground in a flash of a terrific burst. To the astonishment of the men, I got up again unhurt.

After this wild whirligig of shells it became calmer. The fire lifted over us and rested on the Langemarck-Bixschoote road. But we were none the better off in mind, for so far we had not seen the wood for trees; the danger had been so overwhelming that we had no time or power to think of it. Now that the storm had swept on past us, every one had time to get ready for what was inevitably coming nearer. And it came.

The rifles in front were silent. The opposition had been overcome. Out of the haze emerged a thick advancing line. My men fired crouching behind the wreckage. The machine-gun tacked out. As though they had been wiped away, the attacking line vanished into shell-holes and opened fire on us. Strong detachments went on to the left and right. We were soon surrounded by a ring of fire.

The position was pointless, and there was no object in sacrificing the men. I gave the order to retire. Now that they had started, it was difficult to make the men give up the fight.

Making use of a low-lying cloud of smoke, we got away unobserved, partly by wading above the hips along the stream. I was the last to leave the little fort. Lieutenant Höhlemann, whom I helped along, was bleeding from a severe head wound, though he joked and made light of it as we went.

As we crossed the road we ran into the 2nd Company, who had been sent up in support. After a brief consultation we decided to stay where we were and await the enemy. Here, too, we had to compel troops of other units, who wished to carry out retirements on their own, to remain. Stern measures were necessary to persuade artillerymen, and signalers, and so on, that even they in circumstances like these had to take hold of a rifle and get into the firing-line. With the help of Kius and a few quiet folk I soon got matters into order by means of entreaties, commands, and blows with the butt-end.

Then we sat ourselves in a half-dug trench and had breakfast. Kius pulled out his inevitable camera and took photographs. On our left there was some movement on the outskirts of Langemarck. The men began shooting at some figures that were running here and there, until I told them to stop. Immediately after a N.C.O. came up and reported that a company of the Fusilier Guards were taking up a position on the road, and that our fire had inflicted losses.

I gave the order thereupon to advance and occupy the highest part of the road. There was lively rifle-fire, some of the men fell, and Lieutenant Bartmer of the 2nd Company was severely wounded. Kius remained at my side and finished his piece of bread-and-butter as we went. When we occupied the line of the road, whence the ground fell away to the Steenbeek, we saw that the English had been on the point of doing the same. the first khaki uniforms were already within twenty metres of it. As far as the eye could see, the ground to our front was full of troops in line and column. They were swarming round the Rattenburg too.

99

We made full use of the surprise of our sudden appearance and at once opened a steady fire on them. Along the Steenbeek a whole column broke up. One man had a coil of wire on his back of which he was unrolling one end. Others jumped like hares this way and that while our bullets raised clouds of dust among them. A sturdy corporal of the 8th Company rested his rifle with the greatest calm on a shattered tree-stump and shot four of the enemy one after the other. The remainder crept into shell-holes and lay concealed there till nightfall. We had made a good clearance.

At about 11 o'clock aeroplanes tied with streamers came diving down on us and were driven off by a lively fire, which they replied to from above. In the midst of the wild clatter I could not help smiling when a man reported to me and desired to have it placed on record that he had shot down a machine in flames with his rifle.

Immediately after occupying the road I had made a report to regimental headquarters and asked for reinforcements. At mid-day detachments of infantry, engineers, and machine-guns came up in support. According to the time-honoured tactics of Old Fritz all of them were crammed into the already crowded front-line. Here and there the English laid out a few of the men who incautiously crossed the road.

About 4 o'clock a very unpleasant bombardment with shrapnel started. The volleys got the road to a T. It was clear to me that the aeroplanes had ascertained the line on which we were making a stand, and that there were worse times ahead.

And, in fact, we were soon being heavily shelled with shells of all sizes. We lay close to one another in the narrow and crowded ditch of the road. Fire danced before our eyes; twigs and clods whistled about our ears. Close to me on my left a flash flared out, leaving a white suffocating vapour behind it. I crept on all-fours to the man next to me. He moved no more. The blood trickled from many wounds caused by small jagged splinters. On my right, too, there were many hit.

After half an hour it was quiet and we set to digging out the shallow trough of the ditch so as to have at least protection from splinters in case of a second bombardment. Our entrenching tools came against rifles, equipment, and cartridge-cases of 1914, showing that this soil was not drinking blood for the first time.

As dark came on we were given another thorough good do. I crouched beside Kius in a little hole that had cost us some blisters. The ground rocked like a ship's deck under hit after hit at the least possible distances. We were ready for the end.

I chewed my pipe, my helmet pressed on to my forehead, and stared at the pavé whose stones showered sparks under the bursting lumps of metal; and I succeeded in philosophizing myself into courage. The most remarkable thoughts shot through my head. I took a trashy French novel, *La Vautour de la Sierra*, that I had picked up in Cambrai, into lively consideration. I repeated several times to myself a saying of Ariosto, 'A great heart cares nothing for death when it comes, so long when it may be glorious.' It may seem extraordinary, but it helped me to keep control over myself. When the shells gave our ears a little peace, I heard fragments of the beautiful song from *The Black Whale of Askelon* close beside me, and I thought that my friend Kius must have had a drop too much. Every one has his own manner of calming his nerves.

At the end of it a large splinter struck my hand. Kius took out a torch. We only found a scratch.

Hours such as these were without doubt the most awful of the whole war.

You cower in a heap alone in a hole and feel yourself the victim of a pitiless thirst for destruction. With horror you feel that all your intelligence, your capacities, your bodily and spiritual characteristics, have become utterly meaningless and absurd. While you think it, the lump of metal that will crush you to a shapeless nothing may have started on its course. Your discomfort is concentrated in your ear, that tries to distinguish amid the uproar the swirl of your own death rushing near. It is dark, too; and you must find in yourself alone all the strength for holding out. You can't get up and with a *blasé* laugh light a cigarette in the wondering sight of your companions. Nor can you be encouraged by the sight of your friend clipping a monocle into his eye to observe a hit on the traverse close beside you. You know that not even a cock will crow when you are hit.

Well, why don't you jump up and rush into the night till you collapse in safety behind a bush like an exhausted animal? Why do you hang on there all the time, you and your braves? There are no superior officers to see you.

Yet some one watches you. Unknown perhaps to yourself, there is some one within you who keeps you to your post by the power of two mighty spells: Duty and Honour. You know that this is your place in the battle, and that a whole people relies on you to do your job. You feel, 'If I leave my post, I am a coward in my own eyes, a wretch who will ever after blush at every word of praise. You clench your teeth and stay.

All of us held on that evening, all who lay along the dark Flanders road. Officers and men alike showed what they were made of. Duty and Honour must be the corner-stones of every army. And a heightened sense of duty and honour must be inculcated in the officer who fights in the forefront of the battle. For that, suitable material and a fixed mould are required. The truth of this is fully known only in war. . . .

It began to drizzle after midnight; patrols of a regiment which had come up meanwhile in support went forward as far as the Steenbeek and found nothing but mud-filled shell-holes. The enemy had withdrawn beyond the stream.

Worn out by the fatigues of this tremendous day, we got down into our holes, with the exception of the men on guard. I pulled the cloak of my dead neighbour over my head and fell into a restless sleep. As it grew light I was awakened by a curiously cold feeling and discovered that I was in a sad way. It was raining in torrents and the drainage of the road was pouring into the hole where I was sitting. I built a small dam and bailed out my resting-place with a saucepan-lid. In consequence of the ever-increasing volume of water I had to add one course after another to my earthwork, till at last faulty construction yielded to growing weight and a muddy stream gurgled in and filled my refuge to the brim. While I was busy fishing out my revolver and helmet, tobacco and rations were borne away along the ditch, whose other occupants were faring just as I was. We stood shivering with cold and without a dry stitch on our bodies, knowing that when next we were shelled we had no protection whatever. It was a cheerful situation. And here I permit myself the observation that even artillery fire does not break the resistance of troops so surely as wet and cold.

The steady downpour was nevertheless a true blessing in its effects upon the further course of the battle; for the English offensive was just in its first and most critical days. The enemy had to bring up his artillery over a morass of water-logged shell-holes, while we had undamaged roads for the transport of all we needed.

At 11 in the morning, when we were already desperate, an angel appeared in the person of a despatch-rider who brought the order for the regiment to assemble in Koekuit.

We saw on the way how difficult communications must have been on the day of the attack. The roads were packed with men and horses. Twelve horribly mutilated horses lay in one heap near some limbers whose wreckage was scarcely recognizable.

What was left of the regiment assembled in a rain-soaked meadow over which single bursts of shrapnel opened their white balls. It was a shock to see what was left—a body of about the strength of a company with a small groups of officer in the midst. What losses! Of two battalions, nearly all the officers and men! The survivors stood in pouring rain with gloomy faces till quarters were assigned. Then we dried ourselves in a wooden hut, crowding round a glowing stove, and got some fresh courage from a hearty meal.

Towards evening shells fell in the village. One of the huts was hit and several men of the 3rd Company killed. In spite of the shelling we soon lay down to sleep, only hoping that we should not have to counter-attack in the rain or be flung without warning into some gap in the line.

At 3 in the morning orders came that we were definitely to be taken out of the line. We marched along the pavé to Staden. It was strewn all the way with dead bodies and smashed up transport. Twelve dead lay round the crater of one gigantic burst alone. Staden, that had been so full of life on our arrival, now had many houses shelled; the deserted market-place heaped up with household goods hurriedly taken out of the houses. One family was leaving the town at the same time as we were. It led a cow as its only possession. The man had a wooden leg, and the woman led the crying child by the hand. The confused din behind added to the sadness of the picture.

The remains of the 2nd Battalion were quartered in a lonely farm, concealed behind tall hedges in the midst of luxuriant fields. There I was given command of 7th Company. Till the end of the war its fortune and mine were one.

In the evening we sat before an old tiled hearth and refreshed ourselves with a stiff grog while we listened to the thunder of battle breaking out afresh. A sentence from the army *communiqué* suddenly met my eyes in a recent newspaper: 'We succeeded in holding up the attack on the Steenbeek.'

It was odd to feel that our apparently confused doings in the depth of night had won a place in history. The enemy offensive, launched with such tremendous force, had been brought to a standstill, and we had a large share in that result.

Soon we turned in the hayloft. In spite of the profound sleep in which they were sunk, most of the sleepers tossed to and fro in their dreams, as though they had to fight their Flanders battle over again.

On the 3rd of August we set off on the march to the station of the neighbouring town of Gits. We took much of the cattle and produce of the now deserted neighbourhood with us. The whole battalion, in fine spirits again, shrunken though it was, had coffee in the station restaurant. Two buxom Flemish waitresses added to its flavour and to the general contentment by their bold speeches. The men were particularly delighted when they addressed every one, officers included, as 'thou,' as it is the local custom to do.

*          *

*

A few days later I had a letter from my brother in hospital in Gelsenkirchen. He wrote that he was booked for a stiff arm and a shaky lung.

I take the following pages from his diary. They will my own account and give a vivid picture of the impressions made on a young boy who was thrown into the hurricane of modern battle:—

' ". . . Fall in for the attack!" The face of my platoon commander, Sergeant-major Schnell, looked in over the entrance of the little hole covered with branches and boards where we had lain for hours smoking and eating. The three men near me stopped their talk and jumped up cursing. I got up and put on my equipment, set my helmet tight on my head, and went out into the dusk. It was misty and chilly. The scene had altered meanwhile. The shell-fire had moved off and now thundered on other parts of the immense battlefield. Aeroplanes roared through the air and calmed one's anxiously peering eyes with their large iron crosses.

'I went once more to a spring which was still wonderfully clear in spite of the wreckage and rubbish, and drawing up the bucket I drank, and filled my water-bottle.

'The company fell in by platoons. I quickly stuck four bombs in my belt and went to my section, from which two men were missing. I had scarcely time to write down their names before we moved off. The platoons proceeded in single file over the shell-holes, skirting bits of timber, squeezing against hedges, sinking into holes, and making their way with much clatter and rattle to attack the enemy.

'I knew what my task was. The 2nd Battalion of our regiment and a battalion of another on our flank had orders to drive some English detachments, which had pushed on over the canal, back to the other side again. My orders were to take up a position in advance with my section and lie down in readiness to open the counter-attack. While I was going over to see this again, I happened to see the pale, set face of a young N.C.O. "Bachmann," I thought, although I did not know him. It was my comrade, a Fahnenjunker like-wise in Sandvoss's company. I lost sight of him, and looked with astonishment at the scene that had suddenly unfolded.

'The remains of a large wood, black, branchless, and splintered stumps, stuck up in isolation here and there from the scarred Flanders plain. Immense swathes of smoke drifted through the air and hung the sky with a gloomy, heavy pall. Stinking gases, yellow and brown, hung and swayed heavily to and fro over the earth that the shells tore up so mercilessly again and again.

'The order was given to be ready for gas. At this moment a terrific fire came on us like a fit. The soil flew up in fountains and a hail of splinters swept the ground like a shower of rain. For a moment every one stood dazed. Then all broke away like mad. I heard our commanding officer Colonel Böckelmann, bellowing out something, but I could understand nothing.

'My men had vanished and I found myself in another platoon. I pressed on with the rest to the wreckage of a village that the shells had razed relentlessly to the very foundations. We pulled out our masks.

'Without a moment's warning we were in a terrific machine-gun barrage. Every one threw himself down. Near me on my left Lieutenant Ehlers was kneeling up, and near him lay a N.C.O. keeping a look-out. In front there was a yellow, flashing wall of fire. Burst followed burst. Fragments of masonry, showers of soil, brickbats, and splinters rained down on us and struck sparks from our helmets. I stared into this glaring witch's cauldron.

'Compared to this, what was the half-hour's drum-fire that had prepared for this ill-fated attack? For it was as clear to me as a vision that it had failed. Thrice at short intervals a tremendous crash swept through the uproar. Whole rubbish-heaps took the air at once, whirled around and pelted down again with hellish clatter.

'I looked to my right. Ehlers was shouting something. He raised his left hand, beckoned over his shoulder, and with a shout sprang forward. I got up heavily and followed at the double. My feet were burning like fire after the night before, but my socks had soaked up the blood and the pain was not so sharp.

'I had not gone twenty steps when the flash of a shrapnel blinded me as I struggled up out of a shell-hole. It burst not ten paces in front of me at a height of three metres. I felt two dull blows against my chest and shoulder. My rifle flew from my hands of its own accord and I fell backwards into the shell-hole. I could still hear remotely Ehlers shouting as he went by, "It's finished him." He was not to live out another day. The attack miscarried, and in jumping back he was killed and all who were with him. A shot though the back of the head ended the life of this gallant officer.

'When I woke from a long fainting fit all was still. I tried to stand up, but I felt a sharp pain in my right shoulder that increased with every movement. My breath was short and gasping. The lung could not get enough air. "Hit through the lung and shoulder," I thought, and threw away pack and belt and, in a mood of utter apathy, gas-mask too, and hung my water-bottle on the hooks of my tunic.

'After five steps I sank helplessly into a neighbouring shell-hole. After an hour, perhaps, I made a second attempt to crawl on, as a light drum-fire had started. This attempt, too, miscarried. I lost my water-bottle and sank into a state of exhaustion, from which after a long time the sensation of burning thirst aroused me.

'It began to rain gently. I succeeded in collecting a few muddy drops in my steel helmet. I had lost all sense of direction. There was a thunderstorm, but its peals were lost in a new onset of drum-fire. I clung close to the side of the shell-hole. A clod struck my shoulder. Heavy splinters swept over my head. Gradually I lost all sense of time.

'Once two men appeared, hurrying by with long strides. I called to them, but they disappeared in the mist like shadows without hearing me. At last three men came straight towards me. I recognized the middle one was the N.C.O. of the day before. They took me to a little hut near by. It was crammed with wounded, whom two orderlies were seeing to. I had lain thirteen hours among the shell-holes.

'In a corner I saw Bachmann, who convulsively clasped his shattered knee and swallowed down his agony. We spoke in fragments. Now and then when any one pushed against him he suppressed a groan.

'All the while the artillery fire kept at the same pitch. Shell after shell burst close to us, often covering the roof with sand and earth. My wounds were dressed, and I was given a new mask and a piece of bread spread with coarse red jam, and a little water. The orderly looked after us like a father.

'The English began to push forward. They came on by springs and then disappeared in shell-holes, as I could make out from the cries of consternation outside.

'Then my company commander, Lieutenant Sandvoss, came in. He asked me if I could walk, and then was called away by an orderly and vanished. Immediately I heard him giving orders. A machine-gun was mounted and began to tack out.

'Suddenly a young officer smeared in mud from his boots to his helmet, with the Iron Cross of the 1st class on his breast, rushed in. It was my brother, who days before, down the line, was said to be dead. We greeted each other, smiling rather awkwardly in the stress of our feelings. After a minute or two he left me and came back with the last five men of his company. I was put in a ground-sheet and carried away from the battlefield to the thunder of guns.'

# REGNIÉVILLE

On the 4th July 1917 we got out of the train at the famous Mars-la-Tour. The 7th and 8th Companies were quartered in Doncourt, where for some days we lived an almost contemplative life. the only source of conflict for me was the shortage of rations. It was strictly forbidden to forage in the fields, and yet the military police brought me reports nearly every morning with the names of men they caught potato-lifting by night. I had to punish them, for the crime of being caught, as it stood in my (perhaps unofficial) code.

I had to learn, too, during those days that wrong-doing never comes to any good. Tebbe and I had brought with us a princely lord-mayor's coach from an abandoned Flemish mansion, and had contrived to include it in the transport unobserved. Now we planned a magnificent expedition to Metz, in order to taste life at the full once more. So we harnessed up one afternoon and drove off. Unfortunately, the coach had no brakes, since it was designed for the Flemish plain, not for the hills of Lorraine. Before we were out of the village we had already begun to roll, and soon found ourselves embarked on a mad career that boded no good. The first to jump for it was the coachman; then Tebbe, who fell full-length on a heap of agricultural implements, and lay there. I remained alone on the silken upholstery, but certainly not at my ease. A door flew open, and was knocked straight off by a telephone pole. Finally, the coach leapt down a bank and crashed against the wall of a house. I left the wreckage by a window, and ascertained that, with my unusual luck, I was none the worse.

On the 9th the company was inspected by the commander of the division, Major-General von Busse, who praised us for our conduct in the recent fighting. We entrained on the next afternoon for the neighbourhood of Thiaucourt. Thence we marched straight on to our new position in the line. It lay along the wooded heights of the Côte Lorraine, opposite the much-shelled village of Regniéville. It was the first time for a long while that we had the French opposite us.

The trench walls were of chalk, and this withstood the weather much better than the clay we were accustomed to. In places the sides of the trench were even carefully walled, and the floor of it concentrated for long stretches, so that even in the heaviest rain the water could soon run away. the reddish-white rock abounded in fossils. Every time I went to my dugout with a pocketful of mussels, star-fish, and snake-stone. My dugout was deep and drippy. It had a peculiarity very little to my liking, though I am a passionate entomologist. Instead of the usual louse, we had here its far livelier relative. These two varieties appear to have the same enmity to each other as the brown and common rat. It was no good adopting the usual remedy of a change of clothes, for the nimble parasites lay in ambush in the straw palliasses. At last the victim leapt up in desperation, and could have said with Mephisto:

> I give the old rug another shake
> And still one more to flight does take;
> Up! and away! with all my soul
> Go find yourselves another 'ole!

Rations, too, were very poor. Beyond the thin mid-day soup, there was nothing but the third of a loaf, and something infinitesimal to eat it with, usually half-mouldy jam. Most of mine was always eaten by a fat rat, for which I often lay in wait, but in vain.

This sparse living, which left us always half-fed, brought about a most unpleasant state of affairs. The men often suffered literally from hunger, and this led to pilfering of rations. It surprised me to find that I, though used to good and plentiful food, seemed to bear the privation much better than the men. Cabbage soup was their only thought. When it comes to food, the good manners that in Europe are mostly whitewash are soon scratched off. A man shows his real superiority when hunger is part of the meal, not at festive tables. Privation and danger tear away all that has been acquired, and then good form survives only in those in whom it is born.

The companies in reserve and on rest occupied hutments in picturesque situations deeply hidden in the forest. My quarters in reserve were particularly delightful. The camp was in a blind corner on the edge of a narrow forest gorge. My little hut was built half into the bank, and curtained with hazel and cornel bushes. From the window I had a view of the wooded hillside opposite and a narrow strip of meadow traversed by a stream. A collection of bottles of all sorts stacked at the back showed that many hermits had already spent meditative hours there, and I, too, strove to live up to its time-honoured associations. When the evening mist rose from below and mingled with the heavy white smoke of my wood fire, and I squatted in the open door at dusk between the warm fire behind and the keen autumn air in front, it always seemed to me that only one drink was appropriate—red wine and cognac, half-and-half, in a big-bellied glass. These intimate communings consoled me for the fact that a gentleman from the depôt, who had seniority over myself, had come to take over my company, and that I was once more discharging the boring duties of a platoon commander in the trenches. I endeavoured to kill the endless hours on trench duty by frequent warlike excursions in my old style.

On the 24th August the gallant Captain Böckelmann was wounded by a shell splinter. This made the third commanding officer the battalion had lost within a short time. On the 29th, with the N.C.O. Kloppmann, the stoutest fellow of the 7th Company, I paid a visit to the enemy lines.

We crept up to a gap in the enemy wire, cut by Kloppmann the night before. It was an unpleasant surprise to find that it had been mended up again. Nevertheless, we cut it through once more, with a great deal of noise, and climbed down into the trench. We crouched behind the next traverse and listened, lying in wait. After a quarter of an hour we went cautiously on, following a telegraph wire that came to an end at a bayonet stuck in the ground. We found the post defended by wire entanglements of all kinds, and also a trellised door, but unoccupied. After we had taken accurate note of everything we went the same way back, and carefully connected up the wire again across our gap, so as not to betray our visit.

The next evening Kloppmann again reconnoitered the post. However, he was greeted by rifle-fire and the lemon-shaped bombs we called 'duck's eggs.' One of them fell close to his head, which was pressed to the ground— without exploding. He had to take to his heels with all speed. the evening after that there were two of us again, and this time we found the front line occupied. By listening we accurately located four posts. One of them was whistling a very charming tune to himself. Finally we were fired on, and crept back.

When I was standing by myself in the trench again, Vogt and Haverkamp suddenly turned up. They had very obviously been having a jolly time, and the odd idea had come to them of leaving the comfortable reserve camp and journeying through a pitch-black night to the front line, in order to go, as they said, on patrol. I have always made it a rule to let any one carry his own skin to market where he pleases; so I made no objection to them clambering out of the trench, though the enemy still continued in a high state of excitement. It is true that the sole purpose of their patrol was to look for the silk parachutes of French rockets; and that, having found them, they chased each other to and fro in front of the enemy's wire, whirling these white tokens aloft. Naturally, they were fired on; but after a long while they came happily back. Bacchus had them in his tender keeping.

On the 10th September I went for the reserve camp to regimental headquarters to ask for leave. 'I have been thinking of you,' was Colonel von Oppen's reply; 'however, the regiment has to make a raid in force and you are to lead it. Look out the best men and get them into training down in Soulœuvre camp.'

We were to enter the enemy's trench at two points and endeavour to bring prisoners back. The patrol was in three parties, two for attack and one to occupy the front line and cover our rear. I led the left party, Lieutenant von Kienitz the right. The men were all volunteers, and a few who were not required nearly wept when I left them out. My party, myself included, consisted of fourteen men, and among them were the Fähnrich Zglinitzky, the N.C.Os. Kloppmann, Mevius, and Dujesiefken, and two pioneers. The most reckless fellows of the 2nd Battalion found themselves united.

We trained ourselves in bomb-throwing for ten days, and carried out our enterprise against a carefully-built model of the strong-point we were to raid. It was a wonder, considering the excessive zeal of the men, that I had only two wounded with bomb-splinters before the event. For the rest, we were excused all duty; so that when on the afternoon of the 22nd September we proceeded to the second line, where we were to spend the night, I found myself in command of a somewhat wild but very useful band.

In the evening von Kienitz and I made our way through the dark forest to regimental headquarters. We had been invited to a farewell dinner by the commanding officer of the battalion, Captain Schumacher. After that we lay down to sleep in our deep dugout. It is a peculiar feeling when, knowing that next morning you have a fight to the death to go through, you give yourself a last audience before you fall asleep.

We awakened at three, and we got up and washed and had breakfast made for us. I got into a temper at once because my batman had over-salted and so ruined the poached eggs I had treated myself to, both in honour of the day and for my own support.

We pushed back our plates and went through for the hundredth time every detail and contingency. At intervals we offered each other cherry-brandies, and von Kienitz gave us the benefit of several time-honoured jokes. At twenty minutes to five we got the men together and led them to the jumping-off places in the front line. Gaps in the wire had been cut, and long arrows, whitened with lime, pointed to our objectives. We separated with a shake of the hand and waited for what should come next.

I was in full array: two sandbags in front of my chest, each with four stick bombs, the left-hand one having instantaneous, the right-hand with time fuses; in the right-hand pocket of my tunic I had an 08 revolver on a long cord; in my right pocket a small Mauser pistol; in my left tunic pocket five egg bombs; in the left trouser pocket a phosphorescent compass and a policeman's whistle; in my belt spring hooks for pulling out the bomb pins, a dagger, and wire-cutters. There was a pocket-book in my breast pocket and my home address, and in the pocket of the back of my tunic a flat flask full of cherry-brandy.

We had taken off our shoulder-straps and Gibraltar badges so that the enemy should have no information as to our unit. We wore a white band round each arm so as to know each other.

Five minutes before five the division on our left opened fire as a blind. Exactly at five our artillery and trench mortars suddenly opened out. I was standing with Kloppmann in front of the dugout entrance and smoking a last cigar; we had to take cover, however, as many of the shells fell short. Watch in hand we counted the minutes.

Exactly at 5.5 we left the dugouts and made for the prepared gaps in our wire. I ran forward, holding a bomb aloft, and in the half-light I saw the right-hand party rushing on to the attack.

The enemy wire was poor and I jumped over it in two bounds; but I fell over a trip wire behind it and tumbled into a shell-hole. Kloppmann and Mevius pulled me out.

'In!' We jumped into the front line without meeting opposition, while from our right came the sounds of a bombing engagement. Without worrying about that we crossed by the sandbag barricade that blocked the next trench, and jumped from shell-hole to shell-hole till we came to a double row of 'knife-rests' that separated us from the second line. As this trench was in a state of confusion and gave no hope of prisoners, we hurried on without pausing down a communication trench. It was blocked, so I next sent the pioneers forward to clear the way, but time being short I took the lead myself.

At the junction of the third line the red glow of a cigarette-end fell to the ground in front of me. I gave the men a signal, grasped my bomb tighter, and crept warily along the well-built trench, against whose walls leaned any number of abandoned rifles. At such a moment the memory unconsciously fastens upon the most trifling objects, and now the sight of a saucepan with a spoon in it where the two trenches crossed was imprinted on my mind. To this fact I owed my life twenty minutes later.

Suddenly we saw shadowy figures disappear in front of us. We ran after them and came to a sand-bagged sap in whose wall was the mouth of a dugout. I went forward and shouted 'Montez!' A bomb was the only answer. Apparently it was one with a time fuse. I heard the little snap and had time to jump back. It burst at the height of my head against the opposite wall, tore my silken cap, wounded my left hand in several places, and tore away the top of my little finger. The pioneer sergeant standing near me had a hole bored through his nose. We retreated a few steps and bombarded the danger-spot with bombs. One of us, in an excess of zeal, threw a smoke-stick into the entrance and made further attacks on it impossible. We turned back then and followed the third line in the opposite direction, hoping to get a prisoner at last. Arms and equipment had been thrown down everywhere. The question, where were the owners of all these rifles and where were they lying in wait, made a more and more uncomfortable impression on us; but on we hurried all the same, undeterred, on and on through the deserted trenches, with bombs ready and revolver outstretched.

It was only by thinking it out later that I made out our course after this. We had turned without noticing into a third communication trench and by this time were well into the middle of our own barrage, and approaching the fourth line. Here and there we pulled open the boxes of bombs built into the side of the trench and stuck a bomb in our pockets as a keepsake.

After we had gone to and fro and up and down trenches running parallel and across, no one had any longer the least idea where we were, nor in what direction the German lines lay. By degrees we all got the wind up. The needles of our compasses danced in our hands, and when we looked for the Pole-star all we had learned at school evaporated and left us in the lurch. The sound of voices in the next trenches warned us that the enemy had recovered from the shock of surprise. He would be bound soon to realize our position.

After turning about once more I suddenly saw, as I brought up the rear, the muzzle of a machine-gun waving to and fro over a traverse of sandbags. I made a jump at it and came upon Kloppmann and Fähnrich Zglinitzky busy with the gun, while Fusilier Haller was searching a blood-stained body for papers. Without troubling any more about our surroundings we began fiddling with the machine-gun in a feverish haste so that we might at least take back something with us. I tried to loosen the retaining screw, another cut off the loading belt with wire cutters; at last we got hold of the thing, tripod and all, meaning to take it with us without dismounting it. At this moment we heard a voice from a trench running parallel to us. It came from the direction in which we supposed our lines to be. 'Qu'est-ce qu'il y a?" At the same time a black blob flew over towards us, indistinctly seen against the dim sky. 'Look out!' It burst between Mevius and me, and a splinter got Mevius in the hand.

We scattered in all directions, entangling ourselves deeper and deeper in the maze of trenches. With me there were only the pioneer sergeant and Mevius. Our one hope was the Frenchman's alarm; for they did not venture yet to come out of their holes. However, it could only be a matter of minutes before we ran into a strong party of them, who would do us in with delight. I debated whether I would not simply whack the first I met on the head with one of the stick bombs that had an instantaneous fuse. There was no thought of hands-up.

When I had given up all hope of getting safely out of the wasps' nest, a cry of joy escaped me. My eye had fallen on the saucepan with the spoon, and now I knew my direction. As it was now quite light, we had not a moment to lose. We jumped out of the trench and made for our own lives over the top, as the first bullets whistled round us. In the French first line we came on Lieutenant von Kienitz's party. When the cry of "Luttje Lage!' rang out, we knew we had the worst behind us.

Most unfortunately, in jumping into the trench I came right on a man who was severely wounded and lay in the trench among the others. Kienitz hurriedly told me that he had bombed a French working party in the front line and had driven it back, and that at the very start, when advancing further, he had suffered losses in dead and wounded from the fire of our own artillery.

After waiting a longish while, two more of my party turned up, the N.C.O. Dujesiefken and Fusilier Haller. Haller brought me at least some small consolation. He found himself in his wanderings alone in a little sap, and there he had discovered three abandoned machine-guns, one of which he had unscrewed from its stand and brought with him. Now, as it was growing lighter every moment, we hurried over No-man's-land into our own front line.

Of the fourteen men who had gone out with me only four came back, and Kienitz's patrol, too, had heavy losses. I was very crestfallen; but some words of the worthy Oldenburger, Dujesiefken, cheered me up a little. He was recounting his experiences to a group of men in front of the dugout where I was having my hand dressed, and he concluded by saying: 'But Lieutenant Jünger has won my respect; lads, lads, you should see him clear the blocks!' Then we got together again and marched through the forest to regimental headquarters. Colonel von Oppen gave us coffee. He was very much disappointed at our lack of success, but he expressed his admiration all the same for what we had done. then I was put into a car and driven to the division, which required exact information. A few hours before, I was storming shell-shot trenches in forlorn bombing attacks; now I enjoyed to the full at the luxury of leaning back in a powerful car as it purred along over a good road.

The general staff officer received me in his office, and tried in vain to impress upon me that I owed the loss of my men to an ill-considered and over-hasty advance. I thought: 'You can tell me a lot, sitting here twenty kilometres behind the line,' and I gave him to understand that in the enemy's front line I had neither a green table nor the pack of cards upon it. Besides that, all the part I had had was the fighting itself; as for the plan, that had been thrust on me ready-made, though there was much in it to take exception to. I had asked that the objective should be altered to the well-marked line of the paved road, or at least that coloured lights might be fired from our lines in case any of us lost our way. The reply had been that this would draw the enemy's fire. But what the devil did the enemy's fire matter to me? I was used to it. But I was not an owl to see my way in the dark!

The divisional commander was more agreeable, and soon dissipated my low spirits. I sat next to him at lunch in my torn tunic and with my hand bound up, and remembering the saying, 'Only fools are modest!' I took care to put our doings of the morning in their true light.

Next day Colonel von Oppen inspected the patrol again, and distributed iron crosses and gave each of us fourteen days' leave. At mid-day those of the fallen who were brought in were buried in the military cemetery at Thiaucourt. Among these years' graves are some of 1870-1871. One of these old graves had a mossy stone with the inscription: 'Far from our sight but always near our hearts.' Cut on a large tablet of stone were the following lines:—

Heroes' deeds and heroes' graves
Rank themselves beside the old.
How to win and how to keep . . .
Here is told

In the evening I read in the French *communiqué*, 'A German raid near Regniéville failed. We made prisoners.' It was not stated that the prisoners were taken only because we lost our way in seeking an enemy who had fled before us. Had the French defended their trenches as soldiers of courage do, it would have been a different story.

I had a letter some months later from one of the missing, Fusilier Meyer. He had lost a leg in a fight with bombs. After long wanderings he and three others had been engaged by the enemy. When the others, among whom was the brave N.C.O. Kloppmann, had fallen, he himself had been taken prisoner, severely wounded.

I have been in many adventures during the war, but not one was more uncomfortable. It gives me the blues even now whenever I think of our wanderings through those unknown trenches in the cold light of dawn.

A few days afterwards Domeyer and Zürn, both lieutenants, jumped into the French front line with a few men and no more preparation than a few shrapnel shells. Domeyer ran into a French soldier, who replied to his 'Rendez-vous!' with a grim 'Ah non,' and set upon him. After a stern tussle Domeyer shot him through the neck with his revolver, and had to come back, like me, without a prisoner. The difference was that for my attempt as much ammunition was shot away as would have sufficed for an entire battle of 1870.

# FLANDERS AGAIN

On the very day that I came back from leave we were relieved by the Bavarian Reserve Infantry Regiment No. 5. We then went into quarters in Labry, a village in the neighbourhood dirty enough to be typical of it. The vain search for a water-closet is the outstanding memory one has of the villages of Lorraine. Baths appear to be unknown. I have had some strange experiences of this description in France. One has to pass with a smile over certain shady sides of even the most magnificent mansions. Much as I esteem the French, I cannot help thinking that this is a characteristic side of their life. I know indeed that hostile races always call each other dirty, and that we ourselves called 'sales Boches' by the French. Nevertheless, I feel we are fully justified in returning this compliment to the Latin races.

On the 17th of October 1917 we were entrained, and after a day and a half trod the soil of Flanders once more, after an absence of two months. We spent the night in the little town of Iseghem, and next morning marched to Roulers or, in Flemish, Rouselaere. The town was in the first stages of devastation. Things were still for sale in the shops, but the inhabitants were already living in their cellars, and their ordinary life was lost in the streets, being broken up by frequent bombardments. A milliner's window opposite my billet seemed to me to be very much out of place in the tumult of war. By night looters tried to break into the houses of those who had already left.

I was the only person in my billet in the Ooststraat to occupy rooms above the ground-level. The house belonged to a cloth-merchant, who had fled at the beginning of the war and left an old housekeeper and her daughter to look after it. They took care of a small orphaned girl whom they had found during our advance, forsaken by her parents and wandering in the streets. They knew neither her name nor her parents. They had an extreme fear of bombs, and besought me almost on their knees to have no light upstairs, in case of attracting the hateful bombers. However, I found I had laughed once too often. I was standing with Lieutenant Reinhardt at the window and watching an English machine skim low over the roofs in the beam of a searchlight. Suddenly an immense bomb burst close by, and the window panes burst in splinters above our ears.

I was appointed intelligence officer in the coming operations, and attached to the regimental staff. To get my bearings I went, before we took over, to the headquarters of the 10th Bavarian Reserve Regiment, that we were to relieve. I found the C.O. very friendly, though at first he growled something about my 'red band.' By that time I had long given up attaching any importance to a war-worn uniform. The new hand is known everywhere by other tokens than these.

Two orderlies took me to the so-called Meldekopf, which was said to give a very good view of the front. We had scarcely left headquarters when a shell fell near us. I was still, apparently, to be 'the well-beloved son of Chaos.'

Towards mid-day the shells came over in an incessant thunder, but my guides cleverly avoided them by the course they took across a country that was marked by numerous little poplar plantations. They worked their way forward through the lovely autumn landscape, with the instinct of the soldier of modern warfare, who even in the heaviest fire can hit on a path that at least offers even chances.

We arrived at a lonely farm, where there were signs of recent shell-bursts. At the yard gate a dead man lay face downwards.

'Settled him!' said one of the sturdy Bavarians.

'Dirty weather!' said the other, and hurried on after a look at the sky.

The Meldekopf lay on the far side of the much-shelled Passchendaele-Westroosebeke road. It was an intelligence-clearing station like the one I had had in my charge at Fresnoy. Situated near a house that had been shot to a heap of rubbish, it was so little protected that the first honest hit would blow it to pieces. Three officers were leading a sociable cave-life there, but they were very much delighted by the prospect of a speedy relief, and gladly told me all I wanted to know about the enemy, and the front, and the approaches to the line. After this I returned to Roulers by way of Roodkruis and Oostnieuwkerke, and made my report to the commanding officer.

As I went through the streets of the town I read the homely names of the numerous little inns that express the snug Flemish life so well. Who would not be drawn by a signboard with the title 'Die Zalm' (salmon), 'De Reeper' (heron), 'Die Nieu Trompette,' 'De Drei Königen,' or 'Den Olifant'? Does it not echo Teniers and de Coster? At the very outset one is put at one's ease by the homely speech and the confiding 'du.' May this enchanting country get back to its old life again after the frightful wounds of war!

In the evening the town was bombed once more. I went down to the cellar, and found the women huddled in a corner. I turned on my electric torch to comfort the little girl. She was crying for terror in the dark, for a bomb had extinguished the light. Here was another sign of the tenacity with which people cling to their homes. In spite of the violence of their fear, these women embraced the very soil that might at any moment be their grave.

On the morning of the 22nd October I started for Kalve with my troop of four men. It was here that the staff of the regiment was to take over in the course of the morning. There was very heavy shelling on the front, and the flashes gave the early morning mist the appearance of an effervescent blood-red vapour. A house at the entrance of Oostnieuwkerke was hit by a heavy shell, and collapsed with a roar when we were not far from it. Bits of stone rolled along the road. We tried to make a detour, but had to go through the town as we did not know the way by Roodkruis. As I was hurrying by, I asked the way of a N.C.O. who was standing at a cellar entrance. Instead of replying, he dug his hands into his pockets and shrugged his shoulders. I had no time to lose, considering the shells that were coming over; so I leapt upon this blunder of military education and extorted the information at the point of my revolver.

This was the first time I ever found any one in the fighting area who made difficulties, not from cowardice, but just because he wanted to. Though this state of mind naturally grew more general in the last years of the war, yet such an expression of it in the course of operations was extremely unusual, since battle is like an opiate whose immediate effect is to stimulate the nerves, though the subsequent effect is to deaden them. On the other hand, it was when marching out of the line after a 'show' that you found the clearest indications of crumbling morale.

Matters became more serious round Roodkruis, a small farm at a fork in the road. Limbers were going like mad along the shelled road, infantry wound in file through the fields on either side of it, and a string of wounded dragged themselves along to the rear. A young artilleryman had a long jagged splinter sticking out from his shoulder. We turned off the road to the right to regimental headquarters, which were in a ring of shell-fire. Two signalers were laying telephone wire in a field of cabbages near by. A shell went up close beside one of them. We saw him fall, and took it he was finished. However, picked himself up and with admirable sang-froid continued unrolling his wire. As headquarters were no more than a tiny concrete blockhouse, where there was scarcely room for the commanding officer and his staff, I had to seek quarters elsewhere. With the intelligence, gas, and trench-mortar officers I shared a flimsy wooden hut that was scarcely the ideal of a bomb-proof shelter.

In the afternoon I went up the line, as a report had come in that the enemy had that morning made an attack on our 5th Company. My way took me over the Meldekopf to 'Nordhof,' a farm shelled out of all recognition, beneath whose ruins dwelt the commanding officer of the battalion in reserve. Thence a track that was still just to be discerned led to the C.O. of the troops in the line. The vast fields of shell-holes had been turned into a sea of mud by the heavy rain of the last days. Its depths were particularly dangerous in the low-lying field of the Paddebeek. On my zigzag course I passed many a lonely and forgotten corpse. Often only a head or a hand projected from the shell-hole whose circle of dirty water reflected them. Thousands sleep like that, without one token of love to mark the unknown grave.

I crossed the Paddebeek after the utmost exertions, and only with the help of some poplars that a shell had flung across it; and found the officer in command of the 5th Company, Lieutenant Heins, in a giant shell-hole, with what remained of his company around him. Their shell-hole line lay on a slope, and, since it was not entirely flooded, might be called habitable by the unassuming front-line soldier.

Heins told me that the English had come on in line that morning, but had disappeared when fire was opened on them. The enemy had, however, shot a few men of the 164th Regiment who had lost their way and ran for it at their approach. Apart from this all was in order; and I returned forthwith to headquarters and made my report to the commanding officer.

On the following day we were most rudely interrupted at lunch by a few shells planted right in front of the door. Descending fountains of soil beat long tattoos on our tarred roof. There was a rush for the door. I fled to a farm close at hand, and as it was raining I went inside. In the evening the same performance was repeated; only this time, as it was fine, I stood outside the farmhouse. The next shell fell right in the middle of it. Such are the chances of war. Here more than anywhere it is a case of little causes and great effects. Seconds and millimetres make the difference.

On the 28th we were driven from the huts by eight o'clock, and one of those opposite us got a direct hit at the second shot. Others fell in the water-logged meadows. They made less noise, but they scooped out some fine holes. Prompted by the experiences of the day before, I sought out a lonely shell-hole, of dimensions to inspire confidence, in the cabbage-field behind headquarters, and I would never leave it again until a considerable safety margin had elapsed. I heard that next day the news, particularly destressing for me, of the death of Lieutenant Brecht. He had met his heroic death in the shell-hole area to the right of Nordhof, while acting as a divisional observation officer. He was one of those few who were encircled by a nimbus of romance, even in the most material of wars, owing to their insatiable daredevilry. Men like him always stood out from the common run; they laughed every time an attack was ordered.

The morning of the 26th was occupied by drum-fire of unusual intensity. Our artillery, too, doubled its fury when the signals for a barrage went up in the front line. Every little bit of wood and every hedge was crammed with guns, and behind them the half-dazed gunners were kept hard at work.

As the reports of the wounded about an English attack were confused and exaggerated, I was sent forward at eleven with my four men to obtain more exact information. We had to pass through a sharp fire, and met a great number of wounded, among them Lieutenant Spitz, commanding the 12th Company, wounded in the chin. Even before reaching the headquarters of the battalion in the line we were in a direct machine-gun fire, a sign that the enemy must have broken through. This fear was soon confirmed by Major Dietlein, commanding officer of the 3rd Battalion. I found the old gentleman in the act of creeping out of the entrance of his blockhouse, which was three parts under water, and fishing zealously for his meerschaum cigar holder, which had fallen into the mud. The enemy had broken through the front line and taken a ridge from which he commanded the important area of the

Paddebeek and battalion headquarters situated there.

After I had marked the alterations of the front line in blue chalk on my map, I set out on a fresh steeplechase through the mud with my men. We ran at full speed over the exposed ground till a slope gave us cover, and then we proceeded more slowly to Nordhof. Shells were falling to left and right of the boggy ground, and throwing up large mountains of mud surrounded by countless smaller ones. Nordhof was being shelled with H.E. in a nerve-shattering manner, and we had to reach it in jumps. The noise these things made was really most hideous and quite deafening. They came over in groups at short intervals. The only thing to do was to cover the ground in short darts, and then wait for the next shots in the shell-hole. The interval between the first distant howl and the explosion near by is marked by a peculiarly painful emphasis upon the instinct of self-preservation, since the body is reduced to a state of defencelessness and motionless waiting. But I am afraid my insistence on the fact that the war was no child's-play will become burdensome. The picture of every day was at last made up of such experiences.

There was shrapnel, too, among the rest. One of them scattered its bullets with a clatter among us, and one of my men was hit on the hind rim of his helmet and thrown to the ground. After he had lain stunned for some while, he picked himself up and ran on. The ground round Nordhof was strewn with terribly mutilated bodies.

As we carried out our job in a sporting spirit, we were often in places that had just ceased to be possible. In this way the unseen events of the battlefield came to our eyes. We were everywhere pressing on the heels of death. It was almost as though not one living soul was to be found in this desolation. Here lay a group behind a tattered hedge, their bodies covered by the still fresh earth that showered on them after the shell had burst; there, two runners near a shell-hole, from which the suffocating vapour of the explosives still exhaled. At other spots there were many corpses scattered over a small surface—a carrying-party caught in a vortex of shell-bursts, or a strayed platoon coming up in support, had found an end here. We appeared, took in the drama at one glance, and disappeared into the smoke again.

When we had safely crossed the much-shelled bit of ground behind the Passchendaele-Westroosebeke road, I was able to give intelligence to the commander of the regiment.

Next morning I was despatched to the front line at six o'clock, to ascertain whether and where the regiment was in touch with the units on its flanks. On the way I met Sergeant-major Ferchland, who had to take the orders to the 8th Company to advance on Goudberg and fill the gap, if there should be one, between us and the regiment on the left. The quickest way to carry out my task was to go along with him. After a long search we found my friend Tebbe, commanding the 8th Company, in an inhospitable part of the shelled area near the Meldekopf. He was not particularly pleased at the notion of executing the proposed movement in broad daylight. We lit cigars while waiting for the company to assemble, and conducted a laconic conversation in the dreary and oppressive surroundings that the morning light revealed.

Before we had gone a few steps we were under rifle-fire from high ground in front, and we had to go forward by jumps from one shell-hole to the other, each man on his own. As we went across the next rise the fire was so concentrated that Tebbe gave the order to take up a position in shell-holes until night came on. Smoking his cigar, he went with great coolness along the whole length of his front. I decided to go on and ascertain the width of the gap, and first I rested awhile in Tebbe's shell-hole. Soon the enemy artillery began to resent the company's imprudent advance, and got the range of the strip of ground we were on. A bit of shell that struck our refuge, throwing the soil over my map and into my eyes, gave me the tip to go. I bade farewell to Tebbe, and wished him good luck for the hours ahead. He called after me: 'God send the night; the morning will come of itself.'

We made our way cautiously through the low-lying ground of the Paddebeek, which was overlooked by the enemy, taking cover behind the branches shot away from the poplars and using their trunks as a bridge. Now and then one of us sank in mud above the hips and would certainly have drowned but for the rifle-butts that the others stretched out to help him up. I chose as our objective a group of men standing round a concrete blockhouse. In front of us, mobbing in the same direction, there were four stretcher-bearers carrying a stretcher. It made me suspicious to see a wounded man being carried forward, so I took my glasses and then saw a line of khaki-coloured figures with flat helmets. At the same moment the first shots snapped out. As there was no cover to take, we ran, and the bullets spurted the mud up on all sides of us. The chase through the morass was frantically exhausting, and when completely pumped we had to stop a while and give the English a good target; but a few H.Es. soon restored us to our first vigour. All the same, they had the advantage of concealing us from the enemy in their smoke. The worst feature of this run was knowing that a wound would drown one for certainty in a mud-hole. A suffusion of blood on the surface of a shell-hole here and there showed that many a man had vanished thus.

I was dead tired when we reached headquarters. I gave my sketch and made a report of the situation.

On the 28th October we were relieved again by the 10th Bavarian Reserve Regiment, and quartered among the villages behind the line, to be put in again at any moment. The staff moved to Most.

In the evening we were sitting in a deserted inn. We were already in the best of spirits again and celebrating the promotion of Lieutenant Zürn, who had been mentioned in despatches and had just come back from leave. As a punishment for our light-heartedness we were awakened next morning by gigantic drum-fire that blew in my window-panes in spite of our distance from it. Immediately after, the alarm was given. There was a rumor that the enemy had broken through by the gap that still persisted on the regiment's left flank. I spent the day waiting for orders at the artillery observation post, the neighbourhood of which was being sporadically shelled. A light shell went through the window of a small house and drove out three gunners, wounded and covered with brick-dust. The corpses of three others remained beneath the wreckage.

The morning after I had the following orders from the commanding officer of the Bavarians: 'Owing to repeated attacks by the enemy the front of the regiment on the left flank has been still further pushed back, and the gap between the regiments greatly widened. As there was danger of our flank being turned from the left, the 1st Battalion of the 73rd Fusiliers counter-attacked yesterday. Apparently, however, it was dispersed by the barrage and never reached the enemy. This morning the 2nd Battalion was sent forward to close the gap. So far no news has been received. Information is now required as to the position of the 1st and 2nd Battalions.'

I set out, and had only got as far as Nordhof when I met Captain von Brixen, commanding officer of the 2nd Battalion, who had a sketch-map of the disposition of the troops ready to hand in his pocket. I took a copy of it, and with this my task was really completed. However, I went on all the same to the headquarters of the troops in the line, which I found in a concrete block-house, in order to make a personal reconnaissance.

On the way I passed great numbers of recent casualties. The white faces stared out of the brimming shell holes or were already so mud-bespattered that the human face was scarcely recognizable. I was sorry to see the blue Gibraltar badge on most of them. The commanding officer was a Bavarian, Captain Radlmaier, a very energetic officer. He gave me full details of the position that Captain von Brixen had hastily told me of. Our 2nd Battalion had suffered heavy losses, among them the adjutant and the officer commanding the valiant 7th Company. The fate of the adjutant, Lieutenant Lemière, was particularly tragic, as his brother had been killed the April before at Fresnoy, in command of the 8th Company. Both brothers belonged to the principality of Liechtenstein, but they had joined the army out of enthusiasm for the cause of Germany. It is fatal for two sons to be in one regiment in wartime. We had four pairs of brothers among the officers of the regiment. Of these eight, five were killed, and two, one of whom was my brother, was severely wounded. I was the only one to come through in a fairly sound state. This little example shows the losses of the Fusiliers.

The captain pointed to a concrete post about two hundred metres in front of our line, which had been defended with particular heroism the day before. Shortly after the attack began, the commander of this little strong-point, a sergeant-major, saw an Englishman who was taking off three German prisoners. He shot the Englishman and added the three to the strength of his garrison—though it did not appear that he found in them an exactly heroic trio. When they had shot away their ammunition they tied an Englishman in front of the entrance as a peaceful signboard, and at dark succeeded after all in escaping unobserved.

Another strong-point, commanded by a lieutenant, was summoned to surrender. Instead of making an answer, the German leapt out and, seizing the English officer, dragged him inside before the eyes of his bewildered men.

That day, for the only time in the war, I saw small bodies of stretcher-bearers moving about in the open with the Red Cross flag without a shot being fired. Such a sight was unknown to the front-line soldier in this subterranean war except when matters were very desperate. Nevertheless, I heard later on that some of our stretcher-bearers had been shot by English snipers.

This fact may seem astounding, and yet I can explain it to myself. Weak natures are prone to the atavistic impulse to destroy; and it takes hold of the trench fighter in his desolate existence when any one appears above ground.. I have felt it myself only too often.

I had an unpleasant time on my way back owing to the irritant gas of the English shells. The ground was saturated with it. It smelt of rotten apples and made the eyes run. After making my report to headquarters I met two stretchers just outside the dressing-station at Kalve. On each, severely wounded, was an officer whom I knew well. On one was Lieutenant Zürn, in whose honour we had made a night of it only two evenings before. Now he lay half-undressed on a door. His face had that hint of yellow which is the certain precursor of death, and he looked at me with fixed eyes when I went up to take his hand. The other, Lieutenant Haverkamp, had the bones of a leg and an arm so shattered by a shell that an amputation was extremely probable. He was as white as death, and he lay on his stretcher with his features heroically set, smoking a cigarette.

Our losses in young officers were again frightfully heavy during those days. Every time afterwards that I heard prejudice and depreciation on the lips of the mob, I thought of these men who saw it out to the bitter end with so little parade and with so fine an ardour. But after all—what is the mob? It sees in everything nothing but the reflection of its own manners. It is quite clear to me that these men were our best. However cleverly people may talk and write, there is nothing to set against self-sacrifice that is not pale, insipid, and miserable.

On the 3rd of November we entrained at Gits, whose situation was familiar to us from our earliest Flanders days. We found that the two Flemish girls had lost their old freshness. They, too, seemed to have lived through days of battle in the meantime.

Next, we were for some days in rest at Tourcoing, an imposing sister-city of Lille. For the first time and the last during the war, every man of the 7th Company slept on a feather-bed. I occupied a magnificently furnished room in the house of an industrial magnate in the Rue de Lille. The first evening, with an open fire, the indispensable marble mantelpiece, and an armchair, was unspeakably delightful.

The few days were passed by everybody in enjoying life that had been so hardly won. It was still scarcely believable that death had been escaped, and it seemed a necessity to assure oneself of it by enjoying life in every aspect.

# THE BATTLE OF CAMBRAI

The delightful days at Tourcoing were soon over. For a short while longer we were at Villers-au-Tertre, where we were made up to strength by new drafts, and then we went by train on the 15th November to Lécluse, the rest-place of the battalion in reserve on the new front now assigned to us. Lécluse was a fairly large village of Artois, surrounded by lakes. The immense reedy marshes concealed ducks and water-fowl, and the water was alive with fish. Though fishing was strictly forbidden, mysterious sounds were often heard at night. One day, too, I had presented to me by the town-major a few paybooks of men in my company who had been caught fishing with bombs. I wasted no words over that, however; for the good spirits of the men were very much more to me than the protection of French fishing-waters or the dinner-tables of the resident military magnates. After this a gigantic pike was laid on my table nearly every evening by an unknown hand, and on the next day I gave my two company officers a meal, at which the principal dish was 'Pike à la Lohengrin.' (Ask me no more!)

On the 19th I inspected our position in the line with my platoon commanders, as we were going in in a day or two. It was in front of the village of Vis-en-Artois. We were not so soon in the line as we expected, as there was an alarm nearly every night, and on account of an English attack that was supposed to be coming off we were held in readiness by turns in the Wotan line, the reserve gun positions, or in Dury village. Those who had war experience could see that something unpleasant would come of it.

On the 29th November we were, in fact, told by our commanding officer, Captain von Brixen, that we were to take part in a highly-organized counter-attack to strengthen the bulge that the Cambrai tank-battle had made in our front. We were delighted, certainly, to change the part of the anvil for that of the hammer at last; but we had some reservations on account of the men, after their recent exhaustion in Flanders. Nevertheless, I had entire confidence in the spirit of my company and its iron backbone, in my experienced platoon commanders and excellent N.C.Os.

On the night of November 30th—December 1st we were put in lorries. It was in the course of this that my company had its first casualties. One of the men let a bomb fall and for some mysterious reason it went off and severely wounded him and one other. Another man, in the hope of getting sent back, pretended to be mad. I did not know whether to laugh or to storm at him. Finally he recovered his reason at the suggestion of a N.C.O., who gave him a powerful dig in the ribs; and we were all able to get in. We were conveyed, tightly packed together, almost as far as Baralle, and there we waited hour after hour for order sin the ditch by the roadside. In spite of the cold I lay down in a grass field and slept till dawn. We were somewhat disappointed when we were told that the 22nd Regiment were going over the top without our assistance. Pending developments we were to stand by in the park of the château of Baralle.

At 9 o'clock our artillery broke into heavy bursts of fire, and increased between 11.45 and 11.50 to drum-fire. Bourlon wood, which owing to the strength of its defences had been left out of the frontal attack, disappeared under yellowish-green clouds of gas. At 11.50 we saw the attacking waves through glasses, as they emerged upon the vacant expanse of shell-holes; while further back, batteries harnessed up and raced forward to new positions. A German scout shot down an English captive balloon in flames, and the observer jumped out with a parachute.

After enjoying this panorama of battle from the high ground of the park we emptied a dixie of dumplings, and in spite of the cold laid ourselves down on the ground for an afternoon sleep. At 3, orders came through to go forward as far as regimental headquarters, which were concealed in the lock of a drained canal. We covered this distance in detachments under moderate and scattered shell-fire.

From there the 7th and 8th Companies were sent forward to report to the officer commanding the troops in reserve, so as to relieve the two companies of the 225th. The five hundred metres we had to go along the bed of a canal were covered by a band of fire. We ran in one mob and reached our goal without a casualty. There were numerous dead here to show that many a company had paid heavy toll. Reserves were crowded along the sides of the canal and were feverishly digging out holes in the retaining walls to serve as cover. As the whole space was occupied, and as the canal was a landmark that drew the enemy's fire, I led the company off to the right among the shell-holes and gave orders for each of my men to see to himself. A splinter rang against my bayonet. Lieutenant Tebbe had followed my example with the 8th Company, and now we looked out a suitable shell-hole and covered it with a ground-sheet. We then lit a candle, ate our supper, lit our pipes, and talked and shivered. At eleven o'clock I got orders to proceed to the former front line and to report to the C.O. of the battalion in the line, under whose orders the 7th Company was. I gave the order to fall in and led the company forward. There were only isolated shells, but very heavy ones. One of them that crashed in front of us was like a glimpse of hell, and filled the whole canal-bed with black vapour. The men were dumbfounded as though by a blow of an iron fist at the nape of the neck, and stumbled hurriedly on behind me over barbed wire and stone rubble.

A feeling of indescribable discomfort steals upon the nerves, even though the shell-fire is not particularly heavy, when one is traversing an unfamiliar part of the line by night. The strangest illusions play upon the eye and ear, and the menacing walls of the trench inspire a sense of loneliness, like that of a child that has lost its way on a dark heath.

At last we found the narrow mouth of the first line in the wall of the canal, and went on through overcrowded trenches to battalion headquarters. I went in and found a mob of officers and orderlies in an atmosphere that could be cut with a knife. I was told that the attack on the front had not achieved much and that it was to be renewed the next morning. The feeling in the air was not very hopeful. Two commanding officers began a long discussion with the adjutants. Now and then from the height of their bunks, that were as crowded as hen-roosts, the specialist officers threw a few crumbs into the debate. The cigar fumes were suffocating. Batmen endeavoured to cut bread for their officers in the throng. A wounded officer who burst in aroused a passing alarm with the news of an enemy bombing attack.

Finally I was able to take down my orders for the attack. At 6 a.m. I and my companions were to roll up Dragon Alley and as much of the Siegfried line as possible. The two battalions of the regiment in the line were to attack on our right at 7.

This difference in time aroused my immediate and resolute dislike. I raised a number of objections to splitting up the attack in this way, and gained my point. We, too, were to attack at 7. We found out the importance of this alteration the next morning. Fighting experience in an officer commanding troops can often, in cases like this, spare much unnecessary bloodshed.

A company detached from its own unit is not likely to be pampered under alien command. As I had only the haziest notion of the whereabouts of Dragon Alley, I asked, as I was going, for a map. Unfortunately, not a single one could be spared. I made a silent comment and went out.

After I and the men with their heavy packs had wandered up and down the trenches for a long while one of the men discovered a board with the scarcely legible inscription, 'Dragon Alley.' It was at the entrance of a narrow trench branching off to the front and blocked with knife-rests. After entering it, and before I had gone many paces, I heard voices in a foreign tongue. I was very much astonished to find the enemy so close, and indeed almost in our own lines, without having come upon any measures of defence; and I at once posted a section to block the trench.

Close to Dragon Alley there was an enormous pit, apparently a tank-trap. There I collected the whole company and explained the plan of attack and assigned their respective parts to each platoon. My remarks were interrupted several times by light shells. Once, even, a dud hurtled against the rear wall of our pit. Standing on the edge above, I saw a deep and regular inclination of the moonlit helmets at every hit.

I took the precaution of sending the first and second platoons back into the trench, in case of an unlucky direct hit, and remained with the third in the pit. Some men of a party which had come to grief in Dragon Alley the day before put the wind up my men by telling them that fifty metres along there was an English machine-gun that made further advance impossible. In view of this tale, I made it understood with the platoon commanders that at the first resistance we should jump out on both sides of the trench and make a concerted bombing attack. It is more than ever important to keep up a regiment's fighting prestige when attached to another unit. I spent the endless hours squeezed up against Lieutenant Hopf in a small hole. I got up at six and made the final arrangements, in a mood peculiar to the last hour before an attack. There's a lonely, sinking feeling in the stomach as one speaks to the section leaders, tries to make jokes, and keeps running to and fro as if before an inspection by the divisional commander. In short, one tries to be as occupied as possible in order to escape the thoughts that drill into the brain. One of the men offered me a cup of coffee heated in a trench cooker. Its warmth cheered me to the marrow.

At 7 sharp we advanced in single file in the prearranged order. We found Dragon Alley unoccupied; a number of empty drums behind a block showed that the machine-gun must have been withdrawn. Our fighting spirit kindled at this. We went along a narrow sunken way, after passing on our right a well-built trench, where I left a few men posted. The sunken road became shallower and shallower till at last we found ourselves in the open, just as dawn broke. We then turned back and entered the trench on the right. It was full of arms and equipment and English dead. It was the Siegfried line, and suddenly Lieutenant Hoppenrath, the leader of the storming section, snatched a rifle from one of the men and fired. He had come on an English post, which, after a few bombs had been thrown, took to flight. We went on, and a moment later a fresh stand was encountered. Bombs flew on both sides and burst with resounding din. Now the technique of the storm-troop came into play. A chain of bombs went from hand to hand along the trench. Snipers took up positions behind traverses ready to draw a bead on the enemy bombers; the platoon commanders kept an eye out over the top to see a counter-attack in the nick of time; and the light machine-gun section mounted their guns where there was a good field of fire.

After a short fight we heard agitated voices from the other side, and before we understood what was happening the first Englishmen came towards us with their hands up. One after another turned the corner of the traverse and unbuckled his belt while our rifles and revolvers were threateningly levelled. They were all young, well-set-up fellows in new uniforms. I let them pass with the command 'Hands down!' and detailed a squad to take them to the rear. Most of them showed by their confiding smiles that they trusted in us as human beings. Others held out cigarettes and chocolates in order to conciliate us. My enthusiasm and delight when I saw what a bag we had made were unbounded. The procession had no end. We had counted 150 already, and still they came with their hands above their heads. I went up to an officer and asked him how far their positions extended and how many men they had. He answered very politely, but impaired the good impression he made by being so very stiff about it. He then conducted me to the commander of the company, a captain, who was lying wounded in a deep dugout near by. He was about twenty-eight years old, with a clear-cut face. I found him leaning against the timbers at the foot of the shaft with a wound through the calf. I introduced myself, and he raised his hand to his cap, showing as he did so a gold chain. He told me his name and gave up his revolver. His first words showed that I had a man to deal with. 'We were surrounded.' He could not rest till he told his enemy why he had allowed his company to be taken prisoners so quickly.

We had a talk on various matters, in French. He told me there were a number of German wounded in a neighbouring dugout, whom his men had bound up and looked after. When I asked him how strongly held the Siegfried line was further on, he declined to reply. I promised to get him and the other casualties sent back, and we parted with a shake of the hand.

Outside, the men reported that we had taken 200 prisoners, a fine achievement for a company eighty strong. I had guards mounted, and we then looked round the trench. It was bristling with arms and equipment. On the fire-steps were machine-guns, mortars, bombs, and rifle-grenades, water-bottles, sheepskin waistcoats, mackintosh capes, groundsheets, cases of bully beef, jam, tea, coffee, cocoa, and tobacco, bottles of rum, tools, revolvers, Verey-light pistols, clothing, gloves; in short, everything imaginable. Like an old soldier of fortune I allowed an interval for plunder, nor could I resist the temptation myself of having a small breakfast prepared for me by my batman in a dugout entrance and lighting a pipe on the 'Navy Cut' I had so long been without, while I scribbled a report to the commanding officer of the troops in the line. Like a wise man, I sent a duplicate to our own C.O.

After half an hour we proceeded, in an exalted mood to which the English rum may have contributed, and stalked from traverse to traverse along the Siegfried line.

We were fired on from a pill-box built into the trench, and got on to the next fire-step to study the lie of the land. While we were exchanging a shot or two with the inmates, a man was struck to the ground as though by an invisible hand. A shot had pierced the crown of his helmet and torn a long groove in his skull. His brain could be seen throbbing with each beat of his heart, and yet he was able to make his way back alone.

I called for volunteers to carry the place by assault over the top. The men looked at each other in hesitation. Only an ungainly Pole, whom I had always thought weak in the head, clambered out of the trench and stumped off heavily to assault the pill-box alone. But now Fähnrich Neupert sprang over the top with his section, while we at the same time advanced along the trench. The English fired a few shots and ran for it, abandoning the pill-box to us. One of the Fähnrich's men was shot dead half-way over, and lay with his face to the earth a few steps from the goal.

Going further we met with a resolute resistance from some unseen bomb-throwers, and after considerable butchery we were driven back to the pill-box. There we made a block. We, as well as the English, left a number of dead in the disputed length of trench. Among them, unhappily, was the N.C.O. Mevius, whom, in the night of Regniéville, I had learned to value as a daring fighter. He lay with his face in a pool of blood. When I turned him over I saw a big hole in his forehead and knew that nothing could help him.

After the enemy also had retired a little, an obstinate shooting match began. In the course of it a Lewis gun, posted fifty metres from us, forced us to duck our heads. A light machine-gun on our side took the duel on. For half a minute the two murderous weapons rattled on at each other, with the bullets spurting round them. Then our gunner, the volunteer Motullo, was killed by a shot though the head. Though his brain fell over his face to his chin, his mind was still clear when we took him to the nearest dugout. By degrees things calmed down, and the English too were busy making a block.

At 12, Captain von Brixen, Tebbe, and Vogt appeared and congratulated me on the company's success. We sat down in the pill-box and lunched off the English provisions and discussed the situation. Meanwhile I had a conversation in shouts with about twenty-five English, whose heads emerged out of the trench about a hundred metres in front of us, and who apparently wished to give themselves up. As soon as I showed myself, however, I was shot at from further behind them.

Suddenly there was a commotion at the barricade. Bombs flew, rifles pinged, and machine-guns rattled. 'They're coming. They're coming.' We jumped to our sandbags and fired away. One of my men, the volunteer Kimpenhaus, jumped on to the top of the block in the heat of battle and fired into the trench till he fell severely wounded in both arms. I made a note of this hero of the hour, and had the pleasure, fourteen days later, of congratulating him on the Iron Cross of the 1st class.

We had scarcely gone back to lunch after this little interlude when a fresh heathenish alarm broke upon us. There followed one of those extraordinary episodes in which, great and small, the history of the war is so rich. A subaltern of the regiment on our left who had come to get into touch with us became inspired by a boundless pugnacity. It seemed that drink had inflamed his inborn courage to madness. 'Where's the Tommy? At the dogs! Who's coming?' In his rage he pulled down our fine block and plunged on, clearing a road for himself with a roar of bombs. In front of him, through the trench, flitted his orderly, and finished off with his rifle those of whom the bombs had spared.

When a man makes himself the stake with crazy daring his example is always infectious. We were all wrought up and, snatching up bombs, ran to take part in the improvised assault. I was soon up with the fellow, nor did the other officers, followed by most of the company, hang back. The C.O. himself, Captain von Brixen, was among the foremost. He had picked up a rifle, and he shot down several enemy bombers over our heads.

The English resisted valiantly. Every traverse was contested. Mills bombs and stick-bombs crossed and recrossed. Behind each we found dead or still quivering bodies. We killed each other out of sight; and there were losses on our side too. A bomb fell close to the orderly and burst before he could get clear. He fell with over a dozen wounds, from which his blood trickled into the soil.

We sprang on over his body. Thunderous reports gave us our direction. Hundreds of eyes lay in wait in the desolation behind rifles and machine-guns. We were a long way in front of our own lines. Bullets whistled from all sides round our heads or landed with a hard smack on the edge of the trench. One had to have courage here, and every one had; otherwise he would not have ventured on it. Each time that one of the egg-shaped bombs appeared the eye seized it with a precision only possible to a man whose life hangs on the issue. Then one threw a bomb oneself and jumped forward. Scarce a glance fell on the huddled body of the enemy. He was done for, and now a fresh duel began.

A trench branching off to the right was cleared by some of the men of the 225th Regiment who were following us. Caught between two fires, the English tried to escape across the open and were shot down like game at a 'battue.'

Then came the climax. The enemy, hard pressed, and with us always on his heels, made ready to retire by a communication trench that turned away to the right. I jumped on to a fire-step and saw that this trench for a good stretch ran parallel to ours at a distance of only twenty metres. So the enemy had to pass by us once more. We could look right down on the helmets of the English, who stumbled over each other in their haste and excitement. I lobbed a bomb at the feet of the foremost. They started back and crowded on those behind. Now began an indescribable carnage. Bombs flew through the air like snowballs till the whole scene was veiled in white smoke. Two men handed me bombs ready to throw without a moment's pause. Bombs flashed and exploded among the mob of the English, throwing them aloft in fragments with their helmets. Cries of rage and terror were mingled. With the fire in our eyes we sprang with a shout over the top.

In the midst of this tumult I was struck to the earth by a terrific blow. Sobered, I tore off my helmet, and saw with horror two large holes in it. The N.C.O. Mohrmann, who sprang to my help, comforted me by the assurance that nothing was to be seen on the back of my head but a scratch. The shot of a far-distant rifle had pierced my helmet and grazed the skull. I was half-dazed and was forced to give way. With my head bound up I made my way out of the thick of the fight. I had scarcely passed the next traverse when a man ran up behind me and gasped out that Tebbe had been killed by a shot in the head at the very same spot.

This news finished me. I could scarcely realize that a friend with whom for years I had shared joy and sorrow and danger, and who had sung out a jest to me a few minutes before, had met his end from a senseless piece of lead. Unhappily it was too true.

All the leading N.C.Os. and a third of the company had fallen too in this murderous piece of trench; Lieutenant Hopf, also, an elderly man and a teacher by profession, a German 'Ideal-Schulmeister' in the best sense of the word. My two Fähnrichs and many more were wounded. In spite of this the 7th Company held the trench they had gloriously won, and remained there under the command of Lieutenant Hoppenrath, the only officer left, until the relief of the battalion.

Even modern battle has its great moments. One hears it said very often and very mistakenly that the infantry battle had denigrated to an uninteresting butchery. On the contrary, to-day more than ever it is the individual that counts. Every one knows that who has seen them in their own realm, these princes of the trenches, with their hard, set faces, brave to madness, tough and agile to leap forward or back, with keen bloodthirsty nerves, whom no despatch ever mentions. Trench warfare is the bloodiest, wildest, and most brutal of all warfare, yet it too has had its men, men whom the call of the hour has raised up, unknown foolhardy fighters. Of all the nerve-racking moments of the war none is so formidable as the meeting of two storm-troop leaders between the narrow walls of the trench. There is no retreat and no mercy then. Blood sounds in the shrill cry that is wrung like a nightmare from the breast.

On my way back I stopped beside Captain von Brixen, who, with a few of the men, was engaged in a duel with a row of heads sticking up out of a trench running parallel and not far away. I stood between him and another and marked where the bullets struck.

Of a sudden I was again flung down into the trench by a blow on the forehead and my eyes were blinded with blood. The man beside me fell at the same moment and began to cry out. He was shot in the temple through his helmet. Captain von Brixen was afraid he had lost a second company commander in one day. However, there was nothing to be found, on a closer inspection, except two flesh wounds on the edge of my hair, caused, presumably, by the bursting bullet or by a splinter from the wounded man's helmet.

The fresh loss of blood weakened me; so I agreed to return with Captain von Brixen to his headquarters. We passed the edge of Mœuvres village at the double on account of the heavy shelling, and arrived safely at the dugout in the bed of the canal. There I was dressed and injected against tetanus.

In the afternoon I got on to a lorry and went to Lécluse, and there dined with Colonel von Oppen, who received my report with enthusiasm. After I had emptied my bottle of wine, in excellent spirits though half asleep, I took my leave. My trusty Vinke, whose face beamed with joy, had a bed ready for me, and I flung myself into it with a holiday feeling after this tremendous day. On the next day but one the battalion was taken out and came to Lécluse. On the 4th December the divisional commander, Major-General von Busse, addressed the battalions concerned, and mentioned with particular emphasis the services performed by the 7th Company.

I had reason to be proud of my men. A bare eighty of them had taken a long stretch of trench, besides a large quantity of machine-guns, mortars, and war material, and 200 prisoners. Unhappily we, too, had a casualty list of fifty per cent, in which was a large proportion of officers and N.C.Os. I had the pleasure of announcing a large number of promotions and decorations. Lieutenant Hoppenrath, leader of the storm troops, Fähnrich Neupert, the stormer of the pill-box, and also the courageous defender of the block, Kimpenhaus, were given the Iron Cross of the 1st class for their distinguished conduct in the field. As a plaster for my fifth wound I was given fourteen days' Christmas leave, and in the course of it the Knight's Cross of the House of Hohenzollern with swords was sent to me at home. The war ended by giving me peculiar views as to orders and decorations, and yet I confess I was proud to pin the enamel cross with the gold rim to my breast. This cross, my perforated helmet, and a silver cup inscribed 'To the victor of Mæuvres,' presented to me by the three other company commanders of the battalion, are my souvenirs of the battle of Cambrai.

# AT THE COJEUL RIVER

After a few days on rest we relieved the 10th Company in the front line on the 9th December. Our part of the line was in front of Vis-en-Artois, as I mentioned above. My company front was bounded on the right flank by the Arras-Cambrai road, on the left by the marshy bed of the Cojeul river, across which we kept touch with the neighbouring company by nightly patrols. The enemy's lines were hidden from sight by a hill lying between the front lines. Apart from an occasional patrol messing about with our wire at night, and the hum of an electric-light engine set up in Hubert's Farm not far off, we had no knowledge of the enemy. On the other hand, the frequent gas attacks were unpleasant and claimed many victims. They were carried out by means of hundreds of iron cylinders buried in the earth and discharged by electricity in a salvo of flame. As soon as the light showed, gas-alarm was given, and any one who had not his mask on and the flap well tucked in found himself in a bad way. In many spots, too, the gas reached an almost absolute density, that even the mask was useless, since there was literally no oxygen there to breathe. Consequently there were many casualties.

My dugout was in the steep wall of a gravel-pit behind the line, and was shelled nearly every day. Behind, the iron girders of a destroyed sugar-factory showed up in grotesque desolation.

The gravel-pit was an unholy spot. Among the shell-holes, filled with the refuse of war, the crosses of fallen trench-dwellers stuck up awry. At night I could not see my hand in front of my face, and had to stand still between Verey lights in case I fell off the duck-boards into the marsh at the edge of the Cojeul.

I spent the days, when I was not busied over works of construction going on in the trench, in the ice-cold dugout, reading a book or drumming my feet against the dugout framework to get some warmth into them. A bottle concealed in a niche of the chalk served the same purpose, and the remedy was sedulously applied by my orderlies and me.

If the smoke of a fire, however small, had wound up into the still December sky, the place would have become utterly uninhabitable. So far the enemy took the sugar-factory to be headquarters and behaved accordingly. Thus it was not till evening that we came alive. The little stove was then lighted and spread genial warmth as well as thick smoke. Soon the pots and pans of the ration-party, just returned from Vis, clattered down the dugout stairs. They had been long and eagerly awaited. And then when the eternal rotation of swedes, barley, and dried vegetables was interrupted by beans and dumplings, our joy knew no bounds.

As I sat at my little table I used to listen with delight to the racy talk of the men crouching in a cloud of tobacco smoke over the stove, on which stood a pan of grog diffusing a powerful odour. War and peace, battle and home, rest-place and leave, were discussed in the dry Lower Saxon way. Love, too, played a leading part.

On the 17th of December I went on leave, and came back on the 2nd of January.

On the 19th of January we were relieved at four in the morning and marched through snow to Gouy. Here we were to stay some while, training for the great offensive. Ludendorff's marvelously clear scheme of training, which was distributed even to the company commands, foreshadowed the scope of the coming attack.

We practiced skirmishing in line and open warfare and did a lot of shooting with the rifle and the machine-gun. As all the villages behind the line were crammed to the attics, every little slope was in use as a range, so that the bullets whistled about the country very much as in a battle. A machine-gunner of my company shot the C.O. of another unit off his horse while he was reviewing some troops. Fortunately the wound was not mortal, and equally fortunately the deed was not clearly brought home to us.

Sometimes I made practice attacks with the company on complicated trench-systems, with live bombs, in order to turn to account the lessons of the Cambrai battle. Here, too, we had casualties.

On the 24th of January, Colonel von Oppen, who was esteemed by all, left us to take over a brigade in the far south-east. The whole regiment keenly felt the loss. During the long years of the war he had become part of the life of the troops he commanded. Besides the warm sympathy he took in the destiny of those under his command, he had a quality not very common among officers who have grown old in the monotony of peace-time soldiering, the power to adapt himself to the immense innovations brought about by the war. Such a man can effect marvels in war-time. Unfortunately his last words, 'Auf wiedersehen in Hannover!' did not come true. Our beloved colonel saw neither his country nor his proud regiment again. He fell a victim to plague, and lies in foreign soil, far from his own country.

On the 6th February we moved back to Lécluse again, and on the 22nd we spent four days in the shelled area left of the Dury-Hendecourt road, and went on working-parties into the front line at night.

As soon as I saw this part of the line, opposite the slag-heaps that used to be Bullecourt, I was certain that a part of the great offensive, of which the western front was talking with bated breath, would be launched at this point.

Everywhere construction was going forward with feverish haste: dugouts sunk, roads laid down. The shell-hole area was beset with little placards standing in the open and displaying incomprehensible figures that denoted presumably the positions of batteries and headquarters. Our aeroplanes flew to and fro in a phalanx to prevent observation by the enemy. A novelty that interested us on this front was that every day precisely at 12 a black ball was let down from the observation balloons and disappeared precisely at 12.10. This was done to let the troops know the exact time.

Towards the end of the month we marched to our old quarters in Gouy. After further battalion and brigade rehearsals we twice practiced a break-through of the whole division over prepared ground with a whole trench-system marked out. Finally, the general commanding the division addressed the officers in a way that left no doubt that the offensive was to be launched in a few days. The brazen spirit of the attack, the spirit of the Prussian infantry, swept through the massed troops assembled here in the opening spring on the soil of France to go through the ordeal of battle.

If the aim the higher command had in view was not attained, it was certainly not the fault of the officers and the men. After forty-four months of hard fighting they threw themselves upon the enemy with all the enthusiasm of August 1914. No wonder it needed a world in arms to bring such a storm-flood to a stand-still. In the course of time, when the waves of hatred have subsided, history will recognize that we fought as no people ever fought before.

It is a pleasure, too, to recall those evenings when we sat together round the table and talked, hot-headed, of the fresh frolic in front of us—the war of movement. Though our last coins went in wine, what need had we of money beyond the enemy's lines, or, indeed, in a better beyond?

> Who knows but that the world
> To ruin may be hurled?
> But if it last to-day,
> To-day's enough!

On the last evening it needed Captain von Brixen's representation that the staff also had the right to exist, or else we should have smashed glasses, bottles, and crockery against the walls. The men, too, were in good form. It was enough to hear them talk of the coming event as the 'Hindenburg flat-race' in their dry Lower Saxon way, to know that they would take hold as they always did, with an absolute reliability and without a word too much. How could one be behindhand when these sons of the old oak-encircled homesteads went into battle? The gleam of many an ideal that shimmered for me over our war aims had been dashed to earth by war. One remains for ever: this fidelity that cannot be shaken.

On the 17th March, towards dusk, we left the quarters we had now become very much attached to, and marched to Brunemont. All the roads were crowded with columns on the march, eagerly pressing forward, with countless guns and endless transport. Nevertheless, everything went precisely according to plans worked out by the general staff. Woe to any unit whose movements were not up to scheduled time! They were ruthlessly relegated to the ditch and had to wait hours before they found a gap into which they could squeeze. Once we were caught in the scrum and Captain von Brixen's charger was pierced by an iron-tipped waggon-pole and killed.

# THE GREAT OFFENSIVE

The Battalion was quartered in the château of Brunemont. We were told that we were to march up the line on the night of March 19th-20th, and to occupy the dugouts in the line near Cagnicourt, ready to go over the top on the morning of March 21st. The task assigned to the regiment was to break through between the villages of Ecoust-St.-Mein and Noreuil, which we knew from 1915-16, on the first day. I sent Lieutenant Schmidt—who because of his amiability was never called anything but little Schmidt—on ahead to make sure of our quarters.

The regiment marched out of Brunemont at the appointed hour. Their morale was excellent in spite of pouring rain. I overlooked a drunken fellow who reeled bawling between the files of my company, for now any harsh words could only do harm. Training was over; and now we came to business, not a wheel of the machine was to be checked.

From some cross-roads where guides awaited us the companies went forward independently. When we got as far as the second line, where we were to be quartered, it came out that the guides had lost their way. Now began a chase to and fro over the dim and sodden shell-hole area and a questioning of innumerable troops, who knew as little where they were as we did. To prevent the complete exhaustion of the men I called a halt and sent out the guides in all directions.

Sections piled arms and crowded into a gigantic crater, while I and Lieutenant Sprenger sat on the edge of a smaller one. There had been single shells falling about a hundred metres in front of us for some while. Then there was one nearer; the splinters struck the sides of the shell-hole. One of the men cried out and said he was hit in the foot. I shouted to the men to scatter among the surrounding shell-holes, and meanwhile I examined the man's boot to see if there was a hole. Then the whistle of another shell high in the air. Everybody had that clutching feeling: 'It's coming over!' There was a terrific stupefying crash . . . the shell had burst in the midst of us . . .

I picked myself up half-unconscious. The machine-gun ammunition in the large shell-hole, set alight by the explosion, was burning with an intense pink glow. It illuminated the rising flumes of the shell-burst, in which there writhed a heap of black bodies and the shadowy forms of the survivors, who were rushing from the scene in all directions. At the same time rose a multitudinous tumult of pain and cries for help.

I will make no secret of it that after a moment's blank horror I took to my heels like the rest and ran aimlessly into the night. It was not till I had fallen head over heels into a small shell-hole that I understood what had happened. Only to hear and see no more! Only to get away, far away, and creep into a hole! And yet the other voice was heard: 'You are the company commander, man!' Exactly so. I do not say it in self-praise. I might as well say: 'When God gives an office, He gives the understanding for it.' I have often observed in myself and others that an officer's sense of responsibility drowns his personal fears. There is a sticking-place, something to occupy the thoughts. So I forced myself back into the ghastly spot. On the way I ran into Fusilier Haller, he who had bagged the machine-gun on my November patrol, and took him along with me.

The wounded men never ceased to utter their fearful cries. Some came creeping to me when they heard my voice and whimpered, 'Sir . . . Sir!' One of my favourite recruits, Jasinski, whose leg was broken by a splinter, caught hold of me round the knees. Cursing my impotence to help, I vainly clapped him on the shoulder. Such moments can never be forgotten.

I had to leave the wretched creatures to the one surviving stretcher-bearer and lead the faithful few who remained and who collected round me away from the fatal spot. Half an hour before I had been at the head of a first-rate company at fighting strength. Now the few who followed me through the maze of the trenches where I lost my way were utterly crestfallen. A young lad, a milksop, who a few days before had been jeered at by his companions because during the training he had burst into tears over the weight of a box of ammunition, was now loyally hulking one along on our painful way after retrieving it from the scene of our disaster. When I saw that, I was finished. I threw myself on the ground and broke into convulsive sobs, while the men stood gloomily round me.

After we had hastened on for hours and to no purpose, and often menaced by shells, along the trench ankle-deep in mud and water, we crept, dead tired, into some ammunition bays in the side of the trench. My batman spread his ground-sheet over me, but the state of my nerves kept my eyes wide open, and thus, smoking cigars, I waited for daybreak.

The first light of dawn revealed an utterly incredible sight. Countless troops, all over the shelled area, were still in search of their appointed shelter. Artillerymen were humping ammunition; trench-mortar men were pulling their mortars along; signalers were laying wires. There was a regular fair a thousand metres in front of the enemy, who, incomprehensibly, appeared to observe nothing.

By good luck I ran across the commander of the 2nd Machine-gun Company, Lieutenant Fallenstein, an old front-line soldier, who was able to show me the way to our shelter. The first thing he said was: 'What makes you look like that, man?' I led my men to a large, deep dugout that we had passed a dozen times during the night. There I found little Schmidt, who knew nothing of our disaster. The guides, also, were there. After that day, whenever we moved into a new position I always chose the guides myself and with the greatest care. The lessons of the war are thorough but costly.

After settling-in the men who had come with me, I went back to the horrible scene of the night before. It was a ghastly sight. In a ring round the burst were lying over twenty charred corpses, nearly all of them unrecognizably mutilated. Some, indeed, we had to report as missing, as nothing of them was to be found.

I came on some soldiers of another unit busied in extracting the blood-stained possessions of the dead out of the hideous mess, in the hope of booty. I chased the hyænas off, and told my orderly to collect the pocket-books and valuables, as far as could be done, so that we could send them to their people. We had, in any case, to leave them behind when next morning we went over the top.

I was delighted to see Lieutenant Sprenger come out of a dugout near by with a number of men who had spent the night there. I told the section leaders to report, and ascertained that I still disposed of sixty-three men. I had set out the night before in the best of spirits with a hundred and fifty! I succeeded in accounting for over twenty dead and over sixty wounded, some of whom died later from their injuries.

The only grain of comfort was that it might have been worse. Fusilier Rust, for example, was standing so close to the burst that the carrying strap of his box began to burn. The N.C.O. Peggau, who, it is true, was killed the next day, was standing between two men, both of whom were torn to bits, while he had not a scratch.

We spent the day in poor spirits, sleeping mostly. I had to go again and again to the C.O., as there was always something to do with the attack to arrange. Apart from this I lay on a bunk talking to my two officers about trifling matters, in order to escape the torture of our thoughts. The constant refrain was: 'Thank God we can only die once.' I said a few words to the men, who crouched together in silence on the steps, with a view to cheer them up; but it seemed to have little effect. Nor was I myself in an encouraging mood.

At ten o'clock in the evening a runner brought orders to move into the first line. A wild beast dragged from its lair, or a sailor who sees the last plank swept from his grasp, may, perhaps, have feelings comparable to ours when we were compelled to leave the warmth and safety of the dugout. Yet not one of them was tempted to stay behind unobserved.

We hurried along the Felix trench under sharp shrapnel fire and got through without a casualty. While we passed along the trench below, guns crossed by bridges over our heads to take up forward positions. The section of the trench allotted to the battalion was quite narrow. Every dugout was filled with troops in a moment. The rest had to dig themselves holes in the sides of the trench so as to have some shelter at last during the bombardment preceding the attack. At last after much scrambling to and fro every one had found his hole. Once more Captain von Brixen assembled the company commanders for his last remarks. When we had synchronized watches for the last time we shook hands and separated.

I sat down on the steps of a dugout with my two officers to wait for 5.5 a.m., the moment when the artillery preparation was to begin. The atmosphere was slightly more cheerful, as the rain had left off and the clear, starry sky promised a fine morning. We passed the time eating and talking. Every one smoked hard, and the water-bottles went round. In the early hours the enemy artillery was so lively that we were afraid the English had smelt a rat.

Just before zero the following flash signal was given us: 'H.M. the Kaiser and Hindenburg are on the scene of operations.' It was greeted with enthusiasm.

The hands crept on. We counted the last minutes as they marked them off. At last they stood at 5.5. At once the hurricane broke lose. A curtain of flames was let down, followed by a sudden impetuous tumult such as was never heard, a raging thunder that swallowed up the reports even of the heaviest guns in its tremendous reverberations and made the earth tremble. This gigantic roar of annihilation from countless guns behind us was so terrific that, compared with it, all preceding battles were child's-play. What we had not dared to hope came true. The enemy artillery was silenced, put out of action by one giant blow. We could not stay any longer in the dugouts. We got out on to the top and looked with wonder at the wall of fire towering over the English lines and the swaying blood-red clouds that hung above it.

Our delight was lessened by the tears and the burning of the mucous membrane caused by the fumes of our own gas-shells that the wind blew back on us. Many of the men were forced to pull off their masks when the unpleasant effects of our Blue Cross gas threw them into fights of choking and coughing. I felt very uneasy, yet I felt sure that our command could not have made a miscalculation from which our destruction would necessarily follow. Meanwhile I exerted all my energy to keep the first cough back so as not to increase the irritation. After an hour we were able to take off our masks.

It was now daylight. The terrific tumult behind us rose higher and higher. In front stood a blind wall of smoke, dust, and gas. Men we rerunning along the trench and shouting delightedly into each other's ears. Infantry and artillery, engineers and signalers, Prussians and Bavarians, officers and men, were all alike in transports over this elemental expression of German power and were burning with impatience for 9.40, when we were to advance to the attack. At 8.45 our heavy trench-mortars, that stood almost touching one another behind the front line, started up. We could see the great two-hundred-weight bombs fly in a steep trajectory through the air and fall to the earth on the other side with Hephaestean explosions. Their bursts made a close chain of craters in eruption.

The very laws of nature seemed to have lost their validity. The air shimmered as though on a day of summer heat. The changing index of refraction made fixed objects dance to and fro. Black streaks of shadow flitted across the mass of smoke. The roar had become a norm and one heard no longer. One could scarcely hear the thousands of machine-guns in our rear that swept the blue sky with swarm upon swarm of lead.

The last hour of the artillery preparation was unhealthier than all the four preceding ones, during which we had walked about unheeding on the top. The enemy brought a heavy battery into action that landed shell after shell into our crowded trench. I went to the left to avoid them, and ran into the adjutant, Lieutenant Heins, who asked me if I had seen Lieutenant Baron von Solemacher: 'He must take over the battalion at once. Captain von Brixen has just been killed.' I was shocked at this bad news, and went back and sat in a deep burrow in the earth. By the time I left there I had utterly forgotten the news I had heard. My brain had only one link with reality . . . 9.40. It seemed, though, that I was behaving courageously, for everybody smiled approvingly when they looked at me.

The N.C.O. Dujesiefken, a comrade of the Regniéville patrol, came to a stop in front of my burrow and asked me to come out into the trench, as even a light shell bursting anywhere near might precipitate the whole mass of soil on my head. An explosion took the very words from his mouth. He fell to the ground with a leg torn off. I sprang over him and fled to the right, where I crept to earth again in a hole already occupied by two engineers.

The heavy shells were falling in a narrow circle all round us. Suddenly from a white cloud hurtled black lumps of soil; as for the detonation, it was lost in the general roar. Indeed, the sense of hearing was lost. In the piece of trench near us to our left three men of my company were torn to pieces. One of the last hits, a dud, killed poor little Schmidt, who had not left the dugout steps.

I was standing with Sprenger, with my watch in my hand, in front of my burrow, and waiting for the great moment. The rest of the company had collected round us. By jokes of coarseness that unfortunately prevents me from setting it down here, we succeeded in cheering and distracting them. Lieutenant Meyer, who peeped for a moment round the traverse, told me later that he thought us out of our minds.

The officer patrols who were to cover our advance left the trench at 9.10. As our front line and the enemy's were here eight hundred metres apart, we had to move forward even during the artillery preparation and to take up our position in No-Man's-land in readiness to jump into the enemy's front line at 9.40. Sprenger and I climbed out on to the top after a few minutes, followed by the men.

'Now we'll show what the 7th Company can do!'

'I don't care for anything now.'

'Vengeance for the 7th Company.'

'Vengeance for Captain von Brixen.'

We drew our revolvers and crossed our wire, through which the first casualties were already trailing back.

I looked to the left and right. The distribution of the host presented a strange spectacle. In shell-holes in front of the enemy lines, churned and churned again by the utmost pitch of shell-fire, the attacking battalions were waiting massed in companies, as far as the eye could see. When I saw this massed might piled up, the break-through seemed to me a certainty. But was there strength in us to smash the enemy's reserves and hurl them to destruction? I was confident of it. The decisive battle, the final advance, had begun. The destiny of the nations drew to its iron conclusion, and the stake was the possession of the world. I was conscious, if only in feeling, of the significance of that hour; and I believe that on this occasion every man felt his personality fade away in the face of a crisis in which he had his part to play and by which history would be made. No one who has lived through moments like these can doubt that the course of nations in the last resort rises and falls with the destiny of war.

The atmosphere of intense excitement was amazing. Officers stood upright and shouted chaff nervously to each other. Often a heavy trench-mortar fired short and scattered us with its fountains of earth; and no one even bent his head. The roar of battle had become so terrific that we were scarcely in our right senses. The nerves could register fear no longer. Every one was mad and beyond reckoning; we had gone over the edge of the world into superhuman perspectives. Death had lost its meaning and the will to live was made over to our country; and hence every one was blind and regardless of his personal fate.

Three minutes before the attack my batman, the faithful Vinke, beckoned to me, pointing to a full water-bottle. He recognized, in his own way, the need of the hour. I took a long pull. It was as though I drank water. There was only the cigar wanting the usual one for such occasions. Three times the match was blown out by the commotion of the air. . . .

The great moment had come. The fire lifted over the first trenches. We advanced. . . .

The turmoil of our feelings was called forth by rage, alcohol, and the thirst for blood as we stepped out, heavily and yet irresistibly, for the enemy's lines. And therewith beat the pulse of heroism—the godlike and the bestial inextricably mingled. I was far in front of the company, followed by my batman and a man of one year's service called Haake. In my right hand I gripped my revolver, in my left a bamboo riding-cane. I was boiling with a fury now utterly inconceivable to me. The overpowering desire to kill winged my feet. Rage squeezed bitter tears from my eyes.

The tremendous force of destruction that bent over the field of battle was concentrated in our brains. So may men of the Renaissance have been locked in their passions, so may a Cellini have raged or werewolves have howled and hunted through the night on the track of blood. We crossed a battered tangle of wire without difficulty and at a jump were over the front line, scarcely recognizable any longer. The attacking waves of infantry bobbed up and down in ghostly lines in the white rolling smoke.

Against all expectation a machine-gun rattled at us from the second line. I and the men with me jumped for a shell-hole. A second later there was a frightful crack and I sank forward in a heap. Vinke caught me round the neck and turned me on my back: 'Are you hit, sir?' There was nothing to be seen. The one-year's-service fellow had a hole through his arm, and assured us, groaning, that he had a bullet in his back. We pulled off his uniform and bound him up. The churned-up earth showed us that a shrapnel shell had burst at the level of our faces on the edge of the shell-hole. It was a wonder we were still alive.

Meanwhile the others were on beyond us. We scrambled after them, leaving the wounded man to his fate, after we had stuck a bit of wood in the ground near him with a strip of white muslin as a mark for the wave of stretcher-bearers that were following the fighting troops. Half-left of us the great railway embankment in the line Ecoust-Croisilles, which we had to cross, rose out of the mist. From loopholes and dugout windows built into the side of it rifles and machine-guns were rattling merrily.

Even Vinke had disappeared. I followed a sunken road, with its smashed-in shelters yawning in its banks. I strode on in a fury over the black and torn-up ground, from which rose the suffocating gas of our shells. I was entirely alone.

Then I caught the sight of the first of the enemy. A figure crouched, wounded apparently, three metres in front of me in the middle of the pounded hollow of the road. I saw him start at the sight of me and stare at me with wide-open eyes as I walked slowly up to him holding out my revolver in front of me. A drama without an audience was ready. To me the mere sight of an enemy in tangible form was a release. Grinding my teeth, I pressed the muzzle to the temple of this wretch, whom terror now crippled, and with my other hand gripped hold of his tunic. With a beseeching cry he snatched a photograph from his pocket and held it before my eyes . . . himself, surrounded by a numerous family. . . .

I forced down my mad rage and walked past.

Men of my company came jumping down into the sunken road. We were aglow with heat. I pulled off my cloak and threw it away. I still remember that I shouted very emphatically and more than once: Lieutenant Jünger now casts off his cloak,' and made at that the Fusiliers laughed as though I had made the most priceless joke. Above us every one was going for it over the top without the least regard for the machine-guns, which were at the utmost four hundred metres away from us. The same impulse of annihilation drew me into the sheaves of fire. I ran straight for the embankment, spit bullets as it might. In a shell-hole I came upon a figure in a brown waterproof shooting with a revolver. It was Kius, who was in a like mood and stuffed a handful of cartridges in my pocket by way of greeting.

We must have spent a long while running to and fro among the shell-holes and engaged one target after another. In any case I found myself at last at the foot of the embankment, and I saw a dugout window quite close to me covered with a sandbag, from which I could see they were firing. I shot through the cloth. A man near me tore it down and threw in a bomb. A shock and a cloud of smoke welling out showed the result. Two ran along the bank and dealt with the other loopholes in the same way. I raised my hand to warn the men behind, for their bullets at very short range were whistling past our ears. They nodded back delighted. After that we clambered with hundreds more at one rushed up the bank. For the first time in the war I saw large bodies of men in hand-to-hand fighting. The English held two terraced trenches on the rear slope. Shots were exchanged and bombs lobbed down at a range of a few metres.

I jumped into the first trench. Stumbling round the first traverse I collided with an English officer with an open tunic and his tie hanging loose. I did without my revolver, and seizing him by the throat flung him against the sandbags, where he collapsed. Behind me the head of an old major appeared. He was shouting to me, 'Shoot the hound dead.'

I left this to those behind me and turned to the lower trenches. It seethed with English. I fired off my cartridges so fiercely that I pressed the trigger ten times at least after the last shot. A man next to me threw bombs among them as they scrambled to get away. A dish-shaped helmet was sent spinning high in the air.

A minute saw the battle ended. The English jumped out of their trenches and fled by battalions across the open. They stumbled over each other as they fled, and in a few second the ground was strewn with dead. Only a few got away.

A N.C.O. was standing near me gaping at this spectacle with mouth agog. I snatched the rifle from his hands in an uncomfortable need to shoot. My first victim was an Englishman whom I shot between two Germans at 150 metres. He snapped together like the blade of a knife and lay still.

After quite a time had been spent thus, we went on. The spirit of the attack had been kindled by success to a white heat of recklessness in every man. There was no question of leading the several units. Nevertheless, one cry was on everybody's lips: 'On!' Every man went straight ahead.

As my objective I chose a little hill where the ruins of a cottage, the cross on a grave, and the wreckage of an aeroplane were to be seen. I went forward so blindly that I got into the zone of our own fire, and had to throw myself into a shell-hole for cover while waiting for the guns to lengthen their range. I found a young officer of another regiment close to me who, quite like myself, was rejoicing over the success of our first assault. The common enthusiasm brought us as close in those few moments as if we had known each other for years. The next spring forward parted us, never to meet again.

Even during these frightful moments something ludicrous occurred. A man near me whipped his rifle to his shoulder as though he were out shooting, to shoot a hare that suddenly jumped up and ran through our lines. The episode was so bewildering that I had to laugh. There indeed can be nothing so horrible that some crazy fellow cannot cap it.

Near the ruins of the house lay a small length of trench which was being raked by machine-gun fire from the far side. I jumped in it at one bound and found it unoccupied. Immediately after Kius and Wedelstädt appeared. An orderly of Wedelstädt's, who came last, collapsed in mid-jump and lay dead, shot through the eye. When Wedelstädt saw this last man of his company fall headlong he leant his head on the edge of the trench and wept. And neither was he destined to survive this day.

Below us lay a strongly-held position in a sunken road. In front of it were two machine-gun nests, one on each edge of a hollow. The turmoil of our gunfire had rolled on over this strong-point and the enemy seemed to have recovered. At any rate he was pouring out lead as fast as it would leave the barrels. We were separated by a strip of ground five hundred metres wide, and across it the sheaves of fire buzzed like swarms of bees.

After a pause for breath we went on over the top at the enemy with a handful of men. It was a fight to the death. After one or two springs forward I lay opposite the left-hand machine-gun position, alone but for one man. I could clearly distinguish a flat helmet beside a low mound of earth, and close beside it a thin spiral of steam. I approached in quite short springs so as to allow no chance for aim. Each time that I lay down the man threw me a clip of cartridges and I fired a few carefully-aimed shots. 'Cartridges .. cartridges!' I turned round and saw him lying twitching on one side.

When I look back now to that blind dash across the open against a choice and well-furnished position, I see that we must have been inspired by a quite improbable degree of recklessness. And yet, where would be the success of war if it were not for individuals whom the thrill of action intoxicates and hurls forward with an impetus not to be resisted? It seemed often as though death itself feared to cross our path. From the left, where the resistance was weaker, there appeared a few men who were almost in a position to bomb the post. I set out on my last spring forward and stumbled over a barbed-wire entanglement into the trench. The English left their guns and ran, fired on from all sides, and made their escape to the nest on the right. The machine-gun was half concealed beneath a huge heap of empty drums. It was still nearly red-hot and smoking. The corpse of an athlete lay in front of it. A shot through the head had put out one eye, and I could claim the shot as mine. The enormous fellow with his great white eyeball and his smoke-blackened skull looked terrible. I was perishing of thirst and, unable to bear it any longer, I began to look for water. The entrance of a deep dugout seemed promising. I peered in and saw a man sitting at the bottom mending an ammunition belt on his knee. Instead of going for him at once, as in prudence I ought, I called out to him: 'Come here! hands up!' He jumped up staring at me in amazement and disappeared in the darkness. I threw a bomb after him. Presumably the dugout had a second entrance, for a man came from behind a traverse and said laconically: 'We've just shot them. They're done for.'

At last I came to a tin can full of cooling-water. I poured the oily fluid down in huge gulps, filled an English water-bottle, and gave some to the others who suddenly crowded into the trench.

Meanwhile, from the right-hand machine-gun nest and also from the sunken road, sixty metres in front of us, there was still a resolute resistance. The fellows put up a superb show. We tried to turn the English machine-gun on them, but we had no success with it. On the contrary, while I was busy with it a bullet flew by my head, grazed a Jäger lieutenant standing behind me, and wounded a man severely in the shoulder. A light machine-gun section had better luck. They got their gun mounted on the edge of our little crescent-shaped trench and raked the English from the flank.

There was a moment of surprise, and it was turned to good account by the assaulting troops on our right. They charged the sunken road from the front, with our 9th Company, still intact, led by Lieutenant Gipkens. at the head. And now from every shell-hole figures rose, and with a terrific hurrah, brandishing their rifles, rolling their eyes, foam on their lips, they rushed upon the enemy's position, out of which the defenders advanced by hundreds with their hands held high.

No quarter was given. The English hastened with upstretched arms through the first wave of storm troops to the rear, where the fury of the battle had not reached boiling point. An orderly of Gipkens' shot a good dozen or more of them with his 32 repeater.

I cannot blame our men for their bloodthirsty conduct. To kill a defenceless man is a baseness. Nothing in the war was more repulsive to me than those heroes of the mess tables who used to repeat with a fat laugh the familiar tale of the prisoners marched in: 'Did you hear that about the massacre? Priceless!'

On the other hand. the defending force, after driving their bullets into the attacking one at five paces' distance, must take the consequences. A man cannot change his feelings again during the last rush with a veil of blood before his eyes. He does not want to take prisoners but to kill. He has no scruples left; only the spell of primeval instinct remains. It is not till the blood has flowed that the mist gives way in his soul. He looks round him as though waking from the bondage of a dream. It is only then that he becomes once more a soldier of to-day and capable of addressing himself to the next problem of tactics.

This was the state we found ourselves in after the capture of the sunken road. A large body of the men had collected and stood in a mob, shouting confusedly. Some officers pointed out to them the continuation of the hollow ground, and the great battle horde with astonishing coolness lumbered on.

The hollow ran up into higher ground, and from there enemy columns were coming into sight. We advanced, now and then standing still to shoot, till we were held up by heavy rifle-fire. It was extremely painful to hear the bullets striking the ground near your head. Kius, who had come up again, picked up a flattened one that had been stopped half a metre in front of his nose. Making use of a brief pause, we got to a shell-hole. They had already become rare. We found a number of officers of our battalion there. It was commanded now by Lieutenant Lindenburg; for Baron von Solemacher had unfortunately been mortally wounded during the assault on the embankment. On the right side of the hollow Lieutenant Breyer, attached to us from the 10th Jägers, was strolling along the machine-gun fire, to the delight of every one, with a walking-stick in his hand and a long green huntsman's pipe in his mouth, and his rifle hung on his shoulder as if he were out shooting hares.

We told each other briefly our adventures so far, and handed round water-bottles and chocolate, and then the general wish was to go on again. The machine-guns, threatened apparently on the flank, had disappeared. We might perhaps have won three or four kilometres. The hollow was seething with the attacking troops. As far as the eye could see behind us there were men coming on in open order, ranks and columns.

We were unfortunately much too thick on the ground, and it was just as well we did not know in the heat of the attack how many were left behind, either dead or wounded.

We reached the high ground without opposition. A few khaki figures jumped from a piece of trench on our right, and we shot them down out of hand as they ran. Most of them were accounted for. The top of the hill was held by a row of dugouts. From them smoke was rising, and of these we made short work with bombs. From others the occupants emerged with arms uplifted and knocking knees. Water-bottles and cigarettes were taken from them, and as soon as the way to the rear was pointed out they hurried off with great speed. One young Englishman already surrendered to me, and then suddenly turning round he disappeared into this dugout. As he stayed in concealment in spite of my summons to come out, we made an end of his indecision with a bomb and went on. A narrow footpath went off down the other side of the hill. A signpost showed that it led to Vraucourt. While the other still delayed in the dugouts, Heins and I went over the top of the hill.

Down below lay the ruins of Vraucourt. The flashes of a battery in action were to be seen in front, but the detachments fled into the village at the sight of the first wave of storm troops. The occupants, too, of a number of dugouts built in the sides of a sunken road rushed out and fled. I shot one of them as he jumped out of the entrance of the nearest.

With two men of the company who reported to me meanwhile I went along the sunken road. There was a defended position to the right of it from which came a heavy fire. So we withdrew into the first dugout, over which very soon the shots of both sides were crossing. My Englishman lay in front of it, a mere lad. I had shot him right through the head. It is a strange feeling to look into the eyes of a man whom you have killed with your own hands.

We did not worry over the increasing fire, but established ourselves in the dugout and looked through the provisions left behind, as our stomachs reminded us that we had eaten nothing during the attack. We found here white bread, jam, and a stone jar full of ginger-beer. After refreshing myself I sat on an empty biscuit-tin and read some English newspapers that abounded in the most tasteless invective against the 'Huns.' After a while we became tired of doing nothing, so we went back to the beginning of the sunken road in jumps, and there found a large body of men assembled. Thence we could see a battalion of the 164th near Vraucourt. We decided to storm the village, and hurried forward again along the sunken road. A little way before the edge of the village we were brought to a stop by our own artillery, which had the stupidity to go on shooting the same spot till next day. A heavy shell landed among us when we were half-way and killed four men. The others turned and ran.

As I learned later, the artillery had orders to go on shooting at their longest range. This incomprehensible order took the finest fruits of victory from our grasp. Grinding our teeth with rage, we had to make halt before the wall of fire.

In the hope of finding a gap in it we turned away to the right, where at that moment a company commander of the 76th was leading an attack on the Vraucourt line. We joined in with a cheer, but had scarcely got a footing in it before our own artillery shelled us out again. We stormed the trench three times, and three times had to retire again. Curse as we might, we could only occupy some shell-holes, and there a grass fire started by our artillery destroyed many wounded and caused us intolerable discomfort. The English rifle-fire, too, caused casualties, among whom was the volunteer, Grutzmacher, of my company.

Darkness came slowly on. Sporadically the rifle-fire blazed out in a final burst and then was silent all along our front. The men, utterly exhausted, looked round for shelter for the night, and the officers called their own names without ceasing in order to assemble the scattered companies.

Twelve men of the 7th Company had collected round me during the last hour. As it was growing cold I led them to the little dugout in front of which my Englishman lay, and sent them out to collect blankets and cloaks from the fallen. When I got them all settled down I could no longer resist the curiosity I had to visit the gun-pit lying in front of us. I took Fusilier Haller with me, as I had the utmost confidence in his sporting spirit. We walked on with our rifles at the ready towards the pit, over which our artillery fire raged without ceasing, and next explored a dugout that had apparently been recently abandoned by English artillery officers. There was an enormous gramophone on the table that Haller at once set going. The gay musical-comedy song that whirred from the disc made a ghostly impression, and I threw the box to the ground, where after a wheeze and a gasp it lay still. The dugout was furnished with extreme comfort, even to a little open grate and a mantelpiece, on which lay pipes and tobacco, with a circle of armchairs round the fire. Merry old England!

Naturally we took without compunction whatever we liked. I chose a haversack, underclothes, a little silver flask full of whisky, a map-case, and some most charming toilet articles by Roger et Gallet, no doubt tender recollection of a Paris leave.

A neighbouring room served as the kitchen, whose array of provisions filled us with respectful admiration. There was a whole boxful of fresh eggs. We sucked a large number on the spot, as we had long since forgotten their very name. Against the walls were stacks of tinned meat, cases of priceless thick jam, bottles of coffee-essence as well, and quantities of tomatoes and onions; in short, all that a gourmet could desire.

This sight I often remembered later when we spent weeks together in the trenches on a rigid allowance of bread, washy soup, and thin jam. For four long years, in torn coats and worse fed than a Chinese coolie, the German soldier was hurried from one battlefield to the next to show his iron fist yet again to a foe many times his superior in numbers, well equipped and well fed. There could be no surer sign of the might of the idea that drove us on. It is to face death and to die in the moment of enthusiasm. To hunger and starve for one's cause is more . . .

After this glimpse into the enemy's domestic circumstances we left the dugout and went into the gun-pit, where we found that two brand-new guns had been abandoned. I took a lump of chalk and chalked up the number of my company. I may observe that the right of capture was very little respected by the troops that followed after. Each unit obliterated the mark of its predecessor and put its own, till that of some labour battalion survived. This shows how very rudimentary the sporting instinct is among the people.

We returned to the others, as our own guns were throwing metal about our ears all the time. Our front line, dug in the meanwhile by the troops behind us, was two hundred metres in our rear. I posted two men in front of the dugout and gave orders for the others of the guard to keep hold of their rifles. After I had arranged the reliefs, had a little more to eat, and made a note of the events of the day, I went to sleep.

At 1 we were awakened by shouts and lively rifle-fire on our right. We seized our rifles and, rushing outside, posted ourselves in a large shell-hole. A few scattered Germans came back from in front of us and were fired on from our own lines. Two of them fell. Put on our guard by this, we waited till the excitement subsided behind us and calling out to show who we were, we retired to our own lines. There we found the commander of the 2nd Company, speechless with a cold and wounded in the arm, with about sixty men of our regiment. As he had to go back to a dressing-station, I took command of his detachment, among which were three officers. Besides this there were the two companies of Gipkens and Vorbeck, jumbled up like the rest.

The commanding officer of the battalion was Captain Baron von Ledebur; and of the regiment, Major Dietlein, as Major von Bardeleben had been wounded early in the day.

I spent the rest of the night with some N.C.Os. of the 2nd Company in a little hole in the ground, where we were stiff with cold. I breakfasted in the morning from the plundered provisions, and sent a party to Quéant to fetch coffee and rations. Our own artillery began again with its cursed shelling, and, as a morning greeting, sent us a direct hit in a shell hole which accommodated four men of the machine-gun company.

At dawn the platoon commander of my company, Vice-sergeant-major Kumpart, turned up with a few men. I had scarcely got my circulation going again after the cold of the night when I had orders to storm the Vraucourt line further to the right, taking with me what there was of the 76th Regiment as well. This line on our front was already partly in our hands. There was a thick morning mist as we moved off to the jumping-off position, a hill to the south of Ecoust, where many dead of the day before were lying. As is usual when the orders for an attack are somewhat vague, there was a tremendous palaver among the officers of the storm troops, which nothing but the play of an enemy machine-gun was able to bring to an end. Everybody jumped for the nearest shell-hole with the exception of the sergeant-major, Kumpart, who lay groaning. I hurried to him with a stretcher-bearer and bound him up. He was badly wounded in the knee. We extracted several pieces of bone from the wound with a forceps. He died a few days later. I felt it particularly, as he had been my drill-instructor three years before in Recouvrence.

I exposed the folly of a frontal attack in a discussion with Captain von Ledebur, since it was clear that the Vraucourt line, already partly in our hands, could with far less loss be rolled up from the left. We decided not to carry out an attack, and events proved us right.

Such episodes prove the futility of the system of higher command with its headquarters far in the rear, though of course I do not question the necessity. At the same time such orders show clearly a lack of experience of front-line fighting: the time for frontal attacks without preparation has for ever gone by. The common soldier who has been taught his lesson by the enemy's rifles could not fall into such a blunder. It succeeded only where the enemy was weak. The strong parts of the line then fell of themselves.

For the time being we established ourselves in the shell-holes on the higher ground. The sun came through by degrees and English aeroplanes appeared, which sprayed our refuges with machine-guns, but were soon driven off. Below Ecoust we saw a battery drive up, an unusual sight for old trench-soldiers. It, too, was soon shelled. One horse only tore itself free and galloped over the field. It was an uncanny sight—this panic-stricken beast against the wide and deserted stretches of country hung with the drifting smoke of the bursting shells. The enemy fliers had not been long gone before we began to be shelled. At first a few shrapnel broke over us, then light and heavy shells in plenty. We lay as though on a silver salver. Several unquiet spirits drew worse fire by losing their heads and running to and fro instead of lying low in their shell-holes and letting the stuff sweep over their heads. In such situations one must be a fatalist. I took this text to heart as I consumed the really glorious contents of a tin of gooseberry jam that I had carried off as booty. In this fashion the morning slowly drew to an end.

We observed movement for some time past on our left in the Vraucourt line. Now we saw straight in front of us the curved flight and the white bursts of German stick-bombs. This was the moment we waited for. I gave the word to advance. We reached the enemy line without encountering much fire, and jumped in, eagerly welcomed by a storm troop of the 76th Regiment. Headway was slowly made bombing along the trench, as at Cambrai. The enemy artillery soon found out, unfortunately, that we were obstinately eating into their lines. We were pretty sharply shelled with shrapnel and light shells, but the reserves who were streaming up to the trench over the open caught the worst of it. We did our utmost to clear the trench of the enemy so that we could take cover from the artillery fire.

The Vraucourt line was still in course of digging and many stretches of it were only marked out by the removal of the turf. When we rushed these pieces, we had all the fire in the neighbourhood concentrated on us. In the same way we had the enemy under our fire when they crossed these spots as they gave way before us, so that these short stretches of ground were soon heaped with corpses. It was a nerve-scourging spot. We dashed over the still warm muscular bodies, displaying powerful knees below their kilts, or crept on over them. They were Highlanders, and the resistance we were meeting showed we had no cowards in front of us.

After we had gained a few hundred metres in this fashion we were brought to a halt by the bombs and rifle-grenades that fell more and more thickly. The men began to give way!

'Tommy's counter-attacking!'

'Bliew stahn!'

'I'll just see that we're in touch.'

'Bombs forward! Bombs forward!'

'Look out, sir!'

It is just in trench fighting, the fiercest fighting of all, that such recoils are most frequent. The bravest push to the front shooting and bomb-throwing. The rest follow on their heels automatically, in a herd. In the hand-to-hand battle the fighters jump back and forward, and in avoiding the murderous bombs of the enemy they run back on those behind them. Only those in the forefront know what the situation is, while further back a wild panic breaks out in the crowded trench. Perhaps a few even jump over the top and get shot, whereat the enemy of course are much encouraged. Indeed, if they seize their opportunity all is lost; and it is now for the officer to show that he is worth his salt, though he too may have the wind up.

I succeeded in getting together a handful of men, and with them I organized a nucleus of resistance behind a broad traverse. We exchanged missiles with an invisible opponent at a few metres' distance. It took some courage to hold your head up when they burst and whipped up the heaped soil of the traverse. A man of the 76th, close to me, shot off cartridge after cartridge, looking perfectly wild and without a thought of cover, till he collapsed in streams of blood. A shot had smashed his forehead with a report like a breaking board. He doubled up in his corner of the trench, and there he remained in a crouching attitude, his head leaning against the side. His blood poured on the ground as though poured out of a bucket. The snorting death-rattles sounded at longer intervals and at last ceased. I seized his rifle and went on firing. At last there was a brief pause. Two men who were in front even of us made an attempt to dash back over the top. One fell into the trench shot through the head. the other, shot through the body, could only creep after him.

We sat in the bottom of the trench and waited and smoked English cigarettes. Now and then a well-aimed rifle-grenade came arrowing over. The man shot in the belly was a young lad, and he lay between us and almost contentedly stretched himself like a cat in the warm rays of the setting sun. He slipped over to death smiling like a child.

It was a sight that had nothing sad or painful in it. I was touched by nothing but a clear feeling of affection for the dying man. The groaning, too, of his comrade gradually ceased. He died where he lay, after fits of shuddering.

We tried several times to work our way forward by crawling flattened out over the bodies of the Highlanders across the undug part, but we were driven back every time by machine-gun fire and rifle-grenades. Every casualty I saw was a fatal one. In this way the forward part of our trench was gradually filled with dead; and in turn we were constantly reinforced from the rear. Soon there was a light or heavy machine-gun behind every traverse. I stood behind one of these lead squirts and shot till my forefinger was blackened with smoke. When the cooling-water had evaporated, the tins were handed round and to the accompaniment of not very polite jokes and by a very simple expedient filled up again:

> In anxious moments we must bring
> Ourselves to much that's not the thing.

The sun was far from down in the sky. It seemed that the second day of battle was over. For the first time I took a careful look round and sent back a report and sketch-map, overtaken once more by the thought: 'You are not a fighter only, but a soldier!' The trench we were in cut the Vraucourt-Mory road at a distance of five hundred metres in front of us. The road was camouflaged by hangings fastened to the trees. Enemy troops were hurrying over the slope of a hill behind, shells bursting round them. Streamers of black and white and red crossed the cloudless blue of the evening sky. The beams of sunset dipped them in a tender rosy red so that they resembled a flight of flamingoes. We unfolded our trench-maps and spread them out to see how far we had penetrated enemy lines.

A cool evening breeze promised a sharp night. Wrapped in an English trench-coat I leaned against the side of the trench and talked to little Schultz, the comrade of my Indian patrols, who, like a good friend, had turned up with four heavy machine-guns just where there was most need for them. Men of all companies sat on the fire-steps. Their features were youthful and clear-cut beneath their steel helmets. Their leaders had fallen and it was of their own impulse that they were here and in their right place. We set about putting ourselves in a state of defence for the night. I put my revolver and a dozen English bombs beside me and felt ready for all comers, even though they were the most pig-headed of Scotsmen.

Then there came a new outbreak of bombing from the right, and on the left German light-signals went up. From somewhere a faint hurrah came on the wind. That roused us. 'They're surrounded! They're surrounded!' In one of these moments of enthusiasm that herald great exploits, every one seized his rifle and rushed forward along the trench. After a short encounter with bombs a body of Highlanders made hurriedly for the road. There was no holding us now. In spite of warning shots, 'Look out, the machine-gun on the left is still firing!' We jumped out of the trench and in an instant reached the road, where there was a stampede of Highlanders. A long, thick wire entanglement cut off their retreat, so that like hunted game they had to run past us at fifty metres' distance. On our side there broke out a tumultuous hurrah that must have struck their ears like the trump of the last judgment, and a hurricane of rapid fire. Machine-guns mounted in haste made a massacre of it.

While I was cursing at a jam that prevented me firing, I felt a blow on the shoulder. I turned round and saw the face of little Schultz, distorted with rage. 'Look . . . they're still firing, the cursed swine!' I looked where he pointed and saw a row of men in a little trench across the road, some loading, some shooting. In a moment, though, the first bombs were thrown from the right, and the whole trunk of one of them was flung in the air.

Reason bade me stay where I was while we finished off the enemy at our leisure with a few rounds. Instead of this I threw away my rifle and rushed with clenched fists on to the road between the two sides. Unluckily, I was still wearing the English coat and my cap with a red band. In the very transport of victory I felt a sharp blow on the left side of my breast. Night descended on me. I was finished!

I was convinced I was shot through the heart, yet I felt neither pain nor fear as I awaited my immediate death. When I found to my astonishment that I had not fallen, and discovered no hole in my shirt either, I turned on the enemy again. At that, a man of my company rushed up: 'Sir, take off that coat!' and snatched the dangerous garment from my shoulders.

Another hurrah rent the air. From the right, where ever since the morning bombing had been going on, a number of Germans sprang over the road to our help, with a young officer in a brown waterproof at their head. It was Kius. By good luck he tripped over a low entanglement just as our English machine-gun fired its last shots, and the stream of bullets flew by over his head. The Scottish were annihilated in a few furious moments by rifle-fire and bombs. The road was strewn with dead, and what few survived were followed by our fire.

When I was standing talking to Kius in the captured trench I felt a moist feeling in on my breast. Tearing open my shirt I saw that I had been hit just over the heart. The bullet had gone through me just above my Iron Cross, leaving two holes in my body and two in my shirt. There was no doubt that I had been shot for an Englishman by one of our own men (I strongly suspected the one who had torn off my coat) at a range of a few paces.

Kius bound me up and with great difficulty induced me to leave the battlefield at this interesting moment. We parted with 'See you in Hanover!'

I chose myself an escort, looked for my map-case (it contained my diary) on the fire-swept road, and went back through the trench that we had fought our way along.

Our battle-cries had been so powerful that the enemy artillery had broken out at once. Over all the ground beyond the trench, and particularly on the trench itself, lay a barrage of unusual intensity. It was scarcely likely we could get safely through it. We went in jumps from traverse to traverse. Suddenly there was a shattering crash on the edge of the trench close by me. I felt a blow on the back of the head and fell forward stunned. When I came to, I was hanging with my head down over the breech of a heavy machine-gun and staring into a pool of blood that grew larger at an alarming rate. The blood poured so fast that I gave up all hope of survival. As my escort, however, assured me that nothing of my brain was to be seen, I picked myself up and went on. I had paid the penalty for my folly in going into an attack without a helmet.

In spite of the double loss of blood I was in great excitement and implored every one we met in the trench, as though possessed by one idea, to hurry forward and join the fight. We were soon beyond the zone of the light field-guns and slackened our pace, as only a bird of ill-omen need expect to be hit by an isolated heavy.

In the sunken road leading from Noreuil I passed Brigade headquarters, and reported to Major-General Hobel, whom I had already informed of our success, and begged him to send reserves to support the attacking force. The general told me that I had been killed the day before. It was not the first time in the war.

In Noreuil a great pile of boxes and bombs was burning merrily by the roadside. We hurried past with very mixed feelings. Beyond the villages I got a lift in an empty ammunition waggon. I had a sharp encounter with the officer commanding the ammunition column, who wanted to have two wounded Englishmen who had helped me along over the last part of the way thrown off the waggon.

The traffic on the Noreuil-Quéant road was amazing. No one who has not seen it can form any idea of the endless columns of troops that go to make an offensive. Beyond Quéant the throng was incredible. It was a sad sight when I passed the little cottage of Jeanne d'Arc. Nothing but the foundation was left. I went up to an officer with a white arm-band, denoting that he was in control of the traffic, and he procured me a seat in a private car as far as the field-hospital at Souchy-Couchy. We often had to wait half an hour when waggons and lorries got mixed up and blocked the road. The doctors in the operating theatre of the field-hospital were feverishly busy. Nevertheless, the surgeon who attended me could not repress his astonishment at the fortunate nature of my wounds. Even the bullet that had passed in and out of the back of my head had not injured the skull.

After an excellent sleep I was sent the next morning to the casualty clearing-station at Cantin, where I had the luck to meet Lieutenant Sprenger, whom I had never seen again after we went over the top. He had a rifle-bullet through the thigh.

After a short stay in the Bavarian Field Hospital 14 (Montigny) we were conveyed to Douai and there put into a hospital train for Berlin. There, after fourteen days' nursing, my wounds healed up again as well as their five predecessors had done.

To my sorrow I heard in Hannover that little Schultz, among many others I had known, had fallen during the hand-to-hand fighting. Any one who saw us celebrating our meeting in a little Hanover bar would hardly have believed we had parted only fourteen days before to other music than the peaceful click of billiard balls.

# ENGLISH GAINS

On the 4th of June 1918 I joined the regiment again. It was out on rest at Vraucourt, now far behind the line. The new commanding officer, Major von Lüttichau, gave me the command of my old 7th company.

As I drew near my quarters the men ran to meet me and, taking my things from me, led me in in triumph. It was like coming back to a family circle.

We occupied a number of corrugated-iron huts in the middle of neglected grass fields whose green was lit up with sheets of yellow flowers. This waste of ground, that we had christened 'Die Wallachei,' was grazed by herds of horses. If you went out of the hut you experienced the disquieting sense of empty spaces that sometimes grips the cowboy, the Bedouin, and every other dweller of the waste. We went long walks in the evenings in the country road, and looked out for partridges, or for war material hidden in the grass. One afternoon I rode to the sunken road near Vraucourt where there had been such hard fighting two months before. It was thickly edged with crosses, among which I found many a well-known name.

Soon the regiment was put into the line in front of Puisieux-au-Mont. We were conveyed by night on lorries, when the cone of light from the parachute lights of night bombers showed up the road as a strip of white in the darkness. Near or far the rushing swirl of the descending bomb was swallowed in reverberations as it burst. Then the searchlight's quivering arm probed the dark sky for the treacherous night-hawk, shrapnel burst in a scintillating spray, and tracer-shells chased each other in a long chain like fiery wolves.

A repulsive scent of corpses hung about his conquered ground. Whether strong or almost imperceptible, it acted on the nerves as an irritant and wrapped one in a mood of overstrung and eerie foreboding.

'Offensive incense,' I heard a cynic and old soldier say at my elbow, as we were passing for some minutes between rows of dimly-seen graves.

From the Achiet-le-Grand we marched along the embankment of the Bapaume railway line and cut across country into the line. The shelling was lively. Two shells of medium calibre fell close while we were making a brief halt. The memory of the unforgettable night of horror, March 19, drove us onwards. Close behind the front line we came on a noisy company that had been relieved, and chance took us past them just as their mouths were stopped by a dozen or two of shrapnel. Heaping them with abuse, my men jumped head over heels into the next communication trench. Three were hit and had to go back to the field dressing-station.

I was utterly exhausted when at three in the morning I reached my dugout. It was miserably small, and promised little for my comfort during the days ahead.

A candle glowed red in the indescribable atmosphere. I stumbled over a tangle of legs and brought by the magic word of 'Relief,' a string of curses proceeded from a hole like a baker's oven, and then one by one emerged an unshaven face, a pair of battered shoulder-straps, a weather-beaten uniform, and two clods of earth in which presumably boots were concealed. We sat down at a so-called table and went through the business of handing over, in which each tried to do the other in to the tune of a dozen iron rations and a few Verey-light pistols. My predecessor was then disgorged into the open through the narrow entry, prophesying as he went that the rotten hole would not last out another three days. I remained inside—the new captain of Sector A.

I surveyed our trench next morning and found little to cheer me. I had scarcely left the dugout when I met two coffee-carriers bleeding from wounds inflicted by shrapnel bullets in the communication trench. A few steps further Fusilier Ahrens reported to me a hit from a ricochet.

We had the village of Bucquoy in front of us and Puisieux-au-Mont behind. The company was without support in a front line that was both shallow and narrow, and we were separated from the 76th Infantry Regiment on our right by a large unoccupied gap. The left flank of the regimental front comprised a piece of splintered woodland, known as Wood 125. By orders, no deep dugouts were excavated. The men were accommodated two at a time in little dugouts held up by so-called tin Siegfrieds.

As my dugout was situated behind quite another part of our front, the next thing I did was to seek new quarters. A hut-like affair in a length of trench that had fallen in seemed to me to meet the case when I had put it into a defensible state by collecting a few lethal instruments there. Once installed, I lived a hermit's life among fields of green, disturbed only by an occasional runner or orderly, who carried the paper war even into this retired spot.

One was able then to shake one's head between two shell-bursts over many matters of grave importance, such as that the town-major of X had lost a terrier with black spots, answering to the name of Zippi, if one had not lost oneself with savage humour in the suit for maintenance of the servant-girl Makeben against Corporal Meger. The *pro formas* and returns, too, provided us with needful distraction. One was able to keep so fully occupied with the inner organization that time was scarcely left over for the little affair of holding the line. And indeed one was asked little about it. It often appeared that collecting empty cartridge-cases was of far greater importance. Whenever the visit of a superior officer was announced I hurried along the trench collecting paper and cartridge-cases and instructing the men on guard how they were to report themselves and click their heels together. Also that they were not to commit the crime of averting their eyes from the enemy in the course of the operation (though not even the tip of the enemy's nose had been seen for three months past), nor even to let their rifles out of their hands. the sure reward was three days' solitary confinement.

These things were typical of us and did much harm. The letter stifled the spirit. The war was bureaucratized. At the same time, the front-line officer had far too much discipline in his bones to raise these matters, though they were the object of curses in every platoon commander's dugout. Yet it was for him to fuse the old Prussian spirit with the methods of modern warfare.

To return to my dugout, to which I gave the fine name 'Wahnfried House.' Its roof was my only worry; for it could only be described as relatively shell-proof—that is, only so long as it was not hit. However, I comforted myself with the thought that I was no worse off than the men. Every afternoon my batman put a blanket down in an immense shell-hole approached by a sap we had excavated, and there I had a sun-bath. My siesta was, I confess, frequently interrupted by the bursts of shells near-by or the whizz of bomb-splinters when we were bombed from the air.

We were often heavily shelled at night. I lay on my bunk on a mattress of fresh grass and listened with a quite peculiar and quite ungrounded sense of security to the shells falling around, while the soil descended in showers at each shock. Or else I went outside and looked from the fire-step across the sad night landscape, that was in such strange and indescribable contrast to the fiery spectacle whose dance-floor it was.

At such moments there crept over me a mood I had never known before: a certain falling-off of the fighting spirit, a war-weariness occasioned by the length of time I had been exposed to the war's excitements. Nothing but war and danger; not a night that was not convulsed with shells. The seasons succeeded each other. Winter came and then summer, and one was always in the war. Tired of it and used to it, one was all the more dispirited and fed up with it just because one was used to it. One was blinded no longer by appearances. The war had raised deeper problems of its own. It was a singular time.

The front line had comparatively little to suffer from the enemy fire. Otherwise it would have been untenable. It was Puisieux and the hollows near it that were chiefly and almost continuously shelled; and in the evenings the bombardment rose to quite extraordinary intensity. Ration-parties and reliefs were consequently very risky matters.

On the 14th of June I was relieved at two in the morning by Kius, who also had returned and was in command of the 2nd Company. We spent our time on rest behind the railway embankment at Achiet-le-Grande, which gave shelter to our huts and dugouts. The English shelled time after time with heavy low-trajectory shells. The quartermaster-sergeant of the 3rd Company, Rackebrand, fell a victim. A few days before this there had been an appalling disaster. A bomb had been dropped in the midst of the band of the 76th while a crowd stood round listening. There were many of the 73rd too among the casualties.

There was a cluster of shell-shot tanks quite close to the embankment, and I often went to look at them. They bore names that were sometimes humorous, sometimes defiant, and sometimes affectionate, and they were camouflaged with paint; but they were all in a pitiable plight. The little cabin of armoured plate, now shot to pieces, with its maze of pipes, rods, and wires, must have been an extremely uncomfortable crib during an attack, when the monsters, hoping to baffle the aim of our guns, took a tortuous course over the battlefield like gigantic helpless cockchafers. I thought more than once of the men in these fiery furnaces.

On the morning of the 18th the 7th Company had to return to Puisieux on account of the uncertain state of affairs there, to be at the disposal of the C.O. of the troops in the line for carrying-parties or any other purpose. We occupied cellars and dugouts on the edge of the village nearest Bucquoy. Just as we arrived, a salvo of heavy shells went up in the surrounding gardens, in spite of this I did not refrain from breakfasting in a little arbour at the entrance of my dugout. After a while there was another of them; so I made a dash for it. It went up quite close. A stretcher-bearer of my company named Kenziora, who was passing by with some dixies of water, was hit in the lower part of the body. As we bound him up, great drops of sweat stood on his forehead; and when I tried to comfort him, he groaned out: 'It is a mortal wound. I can tell that well enough.' In spite of this prophecy I shook him by the hand half a year later on our entry into Hanover.

In the afternoon I took a solitary walk through Puisieux. The village had already been pounded to a heap of ruins by the Somme battle, and now shell-holes and wreckage of walls wore a mantle of green from which the white disks of the ruin-loving elder shone out on every side. Numerous more recent bursts had made rents in this mantle and once more laid bare the soil of the gardens, so often churned up already.

The village street was fringed with the refuse of the advance now come to a standstill. Shell-shot waggons, abandoned ammunition, the weapons of hand-to-hand fighting, skeletons of half decayed horses, surrounded by the hum of myriad of flies, all told of the vanity of all things in the fight for life. The church that occupied the highest point of the village consisted of nothing now but a dreary heap of stones. While I picked up a bunch of wonderful roses in a waste garden a few shells came to remind me of prudence in this dancing-place of death.

After a few days we relieved the 9th Company in the line of resistance, about 500 metres behind the front line. Three of my men were wounded in the course of the relief. Captain von Ledebur was wounded in the foot next morning by a shrapnel bullet close to my dugout. Though far gone in consumption, he felt that fighting was his vocation. It was his fate to succumb to this slight wound. He died soon after in the hospital. On the 28th, Sergeant

Gruner, who was in charge of my ration-party, was hit by a shell-splinter. This was the ninth casualty in the company within a few days.

After we had been a week in the front line we had again to occupy the line of resistance, since our relief battalion was pretty well disbanded owing to Spanish influenza. With us, too, several men reported sick daily. Influenza was so severe in the neighbouring division, that an enemy flier dropped a pamphlet to say that the English would undertake the relief if the troops were not taken out soon. We heard, all the same, that the malady was spreading more and more on the other side too. With us the effects were worse owing to under-nourishment, and in addition we were kept in constant readiness for an attack, as Wood 125 was being shelled incessantly with an intensity that boded no good. The 6th Company, who were in line there, were many of them down with carbonic-oxide poisoning. Some were only saved by an oxygen apparatus.

One afternoon while walking along the trench I found several buried cases of English ammunition, and blew off the tip of my right forefinger through foolishly taking a rifle-grenade to pieces. The same evening, while I stood talking to Lieutenant Sprenger on the top of my dugout, a heavy shell went up close to us. We argued over the distance it was from us, and Sprenger estimated it at 10 metres, I at 30. In order to see how far I could rely on myself in such matters, I measured it and found the shell-hole 22 metres away from where we were standing. People are very apt to underestimate distances.

On the 20th of July I was again with my company at Puisieux. I spent the whole afternoon standing on the ruins of a wall and watching the front line, where, it seemed to me, something very suspicious was going on.

Wood 125 was often veiled in the smoke of violent shelling, while green and right lights were rising and falling. Often the artillery fire was silent, and the tac-tac-tac of a machine-gun could be heard and the faint reports of distant bombing.

From where I stood the whole thing was like a pretty game. It had not the majesty of the first-class battle, and yet the relentless strife between two brazen forces was there to see.

All over the empty expanse there were hidden eyes fixed on the little wood, round whose shuddering oak tops fountains of brown earth danced in every-changing figures. All round, distributed in trenches, shell-holes, caverns, and ruins, were men and guns, awaiting their turn in the battle for a piece of ground covered with splintered trunks.

Far behind, at opposite poles, two generals are seated at tables spread with maps. there is a report, a brief exposition, a few words to a staff officer, a conversation on the telephone. An hour later a fresh bombardment tears up the old shell-holes and a fresh hecatomb of men bleeds in the suffocating fumes. . . .

Towards evening I was summoned to the headquarters of the troops in reserve, and there learned that the enemy had got a footing on the left flank of our trench system. In order to make a little room in front of us again, the order was that Lieutenant Petersen with the storm company was to clear the hedge trench that ran along the side of the wood, and I with my fellows the communication trench running parallel to it in a hollow of the ground. We moved off at dawn, but before we left our jumping-off place the rifle-fire became so violent that we abandoned the enterprise for a time. I gave orders to occupy the Elbinger Alley, and made up for my broken night's sleep in an immense cavern of a dugout. At 11 in the morning I was awakened by the noise of bombs from the left flank, where we held a block. I hurried to the spot and found the usual scene in this description of fighting. White clouds of bomb-smoke hanging over the trench and a few traverses back, a machine-gun rattling from either side, while in between there were men bending forward and jumping now forward, now back. The little *coup de main* was already beaten off, but it had cost one man, who lay behind the block, torn by bomb-splinters.

Towards evening I had orders to lead the company back to Puisieux, and then, on arrival, I was ordered to take two sections and join in rolling up the trench in the hollow. At 3.40 we—that is to say, Lieutenant Voight of the storm company with a storm troop, and I with my two sections—set off for the starting-point. Our instructions were to roll up the trench from the red point K to red point Z after a five minutes' artillery and trench-mortar preparation.

I cannot deny that both of us considered the artillery preparation, and in fact the taking and occupying of the trench, as unnecessary and ill-judged. The trench lay in the bottom of the hollow and was overlooked from all sides. The decisive point was the hedge trench: if an attack was to be made, it was essential to take it, and it automatically gave possession of the hollow. I cherished the firm suspicion that this operation had been ordered from the rear and by the map, for it could not have occurred to anyone who had seen the lie of the land to give such orders as these. After the artillery preparation—which cost us one man wounded—we advanced and rolled up the trench. Shortly before 2 we encountered opposition and bombed our way through it. As we had gained our objective and were not disposed for further fighting, we made a block and posted a section with a machine-gun behind it.

The only pleasure I had in the affair was the behaviour of the men of the storm troop, who reminded me forcibly of Grimmelhausen's Simplicissimus. These young warriors with great shocks of hair and puttees fell into a hot dispute twenty metres from the enemy because one of them had called the other a rabbit. They cursed like troopers and vaunted themselves with mighty boasts. 'Look here, we are not all such funks as you!' one of them shouted at last, and rolled up fifty metres of trench by himself.

By mid-day the section holding the block came back. They had had casualties and could hold out no longer. I had already given them up for lost, and was surprised that any one at all had been able to pass along this trench and still be alive. That is what comes out of war on paper.

In spite of our counter-attacks, the enemy still had a firm footing on the left flank of our front line and in the strongly barricaded communication trenches, and so threatened our support line.

On the 24th of July I went to the new C sector of the support line to find my way about, as I was to take it over the next day. I got Lieutenant Gipkens, commanding the company, to show me the block at the hedge trench, and sat down beside him on a fire-step. Suddenly Gipkens seized hold of me and pulled me to one side. Next moment a shot flew into splinters on the very place where I had been sitting. By a lucky chance he had seen a rifle barrel slowly pushed out of a loophole in the block only forty metres from us. The keen eye of an artist had saved my life, for any fool could have hit me at that range. I was told later that three men of the 9th Company had already been shot through the head at this apparently harmless spot. In the afternoon I was tempted from my coal-hole by some not particularly violent artillery fire, though I was at the moment comfortably reading, over a cup of coffee. On the front there were signals for the barrage going up incessantly. Wounded men, limping back, told that the English had penetrated sectors B and C in the support line and occupied the ground in front of sector A. Immediately after came the bad news that Lieutenants Vorbeck and Grieshaber had fallen while defending their sectors, and that Lieutenant Kastner was badly wounded. At 8, too, Sprenger, till now in temporary command of the 5th Company, came to my dugout with a splinter in his back. After fortifying himself with a pull at the bottle, he went on to the dressing-station, quoting 'Back now! Back now, Don Rodrigo!' His friend Lieutenant Domeyer followed him, bleeding from the hand.

Next morning we relieved C sector, which had meanwhile been cleared of the enemy. There I found pioneers Boje and Kius with a detachment of the 2nd Company, Gipkens with what remained of the 9th. Eight dead Germans lay in the trench, and two English (cap badge: South Africa, Otago Rifles). All had been roughly handled by bombs. Their fearful injuries were written on their faces, distorted by anguish. Both eyes of two men were shot away.

While I was greeting Boje and Kius in our usual tone of ironical pessimism, I felt the look of horror in the eyes of a new recruit, a seminarist, who was gazing at me. Looking along the channel of his thoughts I had a shock when I realize for the first time how callous the war had made me. One got to regarding men as mere matter.

I had men posted at the block and the trench cleared of the dead. At 11.45, without any warning haven been given us, our artillery opened out on the position in front of us with the utmost fury. The result was more casualties for us than for the English, and it was not long for before the tale of woe opened. The cry for stretchers came along the trenches from the left. Hurrying along, I found what was left of my best platoon commander, a shapeless mess, in front of the block in the hedge trench. He had had a direct hit in the loins from one of our shells. The fragments of his uniform and clothing, torn from his body by the force of the explosion, were hanging above him on the splintered remnant of a thorn hedge. I had a ground-sheet thrown over him to spare the men the sight. Immediately after three more men were wounded at the same spot. One of them had both hands severed at the wrist. He staggered to the rear, covered with blood, both arms resting on the shoulders of a stretcher-bearer. Lance-corporal Ehlers writhed on the ground, stupefied by the explosion.

I sent protest after protest to headquarters, vigorously demanding either the cessation of the firing or the presence of artillery officers in the trench. Instead of any reply, a heavy trench-mortar joined in with the rest and made the trench an utter shambles. Blood and brains and pieces of flesh were everywhere, and at once collected swarms of flies. At 7.15(!) I had orders, from which I learned that at 7.30 the fire would be increased; that at 8 two sections of the storm company were to rush the block in the hedge trench, to roll it up as far as red point A and then to get into touch on the right with a shock troop that was to make an attack parallel with theirs. Two sections of my company were to follow on and occupy the trench.

I made the necessary arrangements with all speed while the artillery fire set in; detailed the two sections, and had a word with Lieutenant Voight, who a few minutes later advanced as ordered. I took the matter more as an evening walk than anything else, and strolled along behind my two sections, wearing a cap, a stick-bomb under my arm. At the moment of the attack every rifle anywhere near was directed upon the hedge trench. with heads bent we made jumps from one traverse to the next. In front of us all went splendidly. the English fled to a line behind, leaving one dead. I was bringing up the rear and had just passed the mouth of a trench branching off to the left, when the man ahead of me, and N.C.O., gave an excited shout and fired past my head to the left. As I could not explain his conduct to myself, I went a few steps back and found myself faced of a sudden by a powerfully-built Englishman, just at the moment when he was lobbing a bomb after the flying N.C.O. At the same time shouts rose to all sides. They were coming on over the top to cut us off. I drew forth the bomb, my only weapon, and dropped it at the feet of the Tommy. Then I took to my heels in the direction of our lines. One man only, little Wilzek of my company, had the presence of mind to run after me. An egg-bomb was thrown after us, and tore his belt and the seat of his trousers without doing him any further injury.

Voigt and the rest of the men who had gone the other way were apparently surrounded and done for. Continued shouts and explosions of bombs showed that they were selling their lives dearly.

In the hope of coming to their help I led Fahnenjunker Mohrmann's section forward along the hedge trench. However we were brought to a stop by a hail of bursting Stokes bombs. A splinter flew against my chest and was caught in the clasp of my braces. Besides this, there was a sudden onset of artillery-fire.

Fountains of earth were sprayed up out of coloured smoke; the blare of flying metal screamed athwart the blunt roar of heavy shell-bursts; the hum of approaching shells came to an end with alarming suddenness; a cloud of splinters sang and whizzed about us. As an attack might be expected, I picked up a helmet and put it on and hurried back with a few men to the trench.

Above we saw figures appearing, so we lay down on the edge of the trench and opened fire. Near me a new recruit was feverishly fingering the trigger of his machine-gun, without succeeding in getting a shot out of the barrel, till I snatched the thing out of his hands. A few English dropped. The rest disappeared in their trenches again, while the artillery fire grew more furious. As for our own—it took sides no longer.

When I was walking to my crib, followed by an orderly, something struck the trench wall between us and, whipping my helmet off my head with enormous force, threw it far away. I thought that I had got the whole charge of a shrapnel shell, and lay half-stunned in my fox-hole. A moment later a shell struck the verge of it and filled the small space with thick smoke. A long splinter smashed a box of gherkins at my feet. To prevent myself being buried I crept out into the trench again, and was able at least to rouse the two orderlies and my batman and put them on the look-out.

It was a really unpleasant half-hour, and the company had many losses. When the worst of it was over I went through the trench to take stock of the damage and ascertain what men I had left. As the count of fifteen men was not enough for holding the trench, I left the defense of the block to Mohrmann and three men, and withdrew the remainder to a giant shell hole behind our line and had all the available bombs collected there. My plan was to let the enemy, if they attacked, enter our trench unopposed and then at a signal blow them to bits from above. However, the battle confined itself to the incessant uproar of light trench-mortars, rifle-grenades, and bombs.

On the 27th of July we were relieved by a company of the 164th Infantry Regiment. We were indeed utterly exhausted. The officer commanding the company was seriously wounded while marching into the line; and a few days later my crib got hit and buried his successor. We all breathed more freely when we had left Puisieux behind us and the rising storm of the final offensive that growled around it.

.  .  .  .  .  .  .  .

**111 INF. DIV.**

DIVISIONAL HEADQUARTERS,
12/8/18.

The 73rd Fusilier Regiment has added in the most brilliant fashion to its high reputation as a brave and war-tried unit in the severe fighting which was renewed against an enemy much superior in numbers. I am all the more glad to recognize this as I know what high demands in endurance and loyalty to duty in our country's cause must have been made on the troops of the division during this long spell in the line on a difficult front.

In particular, Lieutenant Jünger earned fresh recognition. Already six times wounded, he was on this occasion, as always, a shining example to both officers and men.

VON BUSSE,
*Major-General and*
*Commander of Division.*

# MY LAST STORM

On the 30th July 1918 we went into rest at Sauchy Lestrée, a delightful spot in Artois surrounded by water. A few days later we marched still further back to Escaudœuvres, a small, smug working-men's suburb of Cambrai.

I occupied the typical best bedroom of an artisan's house in northern France. The large double bed as its ominous pièce de résistance; a fireplace with hideous red and blue glass vases on the mantlepiece; a round table, chairs; on the walls some of those frightful colour-prints of the *Familistère, Vive le classe, souvenir de première communion,* postcards, and other rubbish. I did what I could to give the right note to my arrival by throwing a pack of cards on the table and my riding-boots on the double bed.

The clear moonlight nights favoured the visits of enemy bombers, who gave us a notion of the overwhelming superiority of material possessed by the other side. Night after night several formations came over and dropped their bombs of alarmingly high explosives over Cambrai and its suburbs. I was not agitated so much by the fine mosquito-like hum of the engines and the series of reverberating detonations as I was by the dash of my host for the cellar. It is true that, one day before my arrival, a bomb had landed in front of the windows and flung the gentleman of the house half-stunned out of the bed in which I slept, broken a bedpost, and bored the walls of the house with splinters. It was precisely this accident which lulled me into the belief that a repetition of it would be unlikely.

After one day's rest the detested but indispensable round of training set in once more. Drill, instruction, roll-calls, lectures, and inspections filled a great part of the day. One entire morning was spent in pronouncing a verdict in a court of honour.

Here, too, we were miserably fed. For a long while there was nothing for supper but gherkins, which the men very drily and aptly named 'gardener's sausage.'

It was by no means easy to weld my decimated company into a unit again. It often went against the grain to be always insisting of the details of the drill in my relations with the men, convinced though I was of the necessity. Drill as the means to an end is indispensable to every army. it cannot be replaced entirely by individual training nor by sporting instinct. A man, unless his inherent worth is beyond all doubt, must have obedience drilled into him, so that his natural instincts can be curbed by the spiritual compulsion of his commander even in the most awful moments.

Above all, I devoted my efforts to the training of a shock troop, as it had become more and more clear to me in the course of the war that all success springs from individual action, while the mass of troops give impetus and weight of fire. Better command a resolute section than a wavering company.

I spent my leisure time reading, bathing, shooting, and riding. On my rides I found vast quantities of literature thrown down from aeroplanes. It was designed to hasten the moral deterioration of the army; among it was even Schiller's poem of Britannia the Free. It seemed to me very clever of the English to bombard us with poetry, and also very flattering to us. A war in which one fought with verses would indeed be a treat. The reward of thirty pfennigs set on the head of each copy by the military authorities showed that they did not undervalue the danger of this weapon. The cost of this, it is true, was laid upon the occupied territory. So it would appear we possessed no longer the wholly pure understanding of poetry.

One afternoon I got a bicycle and rode into Cambrai. The dear old town was a desert. Shops and cafés were shut; the streets seemed dead in spite of the field-grey uniforms that thronged them. M. and Mme. Plancot, who had given me such a fine billet a year before, were delighted by my visit. They told me that conditions of life in Cambrai had got worse in every way. They complained particularly of the frequent visits the night bombers paid them. They often had to run downstairs and up again several times a night, disputing the point as they went whether it was better to die in the first cellar by the bomb itself or in the lower one by being buried alive. The old people's careworn looks made me heartily sorry. A few weeks later, when the town was shelled, they had to leave the house, where they had spent their lives, at a moment's notice.

On the 23rd of August, I was alarmed by a violent knocking at my door at 11, when I had sunk into a happy sleep. It was an orderly with marching orders. Already the day before the monotonous roll and stamp of unusually heavy artillery-fire had surged over and warned us on duty, at meals, at cards, to have no illusions about being on rest much longer. We had coined an expressive front-line expression for this distant thunder of guns: 'es wummert.'

We packed up in haste and were soon marching on the road to Cambrai in a storm like a cloud-burst. Our destination was Marquion and we reached it at 5 in the morning. The quarters allotted to the company were a farmyard, surrounded by demolished farm-buildings, in which each man found shelter as well as he could. I, with my one company officer, Lieutenant Schrader, crept into a little dungeon of brick that had apparently, in more peaceful times, been a goat-shed, but was now occupied only by several large rats.

At mid-day there was an officers' pow-wow, at which we heard that we were that night to take up a position in readiness on the right of the great Cambrai-Bapaume road, not far from Beugny. We were warned that an attack by the new swift and more easily manœuvred tanks was probable.

I paraded my company in battle order in a small orchard; and then, standing under an apple-tree, I said a few words to them as they stood round me in a horseshoe. The expression on their faces was serious and manly. There was little to say. By this time there was not a man who did not know that we were on a precipitous descent, and the fact was accepted with an equanimity that only the moral force which in every army accompanies its armed force can explain. Every man knew that victory could no longer be ours. But the enemy should know that he fought against men of honour.

On such occasions I took care not to be carried away by a spirit of daredevilry. It would hardly have been appropriate to show that one looked forward to the battle with a certain joy in the face of the men whose dread of death was in many cases increased by anxiety for wife and child. It was also my principle not to raise their courage by big words nor to threaten the coward. I spoke rather to this effect:—I know well enough that no one will leave me in the lurch. We are all afraid, but we must fight against it. To be overcome by one's weakness is only human. At such a moment look at your leader and your fellows. While I spoke I felt what I said went home, and the results justified me in this psychological preparation.

Schrader and I had our meal at night on the door laid on a wheelbarrow in the farmyard, and drank a bottle of wine. We then rolled ourselves up in our goat-shed, till the guard woke us at 2 a.m. with the announcement that the motor lorries were in the market-place ready to load up.

In the ghostly light we rattled over the war-torn country of last year's Cambrai battle, through villages in grotesque states of destruction with their streets bordered by billows of wreckage. Just before Beugny we were unloaded and led to our position. The battalion was occupying a hollow on the road Beugny-Vaux. During the morning an orderly brought orders for the company to push on to the road Frémicourt-Vaux. This typical forward movement made me sure that we were in for it till nightfall.

I led my three platoon strung out in file, through a country over which aeroplanes circled, dropping bombs and scattering bullets. When we reached our objective we dispersed in shell-holes, as an occasional shell came over the road.

I felt so bad that day that I lay down at once in a small length of trench and fell asleep. When I awoke I read Laurence Sterne's *Tristram Shandy*, and thus the afternoon went by, while I lay in the sun with the apathy of an invalid.

At 6.15 a despatch-rider summoned the company commanders to Captain von Weyhe.

'I have to make the serious announcement that we are to attack. After half an hour's artillery preparation the battalion will advance at 7 (!) from the western edge of Favreuil and storm the enemy lines. You are to march on the church tower of Sapignies.'

After brief coming and going and a hearty handshake we rushed back to our companies, as the artillery fire began in ten minutes and we still had a good way to march.

'By sections in single file at twenty metres interval. Direction, half left, tree-tops at Favreuil.'

A good sign of the spirit that was in the men now as ever was that I had to detail one man to stay behind and tell the cookers where to go. No one would volunteer.

I walked far ahead of the company with my company staff and Sergeant-major Reinecke. The shots of our guns were bursting out from behind hedges and ruins. Their fire sounded more like a furious yapping than a wave of destruction. Behind me I saw my sections advancing in perfect order. Close to them like dust flew the clouds of shots from aeroplanes; the shrapnel, bullets, empty shells, and driving bands drove with a hellish whirr between the files of the thin human line. On the right Beuquâtre lay under heavy shell-fire, and jagged fragments of iron hurtled heavily overhead and drove with a sudden jab into the clayey ground.

Our advance was still more unpleasant behind the Beuquâtre-Bapaume road. A salvo of H.E. went up madly behind and before and among us. We scattered and threw ourselves into shell-holes. The smoke of shell after shell hung in clouds over the edge of Favreuil, and though it rose and fell again brown fountains of earth, one rapidly succeeding another. I went forward alone, as far as the first ruined houses, to find the way, and then gave the signal with my cane to follow.

The village was fringed with badly-shelled huts, and there detachments of the 1st and 2nd Companies assembled by degrees. A machine-gun had claimed several victims during the last part of the way. Among others, Vice-sergeant-major Balg of my company was hit in the leg. A figure in a brown waterproof came quietly across this fire-swept piece of ground and shook hands with me. Kius and Boje, Captain Junker and Schaper, Schrader, Schläger, Heins, Findeisen, Höhlemann, and Hoppenrath stood behind a hedge that was raked with lead and iron, and held a great council of war. On many a day of wrath we had fought on one battlefield together, and this time, too, the sun, already low in the west, was to gild the blood of all, or nearly all.

Part of the 1st Battalion moved into the park of the château. Of the 2nd Battalion only my company and the 5th had come through the curtain of fire practically without casualties. We worked our way forward under cover of shell-holes and ruins to a sunken road on the western edge of the village. On the way I clapped on to my head a helmet I picked up, a precaution I never took except in critical moments. I was astonished to find Favreuil utterly deserted. Apparently the line of defence had been abandoned by the troops occupying it.

Captain von Weyhe, now lying alone and severely wounded in a shell-hole in the village, had given orders that the 5th and 8th Companies were to form the first attacking line, the 6th the second, and the 7th the third. As there was nothing to be seen so far of the 6th and the 8th, I decided to go ahead without bothering too long over the distribution of the attack in depth.

It was already seven. Looking from between fragments of houses and stumps of trees, I saw an attacking party advance across the open in two waves under moderate rifle-fire. It must be the 5th.

I drew up my men in the sunken road and gave the order to advance in two waves. 'At a hundred metres interval. I myself will be between the first and second waves.

It was our last storm. How often in years gone by had we stepped out into the western sun in a mood the same as now! Les Eparges, Guillemont, St. Pierre Vaast, Langemarck, Passchendaele, Mœuvres, Vraucourt, Mory! Again the carnival of carnage beckoned.

We left the sunken road quite according to programme, only 'I myself,' as the formula ˚of command finely puts it, suddenly found myself near Lieutenant Schrader far in front of the first wave.

Isolated rifle-shots rang out in front of us. My cane in my right hand and revolver in the left, I stumped ahead and, without observing it, left the advancing lines of the 5th Company partly behind us and partly on our right. Meanwhile I found that my Iron Cross had dropped to the ground from my breast. Schrader, my batman, and I began a zealous search for it, in spite of snipers, who seemed to be drawing ahead of us. At last Schrader extracted it from a tuft of grass and I fastened it securely on again.

The ground began to fall. Indistinct figures were seen in motion against a background of brown earth. A machine-gun spat out its bullets at us. A sense of aimlessness took hold of me. Nevertheless, we began to charge at the double. In mid-jump over a piece of trench a piercing shock through the chest took away my breath. I spun head over heels with a loud cry and fell stunned to the ground.

I woke with a sense of great misfortune. I was pinned between narrow walls of earth, and along a row of crouching figures the cry was taken up: 'Stretcher-bearers! The company commander is wounded.'

An elderly man of another company was leaning over with a kindly expression, loosening my belt and opening my tunic. Two blood-red circular marks shone out on the middle of my right breast and on my back. I was crippled and chained to earth, and the close air of the narrow trench bathed me in sweat. My good Samaritan revived me by fanning me with my map-case. My hope as I struggled for breath was for darkness to come soon, so that I could be carried back.

Of a sudden a hurricane of fire broke on us from Sapignies. It was clear that this unbroken roll, this even and regular roaring and stamping, betokened more than a defensive measure against so poorly staged an attack as ours. Above me I could see beneath his helmet Schrader's strong face, as like a machine he loaded and fired, loaded and fired. A conversation arose between us that recalled the tower scene of the *Maid of Orleans*. Humorous as it was, it was all the same hardly in my mood, for I had the clear consciousness that I was done.

Above rose a cry of horror and ran from mouth to mouth: 'They're through on the left! We're surrounded!'

This gave me back my old strength again. I fastened upon a hole that a mole had bored in the trench wall and pulled myself to my feet, while the blood poured from my mouth. With bare head and open coat I stared, revolver in hand, into the fight.

Through whitish swatches of smoke a row of men with packs came on in a straight line. Some fell and lay there, others turned head over heels like shot hares. A hundred metres in front of us the last were sucked down into the shell-pocked earth. They must have been young troops, still unacquainted with the effects of the modern rifle, for they came on with all the hardihood of ignorance.

As though drawn by strings, four tanks crept over the crest of a rise. In a few minutes our artillery had trodden them into the ground. One broke across like a tin engine. On my right the brave Mohrmann collapsed with a cry of death.

It did not seem that all was lost. I whispered to Fähnrich Wilsky to creep to the left and enfilade the gap in our line. He came back almost at once and announced that twenty metres from us the show was up and all were surrendering. It was part of the 99th Regiment there (Zabern). I turned round and saw a strange sight. From the rear there were men coming forward with their hands up. The enemy must already have taken the village from which we went to the attack.

The scene became more and more lively. We were surrounded by a circle of Germans and English and called upon to throw down our weapons. I urged those nearest me to fight it out to the death. Friend or foe were fired on alike. Some who surrounded our little band were shouting, some were dumb. On the left two gigantic Englishmen were using their bayonets in a length of trench from which hands were held up imploring mercy.

Among us, too, there was a tumult of voices. 'It's all up! Throw away your rifle! Don't shoot, Kameraden!'

Looked at the two officers who were with me in the trench. They smiled back and with a shrug let their belts fall to the ground.

There was left only the choice of being taken or being shot. And now the moment had come to show whether all that I had often said to the men when on rest about the fighting spirit was more than empty phrases. I crawled out of the trench and staggered off in the direction of Favreuil. Two Englishmen who were taking a haul of prisoners of the 99th Regiment to their own lines barred my way. I shot the nearest one in the middle of the body with my revolver. He collapsed like a dummy figure. The other blazed his rifle at me and missed. These quick movements caused the blood to be driven clear of the lung in deep pulsations. I could breathe more freely, and set off at a run over the open beside the trench. Lieutenant Schläger was crouching behind a traverse with a section who were still firing. They joined forces with me. Some English who were going over the open stopped to get a Lewis gun in position and began shooting at us. Except for me, Schläger, and two others, not one escaped. Schläger, who had lost his pince-nez, told me that he saw nothing but my map-case flying up and down. The continuous loss of blood gave me the lightness and airiness of intoxication. One thing only bothered me—that I might collapse too soon. . . .

At last we reached a half-moon-shaped earthwork to the right of Favreuil whence half a dozen heavy machine-guns were pumping lead on friend and foe without distinction. Enemy shots were spluttering around the parapet; men danced to and fro in the greatest excitement. A N.C.O. of the Medical Corps attached to the 6th Company tore off my tunic and advised me to lie down at once, otherwise I might bleed to death in a very few minutes.

I was rolled in a ground-sheet and carried past the outskirts of Favreuil. Some men of my own and the 6th Company went with me.

After a few hundred paces we were fired on from the village at close range. The shots went with a smack into the human bodies. The stretcher-bearer of the 6th Company who carried the rear end of my ground-sheet was laid out with a bullet through the head; I was dropped as he fell.

The small detachment had thrown themselves flat on the ground and now crept to the nearest hollow, with bullets dropping into the ground all round them.

I lay by myself, firmly secured in my ground-sheet, awaiting the *coupe de grâce*.

And yet, so long as a man of my company lived, I was not quite forsaken. Near by I heard Lance-corporal Hengstmann's voice: 'I'll take you on my back, sir. Either we'll get through or, at worst, we'll lie where we fall.'

Unfortunately, we did not get through. Too many rifles aimed at us at almost point-blank range. He took me on his back with my arms round his neck, but before we had gone very far there was a metallic report and Hengstmann sank softly beneath me to the ground. I released myself from his arms that were still clasped under my knees, and found that a bullet had passed through helmet and temples. This brave man was a schoolmaster's son from Letter near Hanover.

This evil precedent did not deter another from coming to my aid and venturing on a fresh attempt to rescue me. It was Sergeant Strichalsky of the Medical Corps. He took me on his shoulder and carried me safely to the blind side of the rise of ground.

It was getting dark. The men found the ground-sheet of a dead man and carried me over a deserted stretch of ground over which, far and near, jagged flashes were flaming up. I had to struggle for breath, one of the most painful sensations there are. The smoke of the cigarette that a man was smoking ten paces in front threatened to suffocate me.

At length we reached a dressing-station in charge of a friend of mine, Dr. Key. He made me a divine lemon-squash, and then put me into a refreshing sleep with an injection of morphine.

Next day began the usual journey by stages to the rear. The terrible journey by car to the war hospital brought me to the edge of the grave. Then I was in nurses' hands. Though I am no misogynist, I was always irritated by the presence of women every time that the fate of battle threw me into the bed of a hospital ward. One sank, after the manly and purposeful activities of the war, into a vague atmosphere of warmth. The clear objectivity of the Catholic nursing sisterhoods afforded a welcome exception. I found with them an atmosphere very congenial to soldiering.

My wound was made lighter by many expressions of sympathy; and indeed bodily suffering always increases the sensibility of the inner being. From the Plancots I had a delightful letter, written when the enemy, who were gaining ground very slowly, first began shelling Cambrai. They sent me also a tin of milk they could ill spare, and the only melon their garden had produced. I must not let slip this opportunity of saying that I found many an example among the French civilian population of that internationality of the heart that every decent man and educated soldier ought to uphold. The last of my long series of batmen, too, was no exception to the rest. He stuck by me, though the hospital allowed no provisions to be made for him and he had to beg what he could in the kitchen.

I amused myself once during the monotonous hours on my back by counting the number of times I had been hit. I found that I had been hit in all fourteen times: six times by rifle-bullets, once by a shrapnel bullet, once by a shell splinter, three times by bomb splinters, and twice by splinters of rifle-bullets. Counting the ins and outs, this made precisely twenty punctures, so that I might confidently, with that Roman centurion, Holkschen Reiter, take my place in every warlike circle. Certainly I could at any time assert my claim to belong to one order at least, namely, that of the gold wound-stripes. This honour did in fact come to me at this very time, though the gold, certainly, was only yellow-lacquered metal. Yet I must confess I had it sewn on my coat with a certain pleasure, for if doctors and professors, for all their correctness, do not look askance upon the stamp of an official title, why should the soldier refuse a visible sign of his gallantry. The worth of an order, as of everything else, lies not on but beneath the surface; and who would grudge a heart that has so often beaten fast in the excitement of battle for country's sake the adornment of a bit of enamel as the outward sign? In huckstering times, indeed, when everything turns on money, these things lose their value, for it rests solely within the ideal with which they are bound up.

After fourteen days I was lying on the feather mattress of a hospital train. Once again a German landscape flitted by me, tinged this time with the first dyes of autumn, and once again, as on that time at Heidelberg, I was gripped by the sad and proud feeling of being more closely bound to my country because of the blood shed for her greatness. Why should I conceal that tears smarted in my eyes when I thought of the end of the enterprise in which I had borne my share? I had set out to the war gaily enough, thinking we were to hold a festival on which all the pride of youth was lavished, and I had thought little, once I was in the thick of it, about the ideal that I had to stand for. Now I looked back: four years of development in the midst of a generation predestined to death, spent in caves, smoke-filled trenches, and shell-illuminated wastes; years enlivened only by the pleasures of a mercenary, and nights of guard after guard in an endless perspective; in short, a monotonous calendar full of hardships and privation, divided by the red-letter days of battles. And almost without any thought of mine, the idea of the Fatherland had been distilled from all these afflictions in a clearer and brighter essence. That was the final winnings in a game on which so often all had been staked: the nation was no longer for me an empty thought veiled in symbols; and how could it have been otherwise when I had seen so many die for its sake, and been schooled myself to stake my life for its credit every minute, day and night, without a thought? And so, strange as it may sound, I learned from this very four years' schooling in force and in all the fantastic extravagance of material warfare that life had no depth of meaning except when it is pledged for an ideal, and that there are ideals in comparison with which the life of an individual and even of a people has no weight. And though the aim for which I fought as an individual, as an atom in the whole body of the army, was not to be achieved, though material force cast us, apparently, to the earth, yet we learned once and for all to stand for a cause and if necessary to fall as befitted men.

Hardened as scarcely another generation ever was in fire and flame, we could go into life as though from the anvil; into friendship, love, politics, professions, and into all that destiny had in store. It is not every generation that is so favoured.

And if it be objected that we belonged to a time of crude force our answer is: We stood with our feet in mud and blood, yet our faces were turned to things of exalted worth. And not one of that countless number who fell in our attacks fell for nothing. Each one fulfilled his own resolve. For to every one may be applied the saying from St. John that Dostoievski put in front of his greatest novel:

'Verily, verily, I say unto you, except a corn of wheat fall into the ground and die, it abideth alone: but if it die, it bringeth forth much fruit.'

To-day we cannot understand the martyrs who threw themselves into the arena in a transport that lifted them even before their deaths beyond

175

humanity, beyond every phase of pain and fear. Their faith no longer exercises a compelling force. When once it is no longer possible to understand how a man give his life for his country—and the time will come—then all is over that faith also, and the idea of the Fatherland is dead; and then, perhaps, we shall be envied, as we envy the saints their inward and irresistible strength. For all these great and solemn ideas bloom from a feeling that dwells in the blood and that cannot be forced. In the cold light of reason everything alike is a matter of expedience and sinks to the paltry and mean. It was our luck to live in the invisible rays of a feeling that filled the heart, and of this inestimable treasure we can never be deprived.

I had the good fortune to be taken out at Hanover and sent to the Clementine infirmary. One of my companions there was a young flying-man of Richthofen's squadron, named Wenzel, who had shot down twelve of the enemy. The last of them had first shot him through the shoulder.

On the 22nd of September 1918 I had the following telegram:

'His Majesty the Kaiser has bestowed on you the order of Pour le Mérite. I congratulate you in the name of the whole Division.

'GENERAL VON BUSSE.'

As soon as I was fit enough I celebrated this event with Wenzel, my brother, and a few friends. As a doubt had been expressed whether we should soon be passed out fit for active service, Wenzel and I felt ourselves compelled to jump again and again over a large armchair. We came out of it, however, very badly. Wenzel broke his arm again, and I was kept in bed next morning with a temperature of 104.

In spite of this it was not long before we were in excellent form for another winter campaign. This was deferred for a while; and we soon had to take part in other battles than we ever dreamed.

Now these too are over, and already we see once more in the dim light of the future the tumult of fresh ones. We—by this I mean those of the youth of this land who are capable of enthusiasm for an ideal—will not shrink from them. We stand in the memory of the dead who are holy to us, and we believe ourselves entrusted with the true and spiritual welfare of our people. We stand for what will be and for what has been. Through force without and barbarity within conglomerate in somber clouds, yet so long as the blade of a sword will strike a spark in the night may it be said: Germany lives and Germany shall never go under.

# ABOUT THE AUTHOR

Ernst Jünger (March 29, 1895 – February 17, 1998) was a highly-decorated German soldier, author, poet and philosopher. He received both the Iron Cross 1st Class and the *Pour le Mérite*, one of the highest orders of merit in the Kingdom of Prussia, for his actions during World War I. Jünger later served in the German Army in an administrative role in Paris during World War II. Although *The Storm of Steel* is his most famous book, which he often revisited, he produced other notable works in *Eumeswil*, *On Pain*, and *The Worker*, among many others. Jünger was an atheist for most of his life, though during his later years he converted to Catholicism.

# ABOUT THE TRANSLATOR

Basil Creighton (May 19, 1885 - May 3, 1989) was an acclaimed novelist and translator of German authors. Along with his original novels, including *Medner Hill Farm* and *The Leaden Cupid*, Creighton made many classics of German literature accessible to English audiences. Other than producing the first English edition of *The Storm of Steel*, his major translations included *Der Steppenwolf* by Hermann Hesse and *The Treasure of the Sierra Madre* by B. Traven. Creighton was so esteemed that, according to *The Times of London*, some authors would refuse to have their works translated into English unless Creighton were the translator.

Made in the USA
Columbia, SC
07 March 2024

32860574R00112